TRAUMA AND MASTERY
IN LIFE AND ART

To my parents, in memory.
For my grandchildren, with love.

—— GILBERT J. ROSE, M.D. ——

TRAUMA AND MASTERY
IN LIFE AND ART

Yale University Press
New Haven and London

Published with the assistance
of the F. B. Adams, Jr., Fund.

Lines from "Little Gidding" in *Four Quartets* by T. S. Eliot,
copyright 1943 by T. S. Eliot; renewed 1971 by Esme Valerie Eliot;
reprinted by permission of Harcourt Brace Jovanovich, Inc.,
and by permission of Faber & Faber Ltd. from
Collected Poems, 1909–1962 by T. S. Eliot.

Designed by Nancy Ovedovitz and set in
Garamond No. 3 type by The Saybrook Press, Inc.
Printed in the United States of America by
The Murray Printing Company. Westford, Massachusetts

Library of Congress Cataloging-in-Publication Data

Rose, Gilbert J., 1923–
Trauma and mastery in life and art.
Bibliography: p.
Includes index.
1. Psychoanalysis and the arts.   2. Post-traumatic
stress disorders.   I. Title.
NX180.P7R674   1987   700'.1'05   86–28089
ISBN 0–300–03842–9

10   9   8   7   6   5   4   3   2   1

CONTENTS

The understanding, when not suffused with some glow
of sympathetic emotion . . . gives but a dry, crude
image of the world.
George Santayana, 1896

My aim is always to get hold of the magic of reality
and to transfer this reality into painting. . . . It
may sound paradoxical, but it is, in fact, reality which
forms the mystery of our existence.
Max Beckmann, 1938

The act of writing; like the act of reading, puts one at risk, the risk of opening oneself to asking big questions. It is tempered, at least, by the foreknowledge that one raises large issues not out of the presumption of finding answers but in the hope of stimulating better questions.

The question I address in this book is how the psychoanalytic and the artistic process or experience overlap. Aside from some discussion of parallels between the two (Beres 1957), this area has received little if any examination. Indeed, the situation could hardly have been otherwise, because the very implication that analysis could be viewed to any extent as an artistic rather than a scientific activity has traditionally been deemed by psychoanalysts since Freud to be a form of resistance to the painful scientific truths of psychoanalysis. As Freud wrote of Havelock Ellis in this regard, such an assertion was to be flatly labeled a resistance "disguised in a friendly, indeed in too flattering a manner" (Freud 1920, 263).

Yet art has helped us to realize that some of the sharp dichotomies which appeared self-evident to an earlier age are no longer tenable. Among these is the absoluteness of the distinction between art and science. Freud's oeuvre in particular bridges both areas, perhaps constituting this century's single greatest contribution to the idea of the creative imagination, be it manifested in either art or science.

The overlap between art and psychoanalysis involves the continuing puzzle as to the differences and similarities between everyday thought, psychopathology, and creative imagination. This is not the place to discuss the nature of pathological thought except to say that it has to do with hopes and fears restrained by nothing more than the limits of imagination. Everyday and creative thought, it seems to me, may be distinguished by their relationship to knowledge.

Prosaic thought uses knowledge, or assumptions posing as knowledge, in a circular or solipsistic way to keep verifying itself. It keeps refining what is already there in a closed circuit. Can it ever get beyond itself to discover something new? In mathematics it is said that one needs to get out of the system in order to complete it. Prosaic thought is like percussing the same piece of wood and always getting the same dull thud. As Keats pointed out, this "consequitive reasoning," as he called it, may serve the need for certainty. He conceded that it induced sobriety and propriety. In the search for truth, however, he believed that prosaic thought was not only inadequate but even in the way. The pursuit of truth, he maintained, required the opposite—the capacity for dwelling in uncertainties—what we would refer to, today, as the tolerance for ambiguities.

As for creative thought, it asks the question, "What is the most embracing statement that can be made about something without contradicting known facts?" Imagination in the light of knowledge assumes that imagination is not identical with that which is unreal, but only with that which might be possible, just as it assumes that perception is not the same as the real, but only that which is given to the senses. Percussing that piece of wood again, whatever the elements are that contribute to the difference, creative thought recognizes that the thuddy sound of wood has been transformed into resonance; it leaps into the new realm of tone.

How may one responsibly approach the overlap and contrast between art and psychoanalysis? Their respective domains are the creative process and clinical psychopathology. However, these areas, too, are so vast as to be unwieldy. One needs key concepts that cut across both like a suitable plane for purposes of blunt dissection; they must at the same time lend themselves to being further delimited so as to provide a line of more precise entry or incision.

I have taken the ideas of trauma and mastery as tracing a suitable cross-section to explore clinical and creative process. Focusing down further, I have decided that, among the chief effects of trauma, the phenomena of psychic splitting stand out; and at the heart of mastery lies the matter of reintegration.

The question then becomes: How does the splitting and reintegration of psychopathology compare to that of the creative process? The answer lies in the direction of further questions as to what use they are put: regressive/destructive or progressive/constructive, that is, private/idiosyncratic or public/communicative, reality constricting or expanding?

The second part of this book proceeds to compare and contrast art with psychoanalysis: What is the nature of the reintegrative mastery that is offered by each? How does sensuous form or memory help one to think and perceive more feelingly?

Thus, the fabric of this book consists of two strands running through it like the warp in a weaving: psychopathology/creativity and psychoanalysis/art. They are held together by two other strands—the woof: trauma and mastery.

There is a large literature on trauma, including recent theoretical contributions (Furst 1978; Cohen 1980). Trauma is used here in the general sense of overstimulation, whether due to actual massive flooding from the external world or stemming from the person's own hypersensitivity to stimulation. As is well known, a complementary relationship exists between external overstimulation and inner sensitivity. What is trauma for one person may be challenge for another. Timing is, of course, also crucial. How much stimulation the ego can sustain and what type of fantasies are set off depend largely on the stage of development that has been achieved.

Whether arising from the external world or inner hypersensitivity, trauma and the expectation of trauma results in various types of splitting,[1] which will be defined as we trace them in psychopathology and creativity.

Mastery is in an ongoing process of integration and reintegration, endless in extent and variety. In order to attempt to master past trauma, contemporary reality, and the anticipation of future trauma, both the clinical and the creative imagination split off and repress some aspects of the past and elaborate and reintegrate others. Psychoanalytic mastery has to do with widening the range of inner experience in order to facilitate as broad and deep an integration of mental life as possible.

A basic theoretical matter underlying the question of trauma and mastery is the closed- versus the open-system model of the person. The closed-system model has traditionally held that the process of differentiation of self from other begins in early childhood and, thanks to internalization, is completed with full maturation. There is considerable evidence, however, that the process of distinguishing self from other is never completed, no matter how much internalization has been achieved.

In the open-system model, inner and outer, self and object, are partly matters of fluid processes, with an ever-shifting ratio between externalization and internalization. The emphasis is on the mutual influence of the person and his environment across boundaries that are *permeable* rather than rigid.

With these models in mind, the problem of the nature of mastery in psychoanalysis is contrasted with the form it takes in art and science. Psychoanalysis bears a close relationship to both. The much-valued affinity between psychoanalysis and science needs no restatement. It

---

1. Freud (1894, 46) referred to splitting as a "splitting of the content of consciousness." Later he used it to refer to "splitting of the ego" in fetishism (Freud 1927) meaning that something can be superficially acknowledged but denied in fantasy and behavior. Splitting has also been referred to as dissociation (Glover 1943; Beres 1959; Weissman 1967, 1968, 1969) and as fragmentizing (Peto 1961, 1963). Major contributors to its various meanings include Klein (1948) through Kernberg (1975, 1980).

is based on a shared goal and the means of attaining it: the highest degree of objective truth in the light of the fullest empirical data.

The affinity between psychoanalysis and art requires explication rather than defensiveness. It lies in the fact that each restores the original feelingful matrix of thought and perception; such reassimilation of feeling to thought and perception, whether approached via the psychoanalytic or the aesthetic route, illuminates reality, but from an angle different from that of "objective" science.

The "how" of this is discussed in terms of the open-system model. With continuing openness to the outside, there is no endpoint to internalization. Instead, there is an ongoing cycle of re-externalization and re-internalization. This takes place through the interaction of imagination and knowledge (more microscopically, the interplay of primary and secondary processes). It results in the refinement (sublimation) of primitive imagination (the development of the primary process) and is accompanied by a flow of affect.

Since the interplay of knowledge and imagination, with the associated affect, underlies all perception and thought, there are significant implications: thought and perception are invested with affect from the beginning; affects carry semantic meaning; percepts, being sensuous by their nature, carry an affective charge. In the attrition of everyday life, including the normal and neurotic defenses against trauma and the anticipation of trauma, this affective coloration of thought and perception becomes bleached out. Memories and their affects become disconnected and/or repressed; percepts and their affects are denied. Psychoanalysis, through verbalization, undoes repression; art, through sensuous forms, counteracts denial. Both restore feeling, or, more precisely, awareness of affect to thought and perception, broaden the integrative scope of the ego's reality-testing, and thus contribute to the ongoing mastery of inner and outer reality.

This book draws and expands upon its predecessor, *The Power of Form—A Psychoanalytic Approach to Aesthetic Form* (G.J. Rose 1980). The aim of both is to develop and refine the concept of sublimation by continuing the explorations in art that Ernst Kris began in 1952. The key conception in the earlier book was the recognition that each of the coordinates of orientation to reality—space, time, person—has a double aspect that is harmoniously accommodated in a work of art. To the extent that the work of art does this successfully, it is an idealized model of the task the mind faces in attempting to reconcile the double aspects of space, time, and person. Psychologically speaking, the structure of aesthetic form and of the mind are in resonance, each "imitating" the action of the other. Art and the aesthetic experience would thus appear to have a biological significance: helping to resharpen the coordinates of orientation in the evolving reality of the present.

Trauma and Mastery is also concerned with the problem of mastery in a fluid reality. The earlier work led to a focus on ongoing reorientation; the present one, to overcoming the splitting-off of feeling from thought and perception that takes place in the normal as well as the pathological attrition of daily life.

Trauma and Mastery is addressed to a wide audience, one that is interested in psychoanalysis and the arts, but by no means limited to professionals. This naturally presents problems of exposition. I have attempted to be as specific and as lucid as the material permits, and to preserve both readability and integrity, avoided technical terms or jargon as far as possible, while continuing to confront fundamental issues in specific terms.

In practice, this often turns out to be an impossible ideal. For example, any discussion of music that aims to be more than merely inspirational requires some technical referents. Effort has been made to make them comprehensible. Likewise, such basic principles of psychoanalysis as "primary and secondary processes" demand to be dealt with on their own grounds to do them justice. In the interest of accessibility, however, these concepts are also rendered into such everyday terms as imagination and knowledge.

Toward keeping the text readable for a wider audience, the material unfolds in roughly the order of increasing novelty and complexity. Thus, the opening chapters have a more familiar character. Chapter 1 is largely historical and cultural, and speculates on what personal factors may have influenced Freud to assert (in *Dostoevsky and Parricide*) that art was inaccessible to psychoanalysis. Chapter 2 includes a mini-pathography of Dostoevsky along traditional lines of classical analytic studies of an artist and his work. Both chapters touch on normal and pathological "splitting": Freud's tendency to form spiritual partnerships in the service of creativity is extended to literary "doubles." Dostoevsky dealt creatively with personal problems of love and hate, first by writing *The Double*, the story of a man pathologically "split" by intolerable conflict; then by continuing to work these problems through in contrasting ways in consecutive works.

The third chapter turns from creative to clinical imagination. It makes use of the striking coincidence that both Dostoevsky and a Texan of dull, normal intelligence had almost the same traumatic memory from youth: seeing a horse being beaten to death. In attempting to master this trauma, both obeyed the familiar principle of turning a passive experience into an active one. During a dissociated state, the cowboy acted it out in a brutal murder, after which he was totally amnesic. The novelist wrote *Crime and Punishment*, in which the young Raskolnikov dreams his creator's memory, then awakens with the conviction that he is going to commit murder—and does.

Obviously, there is an enormous difference between committing murder and writing a novel about murder. On the surface there is little relation between unreflective homicidal behavior and the slow, reflective unfolding of creative writing. The former is characteristic of the "short-circuiting" of the primary process that governs the unconscious mental system, and the latter illustrates the typical "long-circuiting" of the secondary process and the conscious system of the mind.

Closer examination, however, reveals an extraordinary similarity in terms of organizational power, that is, the ego's integrative capacity, The degree of *unconscious* integration, on many levels simultaneously, that went into the act of murder was hardly less than the *conscious* craftsmanship that went into the novel. This highlights not only the classic formulation that the ego operates both consciously and unconsciously, but also that the ego's integrative function is capable of an equally high order of complexity on both levels.

This point receives its clearest clinical documentation in chapter 4—a contribution to the sparse analytic literature on multiple personality disorder. The imaginary characters disowned and split off from conscious awareness by their "author," the victim of this disorder, are contrasted in chapter 5 with forms of splitting and reintegration of creative imagination.

Both the imaginary characters of multiple personality disorder and the fictional characters "invited" into the world of literature by the novelist may enter the minds of their originators out of the blue and refuse to disappear. Multiple personality disorder and fiction-writing are further linked by the factors of traumatic overstimulation (external and verified, in the former; internal and postulated, in the latter) and the splitting, integration, and dramatization of part-aspects of the mind. The victim of multiple personality disorder unconsciously creates a world of his or her own in order to escape from an unbearable reality. The novelist, "suffering" from what has been termed an "irritable imagination," consciously fashions an imaginary world. It is postulated that both draw upon the young child's capacity, when first emerging from a sense of psychological unity with the mother, to mold reality as though it were a plastic, malleable medium—creating an individual mixture that reflects inner needs and outer forces.

Chapter 6 continues the theme of trauma and mastery by turning to the wider cultural scene of art and, particularly, modern music. The prevalence of unpredictable violence and senseless death has become a fact of contemporary life. It is no longer possible either to deny its mounting intensity or to view the expectation of imminent disaster as being just a familiar sign of irrational anxiety—of great distress to the person experiencing it but of no wider moment. While most of us manage, by and large, to evade such awareness, recent generations of artists, being sensitive antennae in the world in which we all live, have been mirroring and countering it.

Like contemporary literature and art, some modern music responds to the cacaphony, fragmentation, discontinuity, and, above all, the unpredictability of life by attempting to restructure the sense of time within its own manageable, aesthetic microcosm. By so doing, art offers its audience examples of the creative transformation of stress. The harmonic innovations of Arnold Schoenberg and the rhythmic innovations of Charlie Parker are taken as cases in point—reflections of a major shift in the contemporary sense of time. Without excluding the possibility of personal factors on the part of Schoenberg and Parker, a clinical vignette supplies a possible clue to the cultural meaning and nature of this change: the sudden, totally unexpected death of a woman's young daughter led to the restructuring of her personal sense of time in ways that were analogous to some contemporary music.

In all these examples, the imagination splits and reintegrates in various ways, attempting to master past trauma and the anticipation of future trauma. Bringing this material to bear on the question of how psychoanalysis and art compare and contrast in facilitating reintegrative mastery is the task of the final chapters.

Psychoanalysis and the creative imagination draw together the branches of art and thought into a climate of sensibility. It is therefore not surprising that the writing of *Trauma and Mastery* should have benefited from the interdisciplinary climate of the Yale University Kanzer Seminars in Psychoanalysis and the Humanities, where each participant is a scholar in but one field yet an amateur of many. *Trauma and Mastery* is intended to speak to scholars and amateurs alike who are nourished by a humanistic atmosphere that reflects the interconnectedness of life—a "university" in the original sense of the word.

"BEFORE THE PROBLEM OF THE CREATIVE ARTIST ANALYSIS MUST, ALAS, LAY DOWN ITS ARMS"

With this famous dictum, Freud (1928 [1927], 177) began his paper on "Dostoevsky and Parricide." He never heeded his own caution. Not only did he write a number of important papers on art and artists, but his superb literary style won him the Goethe Prize and led to his nomination for the Nobel Prize in Literature.

What did this contradiction between his prohibition and practice signify? There is much to suggest that, in contrast to his unwavering belief in science, [1] and his admiration, gift, and aspiration for creative writing (Ticho 1986), Freud's feelings about art and artists were profoundly mixed. Placing "the problem of the creative artist" beyond the purview of psychoanalytic investigation was one means by which he distanced psychoanalysis from art. Art was the province of illusion,

---

1. While insisting that psychoanalysis was a science, Freud held that, like astronomy's, its validity stood independent of a fundamental tenet of scientific method—the need for experimental verification. To an experimental psychologist he offered: "Still, it can do no harm" (quoted from a 1934 letter; Rosenzweig 1986, 38).

and however much great art might provide brilliant intuitive insights, psychoanalysis was developed as a science, a science devoted to discovering hidden psychological truths—and Freud's identity was clearly that of a man of science, a seeker of truth.

Given this climate of values, the direction was set for future generations of analysts to emphasize the scientific aspects of psychoanalysis, and downplay the artistic. The application of psychoanalysis to the arts did not keep pace with ongoing developments in the field: applied analysis, when not reduced to a parlor game with "analysands" who cannot talk back (Lewin 1946), was long characterized by either recklessness or avoidance.

Since Freud's attitudes determined the later course of psychoanalytic history, and especially the relationship of psychoanalysis to art, it is appropriate to speculate on the personal meaning of his mixed feelings toward art and artists (in contrast to writers). Needless to say, this is in no way meant as yet another attempt to "analyze" him.

FREUD'S VIEWS ON ART AND ARTISTS

Telescoping their gradual development into capsule form, Freud's views were as follows: Like child's play, art starts out as a form of escape from reality. Thanks to the artist's special gifts, however, it is also a mode of return to childhood and even of triumph. It taps sources of pleasure in the unconscious that make it possible to enjoy and master the most painful experiences. In the process, it may satisfy the highest personal and cultural ideals and even lead to the discovery of new truths.

Among the drawbacks of Freudian aesthetic theory is that it tends to overdichotomize: reality/fantasy, science/art, reality/pleasure, intellect/emotion. And in spite of frequent disclaimers, it tends also to correlate art with neurosis.

In fairness it should be said that the closed system paradigm of the nineteenth century encouraged such categorizing. While Freud's views on art revolved largely around the issue of the relative roles of reality and fantasy, traditional writers on aesthetics at that time were accustomed to drawing a similar distinction—between intellect and feeling. Hanslick (1885, 11), for example, pointed out that "the older writers on aesthetics" kept making a "dilemma" of the contrast between feeling and and intellect in art, "quite oblivious of the fact that the main point at issue lies halfway between."

The contrast between art and science seems to fall easily into the same either/or categories: art as a flight, if often playful and pleasurable, into emotional subjectivity; science exemplifying arduous and altruistic work toward objective, intellectual truth. This dichotomy implicitly involves two others, reality/pleasure and intellect/emotion.

Although Freud well understood from the outset that the relationship between art and neurosis was more complex, he nevertheless tended to link nonverbal art with neurosis, just as he tended to link verbalization with logical, healthy thinking processes. His approach to nonverbal art was to attempt to "understand" it in order to "explain" its effect. If he could not understand and explain its effect, he could not enjoy it. His inability to "explain" the effect that music had upon him rendered him, he stated, "almost incapable of obtaining any pleasure" from it (Freud 1914, 211).

With painting, too, it was almost as if he assumed that painters painted scenes that could just as well be expressed in words. (Delacroix is said to have remarked that a painting that can be thus "explained" was not worth painting.) Perhaps his epochal discovery that the pictorial aspects making up the manifest dream could be "read" like a rebus to unlock the meaning of the latent content led him to assume this.

This overvaluation of verbalization at the *expense* of art contrasts with Nietzsche's remark, for example (in *The Birth of Tragedy*), that art must be seen as the necessary *complement* to rational discourse. Furthermore, depending on language as the key to nonverbal experience is likely to succeed only in breaking the key off in the lock, destroying both.

In line with the high premium he placed on verbalization, Freud greatly admired creative writers and had little use for nonrepresentational art—naturalism, symbolism, impressionism—or for music in any form. In a letter to Pfister (July 21, 1920), he referred to the German expressionists with "aversion" as "cranks" and agreed that "these people lack the right to claim the name of artist" (E. Freud 1960, 330–31). After an evening in an artist's company, he wrote to Jones: "Meaning is little to these men; all they care for is line, shape, agreement of contours. They are given up to the *lustprinzip*" (Jones 1957, 412).

As for music, his indifference to it to the point of aversion was perhaps as heretical in a city like Vienna as was his calling attention to infantile sexuality. He told James J. Putnam that he had no ear for music, and in the Count Thun dream he confessed his inability to carry a tune (Freud 1900, 208). With a few exceptions, music afforded him hardly any pleasure at all (Jones 1957). Most of his references to it are intellectual or literary—for example, attending to the words rather than the music of *The Magic Flute*. It is said that as a youngster he insisted that his sister's piano be removed because her practice interfered with his study. His son Martin relates that none of Freud's children ever studied a musical instrument.

Freud himself attributed his indifference to music and nonrepresentational art (as well as his opposition to certain cultural forms such as religion) to his commitment to science and rationality. Meaning was almost everything to Freud. He ignored nonmimetic, abstract art in the first place because he had no appreciation for its aesthetic qualities of form. Second, he needed a content—a hidden meaning—capable of interpretation by a hermeneutic approach along the lines of psychoanalysis (Spector 1972).

FREUD AND BRÜCKE AND HELMHOLTZ

Ernst Brücke and Hermann von Helmholtz were the important father-figures of Freud's years as a biology student at Brücke's Institute of Physiology. Brücke and the more famous Helmholtz both studied with Johannes Müller, the founder of "scientific" medicine in Germany. All represented the disciplined scientist that Freud hoped to become one day.

Himself a scientist, not a physician, Professor Brücke was also an instructor in anatomy at the Berlin Art Academy. His father had been a successful portrait painter. Like his father, Brücke revered classical line as the mainstay of ideal art. Moreover, it would seem that Brücke believed that the aesthetic ideal could be described by scientific method. Shortly before his death, he published a book on the human figure (Brücke 1891) in which he identifies the objective details that do or do not constitute beauty, for example, in the neck. The book has been characterized as "one of the last significant instances in Europe of the attempt to root artistic expression materially in observed anatomy" (Fuller 1980, 51). Freud's artistic taste, too, it appears, never departed from this same standard, remaining attached primarily to the art of classical antiquity. Helmholtz saw physiology as an extension of physics. He and Brücke stressed that living organisms are phenomena of the physical world: systems of atoms moved by forces the sum of which remains constant in every isolated system, according to the principle of the conservation of energy.

The impact of this closed-system model on Freud was such that he longed to produce a parallel psychology. His "Project" (1895), written shortly after the deaths of Brücke (1892) and Helmholtz (1895), incorporated their principles in its suggestion that the psychic apparatus worked to reduce the level of its own excitation.

Loyalty to these first principles of scientific faith may have played a role in Freud's subsequent break from Jung. For whatever else may have been involved in their complex personal relationship, Jung stood at an opposite philosophical pole from Freud's mentor, Brücke. Aside from his interests in religion, mythology, mysticism, and the occult, (to which Freud also felt dangerously attracted), Jung believed in philosophical vitalism. This is the doctrine that life processes are not explicable by the laws of physics and chemistry alone, that life is not mechanistically determined, but, rather, in some part *self-determining*. Jung held that no psychological fact can ever be exhaustively explained in terms of causality, because, as a living phenomenon, it is continually evolving and creative. Whereas psychoanalysts today might find nothing disturbing about vitalism, it was incompatible with the Brücke-Helmholtzian model on which Freud was constantly struggling to base his science.

Peter Fuller (1980) suggests that it is this personal nexus of father-son conflicts that informs the circumstances and style of "The *Moses* of Michelangelo" (Freud 1914a). Written in a mere matter of days, it was published anonymously in 1914. After long hesitation, during which he referred to the paper as a "joke" and a "love-child," Freud "legitimatized this non-analytical child" by putting his own name to it ten years later (letter to Edoardo Weiss, April 12, 1933, as quoted in Jones 1955, 367). Like Moses, Freud appeared in danger of letting slip the tables of the law—the neurophysiological model— he had received from the hands of his revered father figures, Brücke and Helmholtz. At the same time, he was bitterly fighting to preserve the integrity of psychoanalysis against the revisionism of Adler and of Jung, his designated son.

According to Fuller, "The *Moses* of Michelangelo" represents Freud's attempt to deny that psychoanalysis was abetting the decline of the mechanistic physics of his father figures. The paper expressed Freud's wish to make psychoanalysis less speculative and more scientific, in the spirit of Brücke—that is, based on anatomy, observation, measurement. Thus, though it was written not much later (1913) than the *Leonardo* paper (published in 1910), in style it contrasted sharply with the latter, an imaginative elegant work probably written at the height of the German Expressionist movement in painting (a connection Freud would not have appreciated).

"The *Moses* of Michelangelo," on the other hand, could well pass as a "scientific" document. Full of "objective" data—citations of precedents, attention to measurement and anatomical details—it totally avoids psychological speculation about Michelangelo or his work. In method it resembles the writings of the physician Morelli, which Freud had encountered while studying with Brücke. In his book on bodily beauty, Brücke had pointed out that the ancients had contemplated the human figure daily and hourly. Freud's preparations for the *Moses* paper follwed Brücke's lead: "For three lonely September weeks in 1913 I stood every day in the church in front of the statue, studied it, *measured* it [my italics] sketched it, until I captured the under-standing for it. . . ." (Jones 1955 367).[2]

Fuller suggests plausibly that the style of the *Moses* paper, as well as the ten-year delay in claiming its authorship, reflect Freud's conflicts with his psychoanalytic sons—especially the artistic, speculative, intuitionist inclinations of Jung—and his materialist, scientist father figures, Brücke and Helmholtz. It also seems likely that these aspects of the *Moses* paper reflect a conflict in Freud's mind between art and science, as well as his own mixed feelings about art—his love of literature, attraction to sculpture, indifference to music, and antipa-thy to nonrepresentational art.

What did the artist stand for in his mind? Could this *meaning* have contributed to Freud's declaration that analysis must lay down its arms before the problem of the artist? We will pursue these questions in the rest of this chapter.

FREUD AND DALI

Because Freud's primary identity was as a scientist, throughout his career he struggled to keep psychoanalytic science free of the contami-

---

2. It is interesting to contrast this scientistic approach to art with the attitude of two painters. Picasso (1935, quoted in Chipp 1968, 271): "Art is not the application of a canon of beauty but what the instinct and the brain can conceive beyond any canon. When we love a woman we don't start measuring her limbs." And Matisse (p. 137): "The characteristics of a drawing . . . do not depend on the exact copying of natural forms, nor on the patient assembling of exact details, but on the profound feeling of the artist before the objects which he has chosen . . . and the spirit of which he has penetrated." He discusses four self-portraits, crayon-line drawings, with completely different outlines, yet all expressing unmistakably the same man: "The . . . organic inexactitude in these drawings has not harmed the expression of the intimate character and inherent truth of the personality, but on the contrary has helped to clarify it. . . . In each one . . . the truth of the character is expressed, the same light bathes them all . . .—all impossible to put into words, but easy to do by dividing a piece of paper into spaces by a simple line. . . . L'exactitude n'est pas la vérité" (pp. 138–39).

nants of art, and himself from being seduced by its attractions. *Understanding* was an absolute prerequisite for *experiencing* pleasure from art. "Some rationalistic, or perhaps analytic, turn of mind in me rebels against being moved by a thing without knowing why I am thus affected and what it is that affects me" (Freud 1914a, 211).

This almost automatic recoiling and re-approaching in order to gain mastery through understanding is illustrated by an incident at the end of his life. In June 1938 a meeting took place between Sigmund Freud and Salvador Dali. For Dali, aged thirty-four, the meeting with Freud, then eighty-two, was the culmination of years of pursuit of his idol. Dali had worshipped his father, who, in turn, had treated him as a most precious child—especially so since an older gifted son had died before Dali's birth (Romm and Slap 1983).

How very differently the two men experienced the meeting may be judged by what each wrote about it later. Dali had reason to be bitterly disappointed. He wrote that Freud hardly acknowledged his presence. Freud spoke about him to Stefan Zweig (who had arranged the meeting) as if Dali were not there. When Dali tried to interest him in a paper he had written, "Freud exclaimed, addressing Stefan Zweig, 'I have never seen a more complete example of a Spaniard. What a fanatic!'" (Dali 1942, 24).

Yet the very next day Freud wrote to Zweig: "I really owe you thanks for bringing yesterday's visitor. For until now I have been inclined to regard the surrealists, who apparently have adopted me as their patron saint, as complete fools (let us say 95 percent, as with alcohol). That young Spaniard, with his candid fanatical eyes and his undeniable technical mastery, has changed my estimate. It would indeed be very interesting to investigate analytically how he came to create that picture" (Jones 1957, 235). (Freud was referring to the painting *Narcissus*, which Dali had presented to him).

These totally different perceptions of the same meeting reflected not only personal differences but cultural and historical processes (Rose 1983). Although Dali had already been expelled from the surrealist movement and was turning back toward the High Renaissance of Raphael, he more than any other individual personified

"L'exactitude n'est pas la vérité." Four self-portraits by Matisse. (Photo archives Matisse © SPADEM 1982.) Reprinted from H. B. Chipp, *Theories of Modern Art: A Source Book by Artists and Critics* (University of California Press, 1968).

In a drawing, Matisse said, there is "an inherent truth which must be disengaged from the outward appearance of the object to be represented. This is the only truth that matters" (Chipp, 138). In these four self-portraits, the upper part of the face is the same, but the lower is completely different—massive, elongated, pointed, or bearing no resemblance to any of the above. Yet they all unmistakably represent the same man—attentive and reserved.

surrealism to the general public. It was he who had made surrealism a common term in all languages—as much by his genius for publicity, his moustache, and his quotable utterances as by his paintings. His fashionable flamboyance ultimately raised serious questions about the integrity of his work. But before he turned his way of life into a surrealist publicity stunt, he had sought to make his art a pictorial documentation of Freudian theories. His writing likewise. For example, the article on "paranoia" which he pressed on Freud had to do not with psychiatric paranoia but, rather, with what he referred to as "critical paranoia"—a method of inducing and harnessing multiple images of persecution or megalomania. He would start a painting with the first image that came to mind and go on from one association to the next, attempting to lift the restrictions of control and thus tap a flow of delirious phenomena. He (romantically) assumed that these would lie close to or at the heart of creativity itself.

This assumption of the close correspondence between uncontrolled, passionate, Dionysian spontaneity, on the one hand, and creativity, on the other, was inherent in surrealism. Actually, Dali was borrowing from another surrealist, Max Ernst, and his method of *frottage*. Ernst was making a deliberate effort to exclude all conscious mental guidance, such as reason, taste, and morals, in order to become a spectator at the birth of his own work (Ernst 1948). By restraining his activity and accepting his passivity, he discovered a sudden intensification of visual faculties. What emerged was a succession of contradictory images superimposed on each other, as in a half-sleeping twilight state.

All the surrealists believed, with Freud, in the central importance of the unconscious for art and poetry. The Surrealist Manifesto of 1924 was written by André Breton, a serious student of psychoanalysis. The surrealists conceived of the canvas as a blank tablet on which the artist inscribed the visual associations issuing from the depth of the mind. The element of chance or randomness, of coincidence, like a slip of the tongue or pen, or automatic writing, as well as the dream and the irrational, were royal roads to the unconscious.

It seems apparent now that the surrealists were engaged in a serious study of the conditions of inspiration and creativity. Moreover, they had made two fundamental discoveries: (1) they succeeded in inducing some of the specific ways in which imagination functions, such as by condensation, ambiguity, and the tendency to flash-like immediacy, and (2) they were attempting to harness these to the slow, methodical thinking mode of careful observation and detailed recording.

Two further things should be said about the surrealists: their politics and their origins. Emerging from four years of the bloodiest war in history, many of the post-World War I generation felt betrayed by the institutions, philosophies, and cultural heroes of the Establishment. Since it seemed that tradition and conventional reason had plunged them into World War I, they insisted that nongovernment was better than government, and the irrational superior to reason. Implicit in the surrealist program was the necessity for revolt against institutions. Thus, surrealism was a revolutionary movement of considerable ferocity, not only in literature and art but also in politics. In their revolutionary zeal, many surrealists embraced Communism and (it must have seemed fitting at the time) Freudianism.

Regarding origins. The dadaists had long explored some of the same phenomena as the surrealists. However, there was a growing disillusionment with dada because it, too, was becoming institutionalized. Therefore, the surrealists turned back to the late nineteenth century for their cultural prophets and to the French symbolist poets—especially Rimbaud, Baudelaire, Verlaine, and Mallarmé.

Rimbaud was steeped in Greek and Oriental mystical religious readings. He thought of the poet as one possessed of divine madness, like Prometheus, the thief of the sacred flame. Long before Freud (Rimbaud wrote in the early 1870s), he was explicitly concerned with the as yet undefined unconscious, as well as with the implications of dreams and automatisms. He believed that a rigidly disciplined madness and alienation would lead to the desired visionary state. Confusion and disorder of the senses were to be cultivated by the poet—not self-indulgently, hedonistically, but systematically and patiently, in order to explore an unknown territory of sensuous imagination, using words as magical, mysterious invocations. Thus, the Surrealist Manifesto of 1924 only codified ideas that had been in the air for fifty years, adding a heavy dash of Freudianism as well as the Communist party-line.

French symbolism was not only the chief source of surrealism; more importantly, it was one of the main intellectual currents in Europe at the time of the birth and early years of psychoanalysis (Peyre 1974). Also, like psychoanalysis, symbolism searched the farther reaches of mental life for the many more or less hidden meanings condensed in a single sign. Despite failures and having almost fallen into oblivion, the symbolist movement in France gave rise to similar schools in England, Germany, and other countries and influenced almost all eminent twentieth-century poets, novelists (Joyce, Proust, Stein), dramatists (Maeterlinck), critics, and composers (Debussy).

The symbolist movement in France was at its height toward the end of the nineteenth century. Except for Baudelaire, who died in 1867, its most illustrious figures were flourishing at the time Freud worked at Jean Martin Charcot's clinic in Paris (October 1885 to February 1886) and for the following five years, when Freud was absorbed in the translation of Charcot and Bernheim. Yet, aside from the invisible but powerful influence of zeitgeist, there is little evidence that symbolism influenced Freud. On the surface, the contrary would seem to be the case.

The meeting between Dali and Freud in June of 1938 was remarkable in several respects. What divergent courses these two men had traveled! The young Dali—still intoxicated with the pictorial representations of the Unconscious and the Id; revolting against Western rationalism and its cultural institutions; believing, in keeping with the symbolist tradition of Rimbaud, in the necessity of overwhelming the spectator (or reader, or patient) with explosive shocks to explore in depth the felt mystery beyond consciousness—, was, finally, a supersophisticated aesthete on his way to becoming one of the first proponents of Radical Chic.

By what route Freud had come we well know. Though he studied hypnosis in the respectability of Charcot's clinic, it never lost its taint of black magic and Viennese mesmerism. Nor did Freud, at least in Vienna, every wholly overcome the taint of disreputability. Long rejected by the academic establishment, he was now the founder and patron saint of his own establishment. He had accomplished a revolution in world thought. Yet all the while, Freud remained a thoroughgoing traditionalist in matters of personal taste.

It is all the more remarkable, then, that this ailing eighty-two-year-old man should, on brief contact with Dali, acknowledge that he had to revise his estimate of modern art. One might imagine that that was because he was taken with Dali's enthusiasm for the unconscious, but this was not the case at all. Freud had by now traveled far from the early formulation of the id (which still entranced Dali) to an explication of the functions of the ego. Freud, the systematic explorer of the unconscious, said to Dali, its most flagrant exploiter, "What interests me in your art is not the unconscious but the conscious" (Arnason 1968, 361).

The next day, on further reflection, Freud wrote to Zweig that what changed his estimate was "that young Spaniard, with his candid fanatical eyes and his *undeniable technical mastery.*". . . It would indeed be very interesting to investigate analytically how he came to create that picture" (Jones 1957, 235; italics added).

What elements were operating overnight between the original opinion and its drastic revision the next day? We know what went into the irritated rejection: Dali was a surrealist ("lunatic"), compounded by being a young Spaniard ("fanatic"). Likewise, it is clear what it was that aroused Freud's analytical curiosity about Dali's creativity: Dali's apparent accessibility ("candid eyes"), and the obvious control he exercised over his craft, even in the face of his passionate ("fanatic") nature.

Since all of these factors were apparent at the same time, why did it take until the next day for Freud's analytical interest to manifest itself? My conjectures, in order of increasing speculation, are: (1) The meeting stirred a conflict in Freud between derogatory and idealizing attitudes toward art and artists. (2) He was repelled then fascinated with Dali's combination of passion and control as it echoed similar duel elements in his own nature. It has only recently been elucidated (Vermorel 1986) to what a large extent Freud made use of, and transformed, German *romantic* conceptions ranging from dreams, the unconscious, repression, instincts, bisexuality, to jokes and aesthetics. Did the two sides of Dali—passion and control—remind Freud of a parallel dualism within himself: the depth of the *romanticism* existing alongside his espousal of objective, scientific enlightenment? (3) Since Freud candidly acknowledged unruly elements of bisexuality in other areas of his life, as in his relationship to Jung, did they come into play here too? If he fought his own tendencies to romanticism while highlighting the scientific aspects of his identity, was it because of the feminine connotations romanticism shares with art as contrasted to the masculine implications of science?

Although surrealism and surrealist artists represented something wild and uncontrolled—a bunch of lunatics around the fringe of psychoanalytic science—Freud could still be attracted into attempting to *understand* their art when his attention was drawn to evidence of Dali's technical competence. Perhaps this provided him with the reassurance of structure that enabled him to distance himself from whatever disturbing meanings artist *qua* artist held for him.

For further light on these personal meanings we would do well to turn to literature, which he loved, and his relations with creative writers. A paper entitled "Freud and his Literary Doubles" (Kanzer 1976), is worth summarizing here.

FREUD'S LITERARY DOUBLES

Freud appears to have established several "doubles" relationships with writers, among them Arthur Schnitzler, Romain Rolland, and Thomas Mann. These "doubles" evoked uncanny reactions in him, a mixture of familiar and unfamiliar feelings, that both drew him powerfully toward those persons and also led him to avoid them. For example, to Schnitzler: "I will make a confession which for my sake I must ask you to keep to yourself. . . . I think I have avoided you from a kind of reluctance to meet my double. . . . Whenever I get deeply absorbed in your beautiful creations I invariably seem to find beneath their poetic surface the very presuppositions, interests, and conclusions which I know to be my own. . . . All this moves me with an uncanny feeling of familiarity" (E. Freud 1960, 339). To Rolland: "I may confess to you that I have rarely experienced that mysterious attraction of one human being for another as vividly as I have with you. It is somehow bound up, perhaps, with the awareness of our being so different" (p. 406).

Typically, Freud would point out in birthday messages to these writers that he was older, they younger; that they had an astonishing intuitive grasp of what he could only painstakingly and laboriously discover through research; that they created illusions which provided comfort and refreshment for readers while he destroyed illusions; that, consequently, "my words and ideas strike people as alien, whereas to you all hearts are open" (p. 256); and that "I finally came to the point of envying the author whom hitherto I had admired" (p. 251).

What personal significance did these literary artists have for Freud that they aroused in him what can only be described as intense ambivalence? By analytic detective work, based on Freud's correspondence with these writers and the papers he sometimes included or referred to, Kanzer (1976) adduced a prototypical relationship to a younger brother, Alexander, together with a characteristic fantasy.

It is relevant to recall that Freud had two half-brothers, twenty-four and twenty years older than himself. From the marriage of the elder of these came a nephew one or two years older than Freud, a niece about the same age, and another niece three years younger. Since they lived nearby, uncle, nephew, and nieces were like siblings together. Of Freud's mother's children, he was the oldest, followed by a brother who died at eight months of age, when Freud was nineteen months old; then by five sisters; and, when Freud was ten, by a brother named, following Freud's own suggestion (Jones 1953, 18), Alexander, after Alexander the Great. Thus, Freud was, in effect, the second of eleven siblings born in as many years.

A letter Freud wrote (E. Freud 1960, 432–34) at age eighty to

Thomas Mann, sixty-one, provides a glimpse into the meaning of their relationship. He suggested that Napoleon's older brother Joseph had first been a hated rival who later became excessively admired by the younger Bonaparte. Freud offered this as the theme for a story that Mann might write.

While Mann never followed this suggestion, it is interesting that four years later, only shortly after Freud's death, he did publish "The Transposed Heads" (Mann 1940). Based on an Indian myth, it tells the story of two youths, Nanda and Shridaman, who were sworn to a friendship so intense that their admiration for each other turned to a "yearning of mutual exchange and unity" (p. 5). After having secretly observed a beautiful girl, Sita, bathing nude in a sylvan pool, they sealed their friendship by chewing sweet betel. The younger said to the older: "You are so necessary to me, my elder brother; what I have not you have, and you are my friend, so that it is almost as though I had it myself" (p. 49).

Nanda, the younger, woos Sita successfully on his friend's behalf, and the marriage is consummated. But it turns out that Nanda is also in love with Sita and she with him. Apparently almost having what the other has is not quite the same as having it oneself. The friends decapitate themselves and Sita is about to do likewise when the World-Mother Goddess tells her to place the heads back upon the bodies to bring them back to life. Sita does this, but in her haste transposes the heads.

Shridaman and Nanda are thereupon restored to life, but now which one was the husband of Sita and father of the child stirring within her womb? After a long and unsuccessful effort to resolve this problem a solution satisfactory to all is hit upon: Sita's son puts the torch to the funeral pyre of his mother lying between Nanda and Shridaman, and all three are united on death's fiery bed.

Proceeding now to further clues to the significance of Freud's literary alter egos, what were the papers that Freud alluded to in his correspondence with these younger writers? They were "Group Psychology and the Analysis of the Ego" (1921) and "A Disturbance of Memory on the Acropolis" (1936). The former contains the idea that the younger son, being the mother's favorite, is destined for success in life; it was he who, after the murder of the primal father by the group as a whole, invented the self-serving myth that he had accomplished the deed single-handedly and probably replaced the father; by dint of this lie, the youngest son became "the first epic poet; and the advance was achieved in his imagination. This poet disguised the truth with lies in accordance with his longing. He invented the heroic myth. . . . The lie of the heroic myth culminates in the deification of the hero" (Freud 1921, 136—37).

The later paper was written as a birthday gift to Rolland and has to do with a trip Freud made to Greece with his brother, Alexander, who was, like Rolland, ten years his junior. The theme of jealousy, ambition, and guilt for surpassing all family rivals is again prominent.

In short, the aged Freud appears to set aside hatred and rivalry and relinquish to these younger literary "doubles" the role of mother's favorite son. Responding to the universal "trauma" of failing to win mother's exclusive love, he reluctantly lays down his arms before the problem of younger sibs who seemingly have magical access to mother's love. For himself, not the alluring seductiveness and deception of Art, but the way of the father or the unsung hero—a posture, rather, of lonely but *manly* pride in the arduous and thankless task of advancing the cause of Truth in the teeth of resistance and unpopularity.

If all this sounds like transparent oedipal family romance and literary romanticism, with elements of unconscious feminine identification to compensate for the loss of mother, it should come as no surprise that the world's first self-analysis left important issues unresolved or that some of these issues showed up in "symptomatic" behavior—as, for example, in the aged Freud's sudden swing of attitude from contempt to admiration for the brash, precociously successful young artist Dali.

Nor would it be fitting to decry that he who pioneered so much did not accomplish even more. The discovery of the unconscious left many matters still to be explored. Among these: the establishment of the earliest sense of reality, and the separation of self from (m)other—

issues probably crucial to the psychology of art and the creative imagination.

In order to begin to consider how psychoanalytic and artistic experience may overlap in some ways, it has been necessary first of all to set forth Freud's attempt to project art beyond the reach of psychoanalysis. In this chapter we have tried to understand this "prohibition" by placing it within the framework of his primary identity as a scientist, his mixed feelings about art and artists, and the personal meanings of sibling rivalry and homoerotism that this may have had for him. This has brought us to the fact that Freud was powerfully drawn toward literary "doubles" and, at the same time, felt compelled to avoid them. How are we to view this?

The tendency to discover spiritual kinships, even to the point of sensing one's own double in the other person, might be characterized in several ways. Idealized self-objects, transitional object relatedness, body-ego deformations—all emphasize its rootedness in an early symbiotic stage of development and the intense needs for nurturance this implies. To this extent they all tend to pathologize the phenomenon as regressive.

On the other hand, terms such as "spiritual unity" and "soulmates" tend to romanticize it. Similarly, it is possible to "normalize" the sense of having a double and stress that healthy and ill, gifted and ungifted individuals alike share the need for reassuring confirmation from the external world; some degree of objectification, acknowledgment, positive feedback is necessary to affirm one's sense of self and self-esteem.

As we will discuss in detail later, the sensitivity of many creative individuals seems to express itself as a search for harmony between inner and outer worlds. Involving sensorimotor resonances and affinities, the search may be experienced as both intensely personal and solitary. Thus, supportive partnerships and working alliances along the way may be necessary to sustain creative productivity. What was once invoked as a prerequisite for creative fulfillment—namely, the blessing of the heavenly Muse—commonly has its more earthly equivalents: the need for the generous patron, supportive sponsor, or, at the very least, the encouragement of a colleague—even the constancy of a forgiving spouse. Perhaps the experience of the benevolent double should be seen in that context: it offers the comforting sense that one is not only *not* alone but even has a double.

Yet these supportive relationships often turn out to be double-edged—as fragile as they are necessary. Freud, for example, was drawn to his literary "doubles" and compelled to avoid them at the same time. Earlier, he had also idealized Fliess and then Jung and, for a time, had formed intense working alliances with each of them in turn. These relationships did a great deal to stimulate his creativity. But disillusionment followed and led to falling out.

In the case of the Freud-Jung relationship, there were, of course, many objective and psychological factors to account for the disenchantment and alienation that took place, including the ubiquitous oedipal dynamics of admiration, homoerotism, envy, and hostility. In addition, however, the sheer intensity of the original need and the strength of the attraction might themselves dictate the necessity for distancing sooner or later in order to preserve the sense of one's own separate identity. For example, as J. Gedo (1983) has pointed out, the Freud-Jung letters are full of evidence of Freud's need of Jung: prompt replies had become important, he asked not to be forgotten during vacation, his personality had become "impoverished" through the reduction in correspondence during the holidays. Freud even temporarily entertained an irrational set of beliefs (as he had earlier with Fliess's numerology) in the form of Jung's parapsychological theory of precognition. As we will see later, Freud's fantasy that collaboration with Jung would eliminate any distinction between their respective achievements precisely mirrored the collaboration that actually did take place between Picasso and Braque.

It would seem that the overendowment of creative sensitivity requires affirmation; the capacity to make immediate and intuitive empathic connections is able to provide such affirmation. However, the resulting intensity of the near-merger relationship, together with its homosexual implications, may be such that periodic withdrawals or ruptures become necessary to redelineate self-boundaries and shore up the sense of separate self or identity. In other words, the creatively gifted individual might search for self-delineation in a cyclical fashion: turning in the direction of the outer world for intense, nuturant, close relations that provide confirming reflections; then needing to consolidate and re-establish separateness.

Obviously, any continuing differentiation requires a balance of breathing space as well as support, separateness, and distance in addition to intimacy. The creatively gifted are no different in this regard—only more so. Yet they present us with a paradox: their heightened sensitivity, their wide-ranging search for inner-outer correspondences, together with the ability to discern them and hone in quickly appears to carry with it a susceptibility to problems of permeable, diffuse boundaries and shifting, ambiguous self-image and sexual identity. This same susceptibility is found in individuals whose sense of self is overextended for *opposite* reasons—poor differentiation stemming either from lack of development or neurotic regression.

2

TRANSFORMATIONS OF AGGRESSION;
OR, HOW DOSTOEVSKY CAME
TO LOVE "BIG BROTHER"

The first chapter ended with introducing the discussion that will occupy us for some time—a consideration of the various forms of splitting that occur in clinical and creative processes—in order later to compare the reintegrative mastery that occurs in psychoanalysis and art.

A double is one form of splitting—a conscious or unconscious displacement to the external world of various idealized or despised aspects of the self. Freud experienced it as an uncanny mixture of familiarity and unfamiliarity; he felt a simultaneous attraction for and reluctance to meet creative writers like Schnitzler, Rolland, and Mann. In that they embodied and reflected aspects of himself that Freud valued highly, these were benevolent doubles. Because he also realized that these other men were quite different from him, the displacements were conscious.

For the creative writer, fictional characters, like doubles, also represent aspects of the self, split off and displaced to the outside world. In that they are products of the imagination, they are familiar, like imaginary companions; but because they may surprise even their author by sudden, unexpected motivations and actions, they may at the same time be unfamiliar, like dreams. Thus, for their author they fall midway between imaginary companions—familiar, conscious, controllable—and dream products—strange, surprising, possibly alien. Like doubles in life, dreams, and other displacements, they are at once close and distant.

In *The Double*, Dostoevsky used fictional characters to portray the subjective experience of being harassed by a *malevolent* double—one that represents the existence of *unconscious conflict* with unacceptable aspects of oneself and the wish to extrude them into the outside world. There is reason to believe that this conflict was precipitated by actual traumatic experiences in his life. Using dreams, fantasies, and other displacements, Dostoevsky went on in subsequent works—*Crime and Punishment* and "The Peasant Marey"—to elaborate and work out this intolerable conflict in two opposite ways. Thanks to the act of writing and the creation of fictional characters who could act as proxies for himself, both resolutions were vividly close to, yet at a safe remove from, the feelings associated with his original trauma.

The tradition of the double reaches as far back as ancient Egypt, where every man was believed to have a *Ka*, or soul, that was his exact likeness in miniature.[1] In Egyptian monuments, the *Ka* of a king is represented as a mannikin standing behind him—evidently a precursor of the homunculus, or magic dwarf, of later folklore. Greek mythology offers the related subject of reflections and mirroring. Narcissus's death, hopelessly entranced by his own reflection in the water, was the gods' punishment for his having spurned the nymph Echo, who was cursed with the opposite frustration. Speechless except to repeat the last words spoken in her presence, she can only mirror others.

Dostoevsky's *The Double* falls within a literary tradition studded with well-known titles. Shelley's Frankenstein and Stevenson's Mr. Hyde torment their creators with their untamed passions. Wilde's

---

1. For a classic essay on the subject, cf. Rank (1971). A recent psychoanalytic study of Dostoevsky is that of Dalton (1979).

picture of Dorian Grey reflects the inner corruption of its subject, so well-concealed behind his attractive facade.

These alter egos, who carry on lives of their own quite independent of their counterparts, are by no means always malevolent. Conrad's "secret sharer," Leggatt, is like a trusted and enlightening friend to the young sea captain, who is something of a stranger to himself.

The tradition of the double continues in contemporary literature and includes works by Dostoevsky's compatriot, Nabokov. At least four of his short stories center on this theme. In "A Forgotten Poet," an old man claims to be a young poet who is believed to have died fifty years before. In "Conversation Piece," a writer has a disreputable namesake who causes him all kinds of confusion. "Scenes from the Life of a Double Monster" is about one of a pair of Siamese twins. And "Terror" depicts the attacks of panic that accompany the protagonist's sense of having a double—looking in the mirror and not recognizing himself, suddenly sensing another person's presence in the room with him, abruptly feeling that familiar objects have been robbed of their quality of realness. If the double has a cathartic purpose in art, Nabokov offers another final twist in "Terror"; the double is exorcised. At the end of the story, the protagonist visits his dying mistress. Unseeing, in her delirium, she smiles at his imagined image. "My double died with her," he concludes, "[and] saved me from insanity" (Nabokov 1975, 121).

In Dostoevsky's *The Double*, secret rebelliousness against the authorities and hypocritical fawning are in such intense conflict with each other in the protagonist's mind that they cause his personality to split in two. Dostoevsky wrote the story at age twenty-five, and probably coincided with the period of his underground revolutionary activity.

The tale associated with Dostoevsky's subversive activity is well known. The secret meetings of the group of radical utopianists had been exposed; the existence of their illegal printing press had been discovered. Dostoevsky and his fellow prisoners were already before the firing squad, condemned to death for revolutionary activity when, at the last moment, the Tzar's reprieve arrived, commuting the death sentence. The young author was deported in chains to a penal colony in Siberia, there to serve a four-year sentence at hard labor, followed by four years' compulsory military duty.

The physical and mental pain of the prison experience amid the outcasts and misfits of society brought about a profound change of heart in the young Dostoevsky. He abandoned the liberal atheistic ideologies of Western Europe and turned to religion and the belief that Orthodox Russia was destined to be the spiritual leader of the world.

The detailed images of what went into the transformation of his attitudes toward authority are to be found in *Crime and Punishment*, written twenty years after *The Double* at age forty-five, and "The Peasant Marey," written ten years later. The murderous rage of the twenty-three-year-old protagonist of *Crime and Punishment*, Raskolnikov, refers to the "criminal" Dostoevsky before his arrest and deportation to Siberia. The pious genuflexions of "The Peasant Marey" refer to the penitent Dostoevsky at twenty-nine or thirty, undergoing his punishment in the penal colony.

THE DOUBLE: A ST. PETERSBURG EPIC

Yakov Golyadkin, a titular councilor, wakes up from a long sleep, not quite certain whether he is still dreaming or awake. He runs straight to the mirror, then to the window, then to his pocketbook. He has hired a fancy carriage for the whole day for twenty-five rubles. In full-dress coat, silk cravat, and boots, he goes out for a drive.

Soon a fashionable droshky drawn by a smart pair of Kazan horses drives up rapidly on his right. He is terrified to see that the gentleman inside is Andrey Filippovich, the section head of the office in which Golyadkin is employed as assistant to the chief clerk. (Perhaps Golyadkin was playing hookey.) It is impossible to hide from the astonished gaze of Andrey Filippovich.

"Bow or not? Call back or not? Recognize him or not?" our hero wonders in "indescribable" anguish. "Or pretend that I am not myself, but somebody strikingly like me, and look as though nothing

24

TABLE 1

Abbreviated Chronology of Dostoevsky's Life

Age	
−1 year	Brother Mikhail born
Born, Moscow (10/20/1821)	
1	Sister Varvara born
4	Brother Andrey born
8	Twin sisters born; one died within a few days
	Brother and sister born
10	Summers at Davaroe; episode of wolf terror
15 (2/27/1837)	Mother died. Travel with father and brother to
	St. Petersburg. Courier-horse episode
16	Separated from brother
17 (6/18/1839)	Father killed by serfs at age 50
25	First work published: *Poor Folk*
	Second work published: *The Double*
25−26	First evidence of epileptic fits
	Secret meetings with revolutionaries
27	Arrested, tried for treason, condemned to die
28	Reprieve from execution; sent to Siberia
29−33	Convict in Siberian penal colony
33−37	Service in army in Siberia
37	Married. Wife died. Brother died
39	*The House of the Dead*, memoirs of prison
45 (1866); 46	*Crime and Punishment, The Idiot*
55−58	*A Writer's Diary*, including "The Peasant Marey."
	The Brothers Karamazov
59	Died in St. Petersburg

were the matter? Simply not I, not I, and that's all," thinks Golyadkin, taking off his hat to his superior and keeping his eyes fixed upon him. "I'm . . . I'm all right," he whispers with an effort, "I'm . . . quite all right. I, it's not I—" (Dostoevsky [1846] 1950, 142).

Later, dropping in to see his doctor for no apparent reason, he volunteers: "There's no need for me to conceal it. . . . I'm an unimportant man, as you know; but, fortunately for me, I do not regret being and unimportant man. Quite the contrary . . . I'm proud that I'm not a great man. . . . I'm not one to intrigue, I . . . I don't act on the sly, but openly, without cunning. . . . I set to work . . . by no devious ways, for I disdain them. . . . I've no taste for contemptible duplicity. . . . I only put on a mask at a masquerade, and don't wear one before people every day" (p. 147). He goes on to tell the doctor, darkly, that the mask will drop off the faces of certain others who do lie and deceive. But to two junior clerks in his office he later hints: "You all know me, gentlemen, but hitherto you've known only one side" (p. 156).

The inner turmoil grows in intensity. Mr. Golyadkin wanted only to hide somewhere from himself, cease to exist, and turn to dust.

Just after losing his right galosh in the snow and slush, he has the impression that someone is standing near him, leaning on a railing, as he is, and dressed exactly like him from head to foot. He senses this someone again later, then again, and yet again. Suddenly his strength fails him, his hair stands on end; he recognizes that it "was no other than himself, Mr. Golyadkin himself, another Mr. Golyadkin, but absolutely the same as himself—in fact, what is called his double in every respect" (p. 179). "Who authorized this? Am I asleep, am I in a waking dream?" (183).

In due course, Golyadkin makes the acquaintance of his double. Finding him to be impoverished and without quarters, he befriends him, invites him to his flat, feeds him, lets him spend the night. The double is shy, timid, fearful. They drink together. Golyadkin says: "You and I will take to each other like fish to water, Yakov Petrovich; we shall be like brothers; we'll be cunning, my dear fellow, we'll work together;. . . .we'll get up an intrigue, too. . . . And don't you trust any of them. . . . You must hold aloof from them all, my boy"(196).

The next morning, to Golyadkin's astonishment, his double has vanished without a trace. Moreover, the next time he meets him, the double is cool and distant. Later, he even becomes sly, ridiculing

Golyadkin, and then obscenely familiar, pinching his cheek, flicking his paunch, and making fun of him in front of others.

Our hero is exasperated beyond endurance. All his protests about his own honesty as contrasted to the masks, imposture, shameless-ness, and deception of others are of no avail. The double begins to take over on the job, fawning on everyone, whispering, wheedling, con-niving against Golyadkin, who is driven more and more to distraction by such insolent falseness. Golyadkin tries unsuccessfully to reconcile himself to his double's existence: "It doesn't matter. Granted, he's a scoundrel, well, let him be a scoundrel, but to make up for it, the other one's honest: so . . . that this Golyadkin's a rascal, don't take any notice of him, and don't mix him up with the other . . . [who is] honest, virtuous, mild, free from malice, always to be relied upon in the service, and worthy of promotion; that's how it is, very good. . . . But what if . . . what if they get us mixed up? . . . . What a calam-ity!" (215).

When the double threatens to squeeze Golyadkin out of his posi-tion, with increasingly outlandish blandishments, he finally seeks out his superior, Andrey Filippovich, and begs for an audience. He protests his loyalty and obedience: "I look upon my benevolent superior as a father and blindly entrust my fate to him" (p. 244). Again and again (p. 267) he throws himself upon Filippovich's mercy, as a son on a father's, entrusting his fate utterly to his chief, entreating him to "defend" him from his "enemy" (p. 267). (Twice, during his mounting confusion and excitement, he mistakes a door-way for a looking glass and sees his double reflected there.)

Despite Golyadkin's insistent protestations about his blind devo-tion, his true attitude toward masculine authorities and father figures is by now transparently evident to the reader. It is that of his conniving double: hostile, envious, and venal. His ambition includes owning a carriage like that of His Excellency and even eloping with his superior's daughter. Golyadkin's attitude is, in fact, the *deceitful* version of the way his shiftless, untrustworthy servant *openly* behaves toward him.

At the conclusion of the story, the false double, blowing kisses at Golyadkin, helps push him into a carriage, followed by a doctor. "The carriage door slammed. There was a swish of the whip on the horses' backs . . . the horses started off (p. 283). The horses take him along an unfamiliar, desolate road, through dark woods, on the way to an insane asylum.

In order to examine the transformations of Dostoevsky's attitudes toward authority let us turn for background for what is known about his actual father.

Dostoevsky's father was a stern ex-army surgeon. While he did not believe in corporal punishment for children, he was certainly known for his violence. One of the serfs on the family farm recalled: "The man was a beast. His soul was dark,—that's it. . . . The master was a stern, unrighteous lord, but the mistress was kind-hearted. He didn't live well with her; beat her. He flogged the peasants for nothing" (quoted by Mochulsky 1947, 4).

It is generally believed—and Dostoevsky certainly believed it— that his father was murdered by serfs rebelling against his drunken, violent floggings. It has also been suggested that they murdered him out of revenge for his living with Katerina, the young daughter of a serf, who had borne him an illegitimate child the year before. In either case, if it was murder, including, as some said, castration, most of the male population of the village of Davaroe must have been implicated and kept silence. An official investigation reported only that there were no marks on the body and that the victim appeared to have died of suffocation during an apoplectic fit.

On the other hand, if it were a case of murder, the Dostoevsky family might have hushed it up to preserve the property and avoid scandal. A more recent theory (Frank 1976) is that the murder story is only a rumor originated by the retired mayor of the village. He had a lawsuit against the elder Dostoevsky, and if the murder charge against the Dostoevsky serfs had been upheld, they would all have been sent to Siberia; he could then have snapped up the property for a song.

28

The last time the younger Dostoevsky had seen his father was two years prior to his death. Dostoevsky was fifteen. His young mother had died a few months earlier of "malignant" tuberculosis—probably hastened by the birth of eight children within little more than a decade. Father, Fyodor, and older brother Mikhail were on a long carriage trip from Moscow to St. Petersburg to enroll the boys in the School of Military Engineers.

Waiting in a wayside inn during one of many stops for the carriages to be changed, Dostoevsky witnessed a scene that made a profound impression on him (Dostoevsky 1876a). An official government courier, in full, plumed uniform, dashed into the post coach station, probably had a customary vodka, rushed out, and sat down in a small carriage. A large, red-faced man, he half-rose again, silently lifted his enormous right fist, and gave the coachman's neck a mighty blow. The coachman collapsed forward, lifted his whip, and lashed the middle horse of the troika with all his might. The horses strained forward. But this in no way deterred the courier. He hit the coachman on the neck again and again, not with irritation but methodically , out of long experience. The coachman, in turn, though hardly able to sit up, whipped the horses so that they flew like mad. This continued until the troika disappeared from view.

It is surprising that the well-worked territory of Dostoevsky's life has yielded so little attention to this traumatic episode in his adolescence, especially since he himself dated his sense of social outrage to it and connected it to his joining a revolutionary group opposed to serfdom (Frank 1976). It was his membership in this radical organization that some years later led to another traumatic event in his life—his arrest and sentencing to Siberia.

"This revolting picture remained in my memory for life . . . like an emblem, like . . . cause and effect. Here, every blow that hit the animals sprang forth as though by itself from every blow that fell on the man" (Steinberg 1966, 21). Dostoevsky imagined the chain of cruelty extending still further—to the coachman's wife, who would surely be beaten that night to avenge his own pain and humiliation.

RASKOLNIKOV'S RAGE

The intense affect and visual detail of Dostoevsky's traumatic memory are appropriate to its dramatic content. In this it differs from a screen memory, which, typically, is relatively bland in content. Like a screen memory, however, a traumatic memory may not only conceal allied memories, but also condense key elements of the deeper structure of the person.

There can be little doubt that Dostoevsky saw himself as another victim in the chain of abuses. (His first published work, *Poor Folk*, already showed his characteristic compassion for the downtrodden.) At any rate, this traumatic memory may be taken as emblematic of a whole series of sadomasochistic relationships: his father beating his wife and flogging his serfs; the Czarist authorities terrorizing Dostoevsky with a mock execution, his fellow convicts terrorizing each other.

The courier-horse episode is also directly relevant to *Crime and Punishment*. In his working notebooks for that book (Wasiolek 1931), there are six explicit references to the memory, most of them in the context of reconciling rage against humanity with trying to love it.

A few excerpts from these notebooks will suffice for illustration. Unless otherwise indicated, the thoughts and actions refer to the main character, Raskolnikov. The bracketed material represents interlinear additions by Dostoevsky. Italics are mine.

> p. 54: Main Idea of the Novel. . . . Can one love them? Can one suffer for them? Hate for humanity. [During his wanderings *memories about the horse*.]
>
> p. 64: My first personal insult, *the horse, the courier*. Violation of a child.
>
> p. 81: How low and vile people are. . . . No: gather them up in one's hand, and then do good for them. . . . Hatred choked me, and I lay down. Memories: *horse with a stick*.

In the excerpts that follow it becomes clear that both Dostoevsky and Raskolnikov are identified with the victims—human victims nearly trampled under the hooves of horses, or horses being victimized with the whips, which drive them to the point of trembling, or women as victims of beatings at the hands and boots of men.

p. 137: A driver [of a carriage] gave me a good whack across the back with his whip because I had almost fallen at the feet of his horses. . . . The whip's blow made me so furious.

p. 138: (The significant detail on this page is that Raskolnikov remembers being a student "thirty years ago." Since Raskolnikov is only twenty-three years of age, this must refer to the forty-five year-old author. "Thirty years ago," therefore, recalls Dostoevsky at age fifteen—the time of the courier-horse memory, when, just after his mother's death, he is on the way to becoming a student in St. Petersburg. [G.J.R.])

pp. 139—40: ". . . trembling all over, no longer from the fever but from weakness [*like a driven horse, which I had seen in my childhood*] . . . " (Raskolnikov passes out. He awakens to the terrible screaming of his landlady, who is being beaten, and sits up in terror, paralyzed. [G.J.R.]). "[Soon they will come for me, I thought.]"

One may find a direct reflection of the courier-horse memory in the dream Raskolnikov has early on in *Crime and Punishment*.[2] He had just drunk a glass of vodka in a tavern. On his way home, he feels completely exhausted. He turns off the road into the bushes, where he instantly falls asleep on the grass and has a dream.

Dostoevsky introduces the dream with the following commentary: (1866, 55).

In a morbid condition of the brain, dreams often have a singular actuality, vividness, and extraordinary semblance of reality. At times monstrous images are created, but the setting and the whole picture are so truthlike and filled with details so delicate, so unexpectedly, but so artistically consistent, that the dreamer, were he an artist like Pushkin or Turgenev even, could never have invented them in the waking state. Such sick dreams always remain long in memory and

---

2. This dream, incidentally, occupies an historic place in psychoanalysis, having first come up for consideration at the March 8, 1911, meeting of Freud's Vienna Psychoanalytic Society (Nunberg & Federn 1974).

make a powerful impression on the overwrought and deranged nervous system.

In the dream, Raskolnikov sees himself as a child of seven in the town of his birth. He is holding his father's hand and they stand in front of a tavern. A drunken crowd spills out of the tavern and piles into a cart hitched to a small mare. The crowd cheers and joins in when the owner beats the mare, which is struggling to pull the overloaded cart. She staggers and falls under the rain of blows; the owner bludgeons her to death.

Raskolnikov awakens in terror. He is gasping and soaked with perspiration. " 'Good God!' he cries, 'can it be, can it be, that I shall really take an axe, that I shall strike her on the head, split her skull open. . . . No, I couldn't do it, I couldn't do it. . . . Why, why then am I still. . . ?' " (p. 61).

This dream marks the psychological pivot-point at which Raskolnikov's daydreams of murdering the old woman pawnbroker turn into deliberate plans.

The dream starts peacefully enough. On a holiday evening, the seven-year-old Raskolnikov and his father are walking hand in hand to visit the graves of the boy's grandmother, *whom he had never seen*, and his younger brother, who died at six months of age and *whom the boy did not remember at all*. There is a church in the middle of the graveyard where Raskolnikov used to go two or three times a year with his father and mother.

Since he used to go there with both parents, why is mother not present in the dream for the traditional visit to the cemetery? Because Raskolnikov's dream is no longer about Raskolnikov's childhood but about Dostoevsky. The fictional dream of the mare being beaten to death, based on the memory of the whipping of the horses en route to St. Petersburg, returns us to the time in Dostoevsky's life just after his mother's death. The absence of Raskolnikov's mother from her expected place in the dream affirms Dostoevsky's mother's death. At the same time, displacing the fact to a visit to the grave of the long-since-dead-and-never-seen "grandmother" serves the emotional need to deny this fact.

What about the grave of the "little brother" whom Raskolnikov no longer remembered? This also refers to Dostoevsky's life. When Dostoevsky was about the same age (eight) as Raskolnikov in the dream (seven), a momentous event occurred: twin sisters, Vera and Lyubov, were born. Within a few days Lyubov died. Dostoevsky might indeed have remembered his sister's death almost as well as his mother's because, according to custom, before the burial the child's body had rested in its coffin in the Dostoevsky home, in full view of her siblings.

As is so often the case with dreams, the setting is like the prologue. It says, in effect, "This dream is going to be about the death of my mother and what I imagine happened to her, and perhaps my baby sister before that, and what I am afraid might happen to me." We are then presented with the main body of the dream, bearing its latent unconscious fantasies.

The mare of the Raskolnikov dream was a thin little sorrel beast, gasping, tugging the overloaded cart, feebly kicking under the shower of blows. (At the time of her death, recall that Dostoevsky's mother was emaciated with tuberculosis, after eight pregnancies within ten years.) The master of the mare was Mikolka, "a young, thick-necked peasant with a fleshy face as red as a carrot" (p. 57). He first used a whip to beat her body, face, and eyes, then "a long, thick shaft" on her spine, and finally an iron crowbar to do her in "with measured blows" (59). The drunken crowd of men joined in with whips, sticks, and poles.

If this dream has to do with Dostoevsky's inner image of the cause of his mother's death, as well as fears for himself, it represents this: repeated phallic attacks on an emaciated body, overstrained under the load of multiple pregnancies, until final collapse.[3] In this classically unconscious, sadomasochistic representation of the primal scene, the

3. The unconscious pregnancy and birth/death symbolism of the seven-year-old Raskolnikov is identical to that of Freud's *Analysis of a Phobia in a Five-Year-Old Boy* (1909). The child was afraid to go out into the street lest he see a horse beaten and fall down while pulling a loaded cart.

mare stands for the mother as well as for the seven-year-old Raskolnikov identified with her. Mikolka, the master of the mare, is a sadistic representation of the father. The overloaded cart stands for the many pregnancies. These are also implicated in her death by a telling detail: the number of assailants in the cart, besides Mikolka, is six—exactly the number of Dostoevsky's living siblings.

The dream not only accuses, it alibis. Dostoevsky himself is exonerated from guilty participation in causing mother's death, for he, after all, as the young Raskolnikov, flailed ineffectually at the attackers, received a cut with the whip across his own face, and in the end embraced the dead head "and kissed it, kissed the eyes and kissed the lips. . . . Then he jumped up and flew in a frenzy with his little fists out at Mikolka" (60).

The image of the mother is split. On the one hand she is charged with participating in her own death by behaving like a dumb, abused beast of burden, emaciated and dying under phallic attacks and multiple pregnancies. The other representation of the mother in the dream is that of a jolly participant in the (sexualized) goings-on: "a fat, rosy-cheeked woman . . . cracking nuts and laughing" (57). Again: "The woman went on cracking nuts and laughing." (59).

The father-image is also split. In the form of Mikolka, he is condemned as the chief murderer. In his own person as father, however, he is portrayed as impotent—totally ineffectual at rescuing either mare or son. He is even more helpless, in fact, than the little boy, who at least tries to save the poor mare-mother.

In the rough draft of a letter to his publisher (Wasiolek 1931, 171—73), Dostoevsky stated that the original motive for the murder in *Crime and Punishment* is Raskolnikov's love for his suffering mother and the wish to save her and his sister. The notebooks make it apparent that the actual process of writing forced Dostoevsky to recognize that the relationship between Raskolnikov and his mother is much more complex. While he feels love and pity for mother, he also expresses coldness and hatred for her (pp. 176, 203, 212, 217—18, 220). He fears her judgment (pp. 84, 91), he resents the guilt and shame she makes him feel for failing to live up to her expectations, and he also resents her constantly reminding him of his duty toward her. Thus, her love is a burden (pp. 65–66); and he hurts her (pp. 48, 66, 70, 240), sometimes openly: "He beats his mother" (p. 176). The mutual aggression between them is veiled in the final version of the novel by repeated professions of love.

All this supports what many analysts have contended—namely, that the pawnbroker who preys on the youth of St. Petersburg stands for the mother who preys on Raskolnikov with love and guilt. It also helps explain the impact of the courier-horse memory on Dostoevsky himself. When it was transported into *Crime and Punishment* in the form of the dream of the peasants beating the mare to death, Raskolknikov's horror in the dream was at the glimpse of his own projected murderousness. It was recognized in indirect form immediately on awakening: his shocked realization that he would indeed commit murder—of that other grasping old lady, the pawnbroker. But for a higher good: "Poor mother, poor sister. I did it for you." And, almost immediately after this entry in his working notebook: "Memories: horse with a stick" (p. 81). Identification with his mother's struggle under the weight of eight births and her final succumbing to tuberculosis combined with love and compassion to place upon Dostoevsky a burden of hatred, self-hatred, and guilt. Hatred for her because of her helplessness and his own to rescue her; self-hatred for his impotence and hatred of her; guilt, requiring him to suffer, perhaps die, in order to gain spiritual rebirth and the ability to love again. Basically, he probably hated her because, in her inability to protect herself, he saw himself: helpless in the face of his own sadism, masochism, guilt.

"THE PEASANT MAREY"

Just as love for mother turned to hate and erupted in the murder of *Crime and Punishment*, "The Peasant Marey," written ten years later, performs a similar alchemy on Dostoevsky's feelings of rage toward his father, and people in general. In this autobiographical story, he relates that during his time in the Siberian prison he kept working

35

and reworking memories of his past, "adding new touches to an event that had happened long ago and, above all, correcting it, correcting it incessantly" (Dostoevsky [1876b] 1964, 101). By thus breaking down and reassembling memories, he succeeded in metabolizing his loathing for his fellow-convicts and assimilating it in the form of "love" for the inner beauty of the Russian people, which he felt he had discovered "under impassable alluvial filth" (Dostoevsky [1876a] 1979, 202).

"The Peasant Marey" records another childhood memory in the form of a story. He recalled it, perhaps, during a pilgrimage to the family farm at Davaroe, where he had spent his summers between the ages of ten and fifteen, and where his father had been murdered. Dostoevsky had not been there in the forty years since his mother died and his father retired there. He wandered it step by step and reconstructed long-forgotten scenes. (It was here that he may also have traced in his mind the first outlines of *The Brothers Karamazov*, which appeared three years later. One solid fact is that he gave the name of some woods on the farm, Chermashnya, to a village that plays some part in *The Brothers* [Carr 1931].)

In the story, the childhood memory is described as having been recollected in prison twenty years after the event. It is Easter Monday in the Siberian prison. The convicts are not working; they drink, curse, fight, run amok, lie half-dead. Dostoevsky feels blind fury and disgust toward them (much the same sentiments expressed in his working notebooks for *Crime and Punishment*). A Polish political prisoner, echoing his contempt, hisses, *"Je hais ces brigands."* He goes back into the barracks and sees the drunken Tartar Gazin lying unconscious, having been beaten senseless by fellow convicts. (Gazin is described in *The House of the Dead* as a sadist who lures children to remote places, taunts them, and cuts their throats.)

Lying down himself and trying to sleep, he recovers a vivid childhood memory of an excursion into the forest. He believed he heard the cry, "A wolf is on the loose!" Panicked, he ran up to a thick-set, peasant man of about fifty who was plowing a field with his mare. Marey, the peasant, comforted him "with a slow motherly sort of smile" and "gently touched [his] trembling lips" (Dostoevsky [1876b] 1964, 103).

Dostoevksy never forgot the kindness of the serf to the son of the master who held him in serfdom. Armed with this loving memory, the convict Dostoevsky now was able to look at his fellow-convicts in a different light, without either anger or hatred, as if lifted by some miracle. Indeed, he could even feel contempt for the Pole, who could not appreciate the true Russian soul beneath the coarseness.

A comparison of Raskolnikov's dream of his childhood and the memory of Dostoevsky's childhood recalled in "The Peasant Marey" immediately brings out some intriguing temporal relationships (see table 2). The working notebooks for *Crime and Punishment* connect that book with Dostoevsky's courier-horse memory at the age when his mother died, and thus connect Dostoevsky at that time to his fictional stand in, Raskolnikov. In the case of "The Peasant Marey" there is the possibility of an indirect linkage to that same time in Dostoevsky's life—the time of his mother's death. In "Marey" Dostoevsky is writing of himself when he was a convict in Siberia. He mentions "just as an interesting detail" (Dostoevsky [1876b] 1964, 100), that when he had earlier written of this period of his life as a convict (in *The House of the Dead*) it was in the person of a fictitious character who was supposed to have killed his wife. While he includes this "interesting detail," Dostoevsky does not explain something more central: why the important memory of the "motherly" Marey was *not* included in those earlier memoirs of his experiences as a convict. Might this surprising omission, as well as the gratuitous invention of a wife-killer character, represent unconscious references to his mother's death?

Second, although both *Crime and Punishment* and "The Peasant Marey" were written long after the author's release from Siberia, they stand in a before-and-after relationship to that imprisonment. Raskolnikov was twenty-three when he murdered the pawnbroker woman, not much younger than Dostoevsky when he was involved in revolutionary activity (twenty-five to twenty-six), arrested, tried for treason, and condemned to death (twenty-seven). In "The Peasant

Marey" Dostoevsky was writing of himself in a Siberian penal colony at twenty-nine or thirty, after having been granted a reprieve from execution (twenty-eight).

Finally, both works refer to childhood memories: the Raskolnikov dream to an actual experience at age fifteen ascribed to Raskolnikov at about seven, and "The Peasant Marey" to one experienced between ten and fifteen and fictionalized to age nine. Might these fictionalized ages of seven and nine also stand in a before-and-after relationship to some unspecified "crime"? As mentioned earlier, the one event that did, in fact, occur between ages seven and nine, when Dostoevsky was eight, was the death of one of a pair of twin sisters shortly after birth.

Aside from these similarities, Raskolnikov's dream and the "Peasant Marey" memory are identical in a number of respects. The dream takes place in the town of Raskolnikov's birth, the "Peasant Marey" memory in the village of Dostoevsky's early childhood. It is a holiday eve in one and the second day of Easter holidays in the other. The young Raskolnikov is filled with rage, horror, and pity; the young convict in "The Peasant Marey" is first full of "blind fury" at his fellow-convicts, then remembers his childhood horror of the wolf, the compassion shown him by the "coarse, savagely ignorant Russian serf," and finally his love for "that rascal of a peasant with his shaven head and branded face, yelling his hoarse drunken song at the top of his voice" (p. 105).

The Raskolnikov dream starts peacefully enough: the little boy walks hand in hand with his father to vist the graves of his grand-mother and younger brother. The "prologue" that ushers in the "Peasant Marey" memory is the sight of Tartar Gazin, the child-killer, lying unconscious, without any sign of life, having been beaten into insensibility by fellow-convicts. This leads young Dostoevsky to lie down himself, pretend to sleep, and thus recover the memory of his having been "rescued" as a child by Marey.

Now to the details of that rescue. He recalled that it was a late summer day on the family farm and that he was dreading his return to Moscow, where he would have to spend the whole winter over boring French lessons. This detail deserves a digression at this point. For the fact is that Dostoevsky's tutor for Latin was his father. That his father was a harsh taskmaster we know from his younger brother Andrey, who recalled in his memoirs: "When my brothers [Mikhail and Fyodor] were with my father [for Latin lessons], which was frequently for an hour or more, they not only did not dare sit down, but even lean their elbows on the table" (quoted by Mochulsky 1947, 4).

Dostoevsky recalled that on this particular day in the country, he heard in the distance the voice of a peasant calling "Gee up! Gee up!" to the plough horse. Exactly what had he been doing at the time? "I was too busy, breaking off a switch from a hazel-tree *to strike frogs with*. . . . I was also interested in beetles and other insects . . . but I was afraid of snakes" (101, italics added).

The author then tells us about his love of the woods, its flora and fauna, and its damp smells. Suddenly the child imagined that "amid the dead silence" he "heard clearly and distinctly the shout, 'Wolf! Wolf!' " (102). Panic-stricken, young Dostoevsky screamed at the top of his voice and rushed straight out to the ploughing peasant, Marey, who comforted him.

How might we reconstruct the inner, unconscious dynamics of this narrative? Having seen the brawling, drunken convicts all around and Tartar Gazin beaten into unconsciousness, the young political prisoner Dostoevsky wonders at the real likelihood of being himself attacked, beaten, possibly killed. How easy it would be for these savage peasants to turn the tables and do whatever they liked to the defenseless son of a serf-owner. His father, after all, had probably been killed—possibly even castrated—by similar peasants.

He recalls other times when he felt helplessly dominated. During those long winter lessons his father would not let him sit or rest. The only escape was in the summer. Memories of summer vacations relieve the anxiety temporarily. At those times he was free to roam in the woods. He was not a prisoner of anyone; he was his own master. If he wished, he could cut hazel switches and strike the frogs—be a bully himself.

A peaceful pause of a few sentences, describing the pastoral scene; they mark the attempt to contain the mounting anxiety at the perception of his own sadism. Then it breaks out in a full-blown attack: the sadism is projected in the form of an auditory hallucination that a wolf is on the loose. Again, the fear of being attacked. He rushes into the clearing and clings, pleading, to Marey.

The story of Marey is successful in keeping sadism, both his own and that of others, largely at bay, like the imaginary wolf. Tartar Gazin had already been attacked; we never see it. And, being a child-killer, he probably deserved it. The boy Dostoevsky was about to strike the frogs but did not actually get to it because of the imagined wolf, which never materialized.

In sharp contrast to this carefully distanced sadism, the Raskolnikov dream of childhood is full of raw violence. The mare of the dream is a thin little beast, gasping, tugging the overloaded cart, feebly kicking under the shower of blows. Her master was Mikolka, of the fleshy carrot face, with crowbar in his fist, beating on her spine.

How different from Marey, that other father figure (who, like Dostoevsky's father at the time of his death, is fifty years of age). Marey is a grizzled, benevolent master who encourages the mare in her efforts to plough up the steep slope of the hill.

The seven-year-old Raskolnikov had manfully torn himself from his father's hand and rushed in to try to protect the mare from Mikolka, only to receive a cut with the whip across the face. The fictionalized nine-year-old Dostoevsky had screamed, terrified, and clutched pleadingly at Marey's sleeve. In return he received compassion, protection, and a blessing.

Since everything has a price, at what cost such protection? "He [Marey] quietly stretched out his thick finger with its black nail, smeared with earth, and gently touched my trembling lips." (Dostoevsky [1876b] 1964, 103). Again: "I remembered . . . particularly that thick finger of his, smeared with earth, with which he touched my twitching lips so gently and with such shy tenderness" (p. 104). The answer appears to be submission to a man.

And if it is to be submission to a man, better to a loving, "motherly" one, with the power to invoke religion ("he made the sign of the cross over me, and then crossed himself, too" [p. 103]), than to the "devil" Mikolka. Of course, the sexual implications of such submission remain in either case. But if one is to be feminized anyway, better through an act of love than by lethal rape—better to be a mare hitched to Marey's plough than to Mikolka's overloaded cart, felled under his crowbar.

Fear and hatred of Tartar Gazin, the child-killer, reminded Dostoevsky of his childhood fears of being consumed by his own aggression, projected in the form of the imaginary wolf. Back then, his submissive pleading had transformed a potentially murderous father

TABLE 2

Comparison of Raskolnikov's Dream of Childhood
and
"The Peasant Marey" Memory of Childhood

	Raskolnikov's Dream	Peasant Marey Memory
Dostoevsky's age at time of writing:	45	55
Age at actual memory:	15	10−15
Protagonist's age:	23 (pre-Siberia)	29−30 (in Siberia)
Age at fictionalized memory:	7+/−	9
Location:	Town of birth	Village of childhood
Time:	Holiday eve	2d day of Easter
Onset of Memory:	En route to visit family graves	About to strike frogs
Atmosphere:	Drunken noise and singing	Same
Victim of beating:	Old mare killed	Childkiller beaten
Affects:	Horror, rage, pity	Same
Action of mare:	Straining to pull overloaded cart	Hard plowing uphill
Caress:	Raskolnikov kisses mare's lips	Marey touches child's lips
Mother:	Absent	Absent
Father:	Split-image: Ineffectual/murderous	Split-image: Nurturant/murderous

figure into a protective, motherly one. Submissiveness to the power of Marey, who could have inflicted abuse but chose not to, transformed the boy's hatred and fear into gratitude and love; it protected him from anxiety stemming from his own sadism.

One might ask why such love of the peasantry no longer led Dostoevsky to continue to work to improve their lot in life. On the contrary. What had begun as revulsion against the chain of injustice which he saw passing from the uniformed government courier to coachman to mare and to wife and which had at first turned him to revolutionary activity, finally became remorse and apology, submission to Czar and God. He even came to believe in a higher purpose that justified, indeed necessitated, suffering and submission.

As Freud ([1928] 1961, 177) concluded: "He landed in the retrograde position of submission both to temporal and to spiritual authority, of veneration both for the Tzar and for the God of the Christians, and of a narrow Russian nationalism—a position which lesser minds have reached with smaller effort."

Dostoevsky ends "The Peasant Marey" on a note of complacent superiority toward the Polish political prisoner who was unable to do what Dostoevsky succeeded in doing in prison: convert his earlier rebellion against injustice, like that of the boy Raskolnikov, into a quasi-religious acceptance.

A century before Orwell's *1984* he anticipated the history of his country: he learned to love "Big Brother."

3

DOSTOEVSKY IN TEXAS

Dostoevsky's oeuvre obviously transcends his own traumatic memories and has had a major impact on twentieth-century sensibility. It provides a text for the depth psychologist as well as the present-day utopian terrorist.

His appeal is such that he has always presented something of a dilemma for the Soviet control apparatus. Though far removed from the spirit of social realism, his works have been tolerated rather than suppressed—untaught and often unavailable, but not forbidden. Even in the USSR, however, his collected writings are finally scheduled to appear in thirty volumes—spurred by a hefty advance from a Japanese publisher for a translation.

As we have seen, Dostoevsky's traumatic memory—seeing a courier beat a coachman who in turn whipped the horses—stood in his mind for a whole chain of abuses involving father over mother, masters over serfs, authorities over prisoners, convicts over each other. During the course of his life, his attitude toward power and authority underwent a profound metamorphosis and was elaborated and reflected in *The Double, Crime and Punishment* (where the memory formed the substance of Raskolnikov's dream of childhood), and "The Peasant Marey."

Two questions might be asked at this point: (1) exactly what made the courier-horse memory traumatic, and (2) how did writing these particular works help Dostoevsky master the trauma? The answer in both cases stresses the importance of aggression.

Bearing in mind that the courier—horse act of abuse was emblematic of many others, the single effect of any one of these, and surely the cumulative effect of all of them, must have been that Dostoevsky was flooded from an early age with aggressive-sadistic stimulation. The act of writing itself helped transform these passive experiences of being overwhelmed into an active one in which unwelcome affects could be attributed to fictional characters, elaborated, and transmuted.

Above all, it was aggression that was split off and projected. The story of Golyadkin projects it only as far as a fictional double. *Crime and Punishment* intensifies it and places it farther away—in the drunken killing of the mare by the uncontrolled Mikolka of the dream of childhood, and later in Raskolnikov's planned, intellectually rationalized act of murdering the pawnbroker woman. By the time he wrote the autobiographical "The Peasant Marey," Dostoevsky acknowledged aggressive impulses to be his own. But they are only those of his childhood, when he was about to strike some frogs but never did. The dangerous wolf is imaginary and never materializes, and the potentially hostile Marey turns out to be motherly and protective. As a result of all these displacements over time, aggression has been dispersed, tamed, and its direction reversed: the originally murderous counteraggression has been transformed into submissive humility.

At the opposite extreme from Dostoevsky's transformation of personal trauma into creative literature are the legions of clinical examples of attempts at mastery of trauma which never achieve significance. Both creative and clinical processes follow the fundamental psychic principle of attempting to master passively experienced trauma by active repetition, yet one illuminates an area much beyond itself, whereas the other is seldom of more than private interest.

In the Freudian spirit that "a most important piece of information is often . . . disguised as a beggar" (Breuer and Freud [1893–95] 1955, 279), this chapter presents a clinical case history. Instead of a masterpiece of creative imagination, one hundred years after Dostoevsky and half a world away, in the attempt to master a strikingly similar childhood beating memory, a dull Texan farm boy committed a brutal act of child-murder.

What possible relevance to the present context can this case offer us? The differences are glaring. In the personal realm, Dostoevsky went from being overstimulated with murderous counteraggressive impulses to a characterological submissiveness to authority—achieving in this way some degree of mastery over his own traumatic history. Thanks to his gift of creative imagination, in his writing he was able to work through displacements consciously; he identified with his fictional characters yet distanced himself from them. His legacy of work broadens the reader's capacity for compassionate understanding of human characters and experiences far removed from one's usual life sphere. Our clinical protagonist, on the other hand, did the opposite. He went from his customary adaptive docility to an outburst of murder; he lost safe distancing from past victims and villains and regressed from memory and thought to unconscious identifications, repetition, and acting out.

The differences between unthinking, impulsive, psychotic action and thoughtful delay, elaboration, and working through are not only glaring but together constitute the familiar signs of ego weakness as against ego strength. Whatever Dostoevsky's personal psychopathology—and even a casual reading of his biography reveals it to have been considerable—his talent and ability to work at it reflects only ego strength. Yet such creativity, while reflecting ego strength, cannot merely be equated with ego strength; many are graced with strong egos but no creativity.

What, then, is the nature of creative, artistic ability? What does it consist of? Surely the power to integrate many diverse elements into coherent patterns—another aspect of ego strength—must be part of the answer to "the problem of the creative artist"?

The following case, and the chief reason for presenting it, suggest otherwise. As we shall see, the criminal act and the events surrounding it involved an exquisite degree of coordination, both of different levels of functioning—for example, somatization, fantasy formation, and organized action—and of different time frames. However, all of this synthesizing organization took place *unconsciously*. Moreover, it is of such a high level that it impresses one as being quite comparable in scope and complexity—perhaps superior?—to the *conscious* craftsmanship of creative writing.

Needless to say, this is not meant to imply that conscious and unconscious processes are to be equated; or that the creative artist is necessarily ill, any more than that psychopathology confers creativity. Rather, because high levels of integrative power are to be found in both creative and uncreative individuals, integrative capacity per se cannot be considered the hallmark of creativity. This will be expanded upon at the end of the chapter.

It was the eve of the Fourth of July in San Antonio, Texas.[1] Three heavy-equipment construction workers, low on money and out of jobs, were preparing to spend the night in a car parked near a gravel pit when a man appeared, unexpectedly, out of the brush. In the words of one of the construction workers, "He walked towards us. Not fast. Not slow either. Just sort of casual. Except he's sweating and out of breath, and kind of unsteady on his feet. I yelled, 'Hey, boy, where are you going?' But he doesn't answer, just comes up towards our lights looking sort of dazed and says, 'What's going on here?' We say we don't know but let's find a policeman, and just then one came up."

The patrolman who came up was a deputy sheriff. He pointed a pistol at the man, whose name was Jimmy Shaver, told him that a little girl had been raped and killed, and asked whether he knew

---

1. This case presentation is an expanded version of Gilbert J. Rose, "Screen Memories in Homicidal Acting Out," *Psychoanalytic Quarterly*, 29:328–43 (1960a).

anything about it. Shaver said that he had just been beaten up by some stranger and had run off into the brush to hide.

By then word of the rape-murder of the three-year-old child in a gravel pit had spread, and a large, angry crowd was gathering. A constable soon appeared on the scene. He was from a neighboring precinct and this was not his jurisdiction, but he was running for re-election in a close contest. He quickly handcuffed Shaver, whisked him off to the county jail, phoned a reporter, and returned to the crowd.

During the ensuing jurisdictional dispute between the sheriff's and the constable's offices, the defense attorneys turned to the nearby Air Force base and its department of psychiatry for a psychiatric evaluation of their client, Shaver. This was necessary for two reasons. First, Shaver was on active duty with the Air Force; and second, at that time, if a defendant's sanity was in question in the State of Texas, it had to be determined in court by a jury trial before the criminal matter itself could come to trial.

Hence, Shaver was brought to the psychiatrist's office, where I examined him. His appearance was totally unremarkable: he was a pale man of thirty-two, of medium height and slight build, dressed in a short-sleeved sports shirt, plaid slacks, and plastic sandals. His manner was passive, his expression somewhat dull and apathetic. He said that when he was picked up by the police he believed that he had run into the brush to escape being beaten up by some man. Later he had remembered a bit more. He had been in charge of some military recruits. At the end of the day he had illegally released one of them, Brawley, from disciplinary restrictions, and together they had gone out drinking at the Lazy-A Bar. Shaver's plan was to kill time in this way until his wife, a waitress, got off from work at midnight.

At first he said this was all he could recall. But a few days after being taken into custody he struck his head while in his prison cell and was thereafter able to "recall" something further. He and Brawley had been drinking heavily at the Lazy-A. There had been a little girl there, playing shuffleboard with her brother while her parents sat and drank with the owner. Shaver had driven Brawley back to the barracks and returned to the Lazy-A. A strange man and a girl came up to him as he stood by his car at the side of the road; the man kicked him in the genitals and hit him in the stomach. Shaver vomited, then fainted, and when he regained consciousness he found himself lying in a gravel pit without his clothes. He could not understand how he got to the gravel pit and why he was undressed.

When he was asked about his past, he spontaneously began to talk about his father: "He was brutal, just brutal. You know what he did? Beat a horse to death with a chain just for stepping on a pig. He beat him around the head till he hardly had a head left. He beat me, too, and cursed me out, for chucking corncobs at the chickens and stuff like that. I fell down and couldn't get up. Black and blue. I tried to run away that night but he caught me and put me back to bed. Later on I took off and went to my mother's home. I must've been about ten. Hardly ever saw him after that."

With little encouragement he began to talk about his experiences with women. He had married "on the spur of the moment to the kind of girl you'd mess around with." He had difficulty getting or maintaining an erection. "Sex just didn't mean much one way or the other. I could always take care of myself that way, y'know? I'm still that way. It's better like that." His wife was unfaithful, became pregnant by another man, and would slap, kick, and curse him, as did her mother sometimes. "So one day I suddenly turned and slapped her in the face. She screamed. That's when I left."

He was asked if women other than his wife and mother-in-law had treated him that way. He immediately answered, "My cousin, Beth. We were about nine or ten. She hit me with a rock on the head at the swimming hole. She got the older boys to throw me into the swimming hole before I could swim. I almost drowned. She'd tease me about being afraid to dive and do things like that.

GR: Do things like that?
SHAVER: Well, the older boys would have sex with her, y'see. I'd watch them do it. I was scared to touch her. But she teased me into it.

48

They'd watch. I was ashamed. Couldn't do much. Then she'd get mad at me afterwards.

GR: Was it one of those times she hit you with a rock on the head and got the older boys to throw you into the swimming hole and you almost drowned?

SHAVER: Yes.

Beginning at about the same age, ten, Shaver had nightmares about twice a week of a black cloud coming down on his head and suffocating him, or of being chased and killed by his father. Childhood enuresis continued until adolescence. He was frequently truant from school, ran away from home five or six times, and left school after the eighth grade. His father abandoned the family at about this time and was said to have been killed in a fight. Little is known of Shaver's relationship to his mother except that he would sometimes go out on double dates with her and her boyfriend. His marriage at eighteen lasted for one month. When his mother remarried, he enlisted in the military service, was in active combat as a tailgunner, and earned the Bronze Star.

When he returned from overseas, the childhood nightmares of suffocation recurred. He would wake up in a cold sweat screaming. There were compressive headaches which sometimes assumed the character of a migraine, and a strange taste in the mouth associated with vomiting.

During the next several years he had many jobs. His relations with women were chaotic; the women often became pregnant by some other man; there would be fights followed by reconciliations. He married a second time and the following day re-enlisted in military service.

He never trusted anyone, never had a close friend, was shy, passive, and reclusive. He was afraid of being hurt and avoided fights. He especially feared guns and knives. He had difficulty concentrating, would become depressed and wander off "in a daze." He drank heavily on weekends and subsequently had difficulty recalling events. He suffered increasingly from headaches and would dip his head in cold water to seek relief.

This information came forth with little reluctance over the course of a few interviews with me. Shaver seemed eager to talk about himself. Several times he turned back to his father and the fear of his beatings. There were also almost gleeful recountings of how he had cheated women out of money or otherwise tricked them.

At the end of the last session, the following exchange took place:

SHAVER: Can I tell you something, Doc?
GR: Sure, Jimmy. Anything.
SHAVER: You won't laugh or nothing?
GR: No, I won't.
SHAVER: I write.
GR: You're *right*?
SHAVER: I *write* . . . like poems.
GR: Poems? You write poems? About what? Tell me.
SHAVER: About God. Things like that. I think about it a lot.
GR: You do?
SHAVER: Would you like to see one I did yesterday?
GR: Yes, I would.
SHAVER: Here. You can keep it.

He took a scrap of lined paper from his shirt pocket and handed it to me. There was a penciled poem in block letters. It began:

Like father, like son,
Like horse, like cart . . .

The conviction instantly flashed hot: "So, he *did* do it. And I know why." Modified in some moments by the cooler thought: "Or, *if* he did it, I'll bet I know why."

Amnesia: "The inability to recall past experiences. . . . Often the onset is acute, following a psychical or physical trauma severe to the individual. It may develop subacutely (as sometimes occurs in idiopathic epilepsy) or chronically (as in dementia praecox)" (Hinsie and Shatzky 1940, 26).

Amnesia, feigned: "Amnesia is more frequently alleged [that is, feigned] than any other mental anomaly. It is obviously a convenient defense, and it is a simple matter for a person accused of a serious crime to assert that he has no memory whatever concerning it. The first thing to decide in such a case is the presence or absence of those disorders which experience suggests may be associated with some degree of amnesia: alcoholism, epilepsy, hysteria, melancholia, mania, confusional insanity, dementia praecox, dementia paralytica, senile dementia, and amentia" (East 1927, 354).

Even without these classical definitions and traditional cautions, laymen and professionals alike are often skeptical about the existence of amnesia, let alone of fugue states of altered consciousness during which any kind of behavior can take place over extended periods of time without subsequent recall. If the claim of amnesia is made to support one's innocence of criminal behavior, the disbelief becomes almost insuperable.

Shaver, however, did not insist on his innocence. He simply could not account for being at the gravel pit beyond vaguely "remembering" someone's attacking him. His attitude was one of puzzlement and passivity. "They showed me my car and they showed me these panties in my car all torn to Hell. They told me some little girl had been killed and raped. I didn't know anything about it because at that time I figured I had been beaten up by some guy and I run off into the brush to hide. But the next day I remembered I let my buddy off and I come back to the Lazy-A, and that little girl. If it happened, what they say happened, I must've done it. . . . I was the only one."

A full battery of tests was carried out. The results of a physical examination were negative. Although the electroencephalogram was within normal limits, temporal lobe epilepsy could not be ruled out. On psychological testing his intelligence was rated dull normal, and while responses to various tests indicated poor control of strong emotions and marked inner conflict with fear of being injured, there was no gross evidence of psychosis.

Therefore, on the basis of this material a psychological hypothesis was formulated. If Shaver had committed the rape and murder, it represented an acting out of a series of memories of such passively experienced incidents as seeing his father beat a horse to death, being beaten by his father, being seduced (raped?) by his cousin, then struck on the head and almost drowned. The innocent three-year-old victim of the rape and murder represented the girl cousin, Beth, his childhood tormentor. In other words, if Shaver was the murderer, he had beaten the little girl the way he saw his father beat the horse's head, the way he feared his father would beat him, the way he kept dreaming that his father beat him, and finally the way cousin Beth had struck him on the head.

A so-called truth serum interview under sodium amytal was then conducted by the chief of the psychiatric service, who was most skeptical of this formulation.[2]

> EXAMINER: O.K., Jimmy, I have given you a shot that is going to bring back your memory of that night, July 3rd. . . .You're driving down the road now, Jimmy. . . . You come to the Lazy-A. Now you are in the Lazy-A. You are sitting at the bar drinking beer. . . . Tell me, Jimmy, who is with you?
> SHAVER: Brawley.
> EXAMINER: See anybody else inside there?
> SHAVER: Yes, I see a little boy and a little girl.
> EXAMINER: Yes? What does the little girl look like? What color dress does she wear?
> SHAVER: Well, I never mess much about clothes anyway.
> EXAMINER: Well, now what are you going to do?
> SHAVER: Well, it's about time to go back to the base. It's late.
> EXAMINER: O.K. You're on your way back to the base, Jimmy. You going to let Brawley off?
> SHAVER: Yes. I let him off at the barracks.
> EXAMINER: Sure. Now where are you going to go?
> SHAVER: Oh, now I'm to pick up my wife at one o'clock.
> EXAMINER: Got some time left, have you?
> SHAVER: Not much. I'd better get down there right away.
> EXAMINER: O.K. Now you're driving down the highway. Where are you going?
> SHAVER: Now I start to go back to the Lazy-A.

2. Dr. L. Jolyon West. Permission to use this material is gratefully acknowledged.

EXAMINER: You go back to the Lazy-A?

SHAVER: Yeah.

EXAMINER: O.K., are you there?

[Shaver becomes agitated, gets up, looks around, frightened.]

EXAMINER: Back at the bar, Jimmy? Just close your eyes. Don't worry. You'll be all right. Tell me what happens now. Just keep your eyes closed. Keep your eyes closed. You're back at the Lazy-A. What's happening?

Shaver [entranced]: Now I see . . .

EXAMINER: Do you go back in?

SHAVER: Now I see . . . The same cars are there as when I left.

EXAMINER: Same cars?

SHAVER: Studebaker.

EXAMINER: O.K. So what do you do now?

SHAVER: Well, I walked around to the juke box and played a song, you know, and stood looking over the place. Then I started outside, and here's this little girl. So the little girl wants to go for a ride, you know?

EXAMINER: Sure.

SHAVER: I figured no harm in that.

EXAMINER: That's right.

SHAVER: She says, "Please, sir, mister, will you take me for a ride in your car?" I says, "Why sure honey." You know I love children.

EXAMINER: Sure. Then what happens, Jimmy?

SHAVER: Well, we get in the car and drive down the road there. I always was an impulsive guy. I wonder, Doctor, if there's anything for that?

EXAMINER: Well, we'll see, Jimmy. What happened next?

SHAVER: Well—I mean—I—you get times that are right. You know, at that moment—you know what I mean? And I can't understand it.

EXAMINER: Tell me, Jimmy.

SHAVER: Well, when I got down there I turned the corner on Frio Road . . . and I went on up there and I didn't know nothing about that place up there but the girl did so we went in . . . and after I got her out there, I—don't know!

[Starts up—looks frightened—presses both his hands tightly over his mouth.]

EXAMINER: Yes, Jimmy. It's all coming back to you.

SHAVER: I could—

[Agitated, thrashing about].

EXAMINER: Yes, Jimmy. It's all coming back to you.

SHAVER: Hey! Hey! Let me out of here! Let me out! Let me out of here! PLEASE LET ME OUT!!

[Screaming and thrashing about.]

EXAMINER: Don't worry. You remember what happens, Jimmy. Tell me. What were you thinking about? What did you do?

SHAVER: IT WAS THAT GIRL BACK HOME!

EXAMINER: The same thing happened?

SHAVER: And I beat her until she was a pulp and I was glad! [Sobbing].

EXAMINER: Which girl back home was it, Jimmy?

Shaver [Weeping]: Back where they used to go swimming with us. They was always treating me so mean.

EXAMINER: The one who always treated you so mean? Was that who it was? Is that who you thought it was?

SHAVER: Yes, sir. [Weeping]. I could have killed her!

EXAMINER: You could have killed her. For what she did to you?

SHAVER: Yes. She was always doing things. Hit me in the head with a rock. Almost had me drowned—knocked me out—you know they had me drowned, Joe?

EXAMINER: Yeah. I know.

SHAVER: Almost had me drowned. [Groaning]. My father. My father! I'm telling you he was the most rotten, the most deceiving man there ever was. [Weeping]. I hated his guts. Abosulutely hated his guts! Whip a horse to death with a chain 'cause it stepped on a little pig. Pig wasn't worth two cents. He beat me—do you know, Joe?—he beat me with a lariat rope. A lariat rope!

EXAMINER: Jimmy, what was the girl's name down in the swimming hole?

SHAVER: It's been a long time. Now let me think. Oh! Beth! She's dead now. She had an auto accident—a truck. She used to work in these places, you see. Truck drivers come there and she used to take a trip now and then. Well, that was all right with me—that's been some years back. I hated her guts.

EXAMINER: And the little girl in the car?

SHAVER: If you want to hear it, got any more stuff you can put in my arm? Kind of makes me feel like I was about half high.

EXAMINER: Yes, that's the way it feels all right.

[injecting more amytal intravenously].

SHAVER: I'm here to cooperate, you know. . . . I never was afraid of the needle before but that's quite a needle. . . . You sure I'm getting it, Doc?. . . . Hey, it's those blood veins right there, hmm . . . private property . . . can I have a cigarette?

EXAMINER: You were telling me about that night out at the gravel pit. How mad you got.

SHAVER: You see, I didn't have no sexual desire for this little runt of a kid. She wasn't nothing to me. And rightfully . . . they didn't do nothing to me. I never seen the people before. I didn't think anything about it. I walked outside and that little girl was standing by my car. Just throwing stones, you know. Just throwing stones at my windshield and at my body.

EXAMINER: Your body?

SHAVER: *My car body.*

EXAMINER: How did you feel?

SHAVER: I thought it probably wouldn't hurt it. But then she got to picking up bigger rocks and hitting it in the body and knocking paint off. I told the little girl to go home and leave. Well, she could talk a little bit, but not too plain. She says, "I ain't gonna do it." Just like Beth.

EXAMINER: Just like Beth used to say?

SHAVER: I don't know what got ahold of me at that time. I just don't realize how in the world I could do such a thing as I did.

EXAMINER: Right then and there you did something?

SHAVER: I slapped the little girl down. And then—she said she wanted to go for a ride. Sure, why not? I left. I would—the only thing I was going to do, Doc, see, I was going to take her right around this parking lot, you know, like that, and back. A little girl like that. But I mean, you know, I thought it might feel better, Doc, to do something like that. I didn't have anything on my mind at that time. But then later on an *evil* come up over me.

EXAMINER: An *evil* came up over you?

SHAVER: And even *more* of an *evil*! I don't know. I was sick already, Doc. I have headaches. Seven to eight hours at a time, Doc, you know?

And they drive you to do anything to get away from them. I've ducked them in almost solid ice, and drank, and done everything. . . . I went to the doctor and he says I have migraine headaches and wanted to give treatment for two years. Ain't that a kick, Doc?

EXAMINER: You thought it might feel better to do something with the little girl? Before you put her in your car you said you slapped her down?

SHAVER: Yes, sir. I knocked her out.

EXAMINER: Why did you do that, Jimmy?

SHAVER: Because I hated her. I thought she was someone else. Beth, when we were kids.

EXAMINER: What was the little girl doing to make you think such a thing?

SHAVER [Weeping]: Throwing rocks at my car.

EXAMINER: That made you think of Beth?

SHAVER: She hit me in the head once with a rock when we were young. Real small kids.

EXAMINER: After you knocked the little girl out, then what did you do, Jimmy?

SHAVER: Put her in the car. Then I drove down this country place, to this gravel pit. I'd never been there before but I knew just about where it was.

EXAMINER: On the way out, how were you feeling toward the little girl?

SHAVER: Well, I—I didn't like her because she was *past*, but she was *still* coming up on me. She was still grasping me. She was still trying to take things away from me like she always had. She was *evil*.

EXAMINER: How did you know she was evil?

SHAVER: God told me she was from the devil.

EXAMINER: He told you? What did he say exactly?

SHAVER: He told me to find Beth and destroy her, because she— come back to me, and was going to take all my things away again. Everything.

EXAMINER: So you got out to the gravel pit. Then what?

SHAVER: Well, then I took her and I beat her and I beat her and I beat her and I beat her some more.

EXAMINER: How did you feel at that time, Jimmy?

SHAVER: Well, I didn't want to do it. I knew that it was God's will. He sent an angel and told me.

EXAMINER: What did you do after you beat and beat on this little girl?

SHAVER: Then I run my finger up in her real far because I wanted to hurt her. For the way she hurt me so many times.

EXAMINER: Who was she then?

SHAVER: She was Beth.

EXAMINER: What did you do with her then?

SHAVER: Just left her there. And run out through the brush.

EXAMINER: Did you think you'd done something wrong?

SHAVER: No, sir.

EXAMINER: Then why did you run?

SHAVER: Well, I just run. I run and the grass began to scratch me, and then I put on my clothes and started walking towards the lights. I walked up there in front of the lights and the cops put handcuffs on me.

EXAMINER: How do you feel about what happened, Jimmy?

SHAVER: All right.

EXAMINER: Jimmy, don't you know that you made a mistake?

SHAVER: When?

EXAMINER: That little girl you killed. She wasn't Beth, Jimmy.

SHAVER: Who was she?

EXAMINER: She was just a little girl that you'd never seen before.

SHAVER: You mean that I didn't kill the right one. Huh? [Weeping].

EXAMINER: She was just a little girl that you'd never seen before, Jimmy? How does that make you feel?

SHAVER: It makes me feel terrible. [Weeping.]

EXAMINER: How do you think God will feel about that, Jimmy?

SHAVER [Weeping]: He sure won't like it. I'll have to pray and pray that he'll forgive me. But I'm afraid it's too late for that now.

EXAMINER: Jimmy, look up here a minute, boy. What do you think is going to happen now?

SHAVER: I'll go to the electric chair, I guess.

EXAMINER: Are you afraid to go to the electric chair?

SHAVER: I don't know. I've never been there.

EXAMINER: Do you think you deserve to go to the electric chair?

SHAVER: Yes, sir. I guess I do.

EXAMINER: Why?

SHAVER: You just said I killed the wrong girl.

EXAMINER: Would it be because you killed the wrong one? Let me ask you this, Jimmy. If you had killed the right one, then would you have had to go to the electric chair?

SHAVER: Oh, no. She was evil. She was evil. *Nobody* would send me to the electric chair for her.

How is one to look at this story? From the point of view of a jury, central issues would involve both the rights of the accused and the concern that society be protected from a repetition of such violence. Questions having to do with the defendant's legal sanity, such as his responsibility at the time of the crime and current ability to stand trial, hinge on the existence of free will. The extent to which he was able to exercise free will would be estimated by traditional judicial tests of sanity—for example, the ability to know right from wrong, adhere to the right, and participate in his own defense (McNaughten's Rule).

Far removed from the doctrine of free will is the clinician's experience that pyschic determinism operates along the entire gamut of human behavior. From the amytal interview it is apparent that this rape and murder represented the reenactment of consciously remembered, severely traumatic events in Shaver's childhood. A close examination of the data might even support the further supposition that forgotten memories of primal scene experience unconsciously, yet decisively, helped shape Shaver's life. For example, his lifelong neurotic adaptation could be seen as based predominantly on *masochistic* identifications with both parents in the sexual act, and the rape-murder was based on an eruption of repressed *sadistic* identifications with both parents in the primal scene (Rose 1960a).

Setting aside both frames of reference, legal and clinical, let us look at the story primarily as a *story*, having a narrative line and an integrated thematic development. There is obviously the theme of violence, closely interwoven with that of revenge. The traumatic historical elements from the past are represented on many levels simultaneously: they are symbolically represented in the form of physical symptoms, ritualistic reenactments, the murder and rape, and the confabulating attempt to account for himself at the scene of the crime. Also, these historical elements are recapitulated and integrated in differing time frames: momentary percept, structured symptom, patterned episode, lifetime style.

Regarding lifetime style, Shaver's characteristic behavior pattern was one of passive submission to abuse, leading, finally, to a sudden about-face and turning against the persecutor in a single act of revenge. Character being fate, he repeatedly let himself be taken advantage of by women before suddenly getting even.

With this sadomasochistic character structure as background, Shaver's long-standing neurotic symptoms may be considered as middle-ground. Among the symptoms, his sexual impotence and marked passivity, compulsive masturbation and enuresis all testify to the fear of bodily, probably sexual, injury and possibly death. The attacks of migraine may symbolically repeat his experience with violence directed especially to the head: the horse against the pig, father's demolishing the horse's head, Beth striking Shaver on the head with a rock, and so on. Likewise, the nightmares of smothering, the excessive drinking, and the attempts to cure headaches by dunking the head in water may refer to the memory of almost drowning after being impotent with Beth. (At the same time they may also represent castration threats displaced upward to the head.)

The events of the day of the murder recapitulate the characteristic pattern within a tighter time frame. It is a holiday eve, but Shaver is alone, deprived of his wife, who, as a waitress, is off feeding others. We may guess that resentment and rebellion are brewing since he illegally releases Brawley from disciplinary restrictions. Seeking further for a sense of release, and perhaps even hearing preliminary Independence Day fireworks already being set off in the hot summer night, he goes off with Brawley for some heavy drinking. This culminates in the explosion of rape and murder, which, as he made clear, was an act of revenge against his childhood tormentor.

A few days after his apprehension by the police, he struck his head while in his cell and thereafter felt he could "recall" something of what had happened. The content of this "recall" was a confabulation. It is significant that it was ushered in by a blow to the head, just as the murder episode had been precipitated by blows to the body of his car. As is so often the case with organic confabulations (Williams and Rupp 1938), the content also contained elements of truth. In the confabulation, he said he had been hit on the head and genitals by a man, knocked out, and stripped. Once again the theme of assault by Beth and father is recapitulated. Again, too, one could theoretically posit sadomasochistic identifications in an unconscious memory of the primal scene.

We move, finally, to the specific precipitant of the murderous violence, the single moment when Shaver perceived the little girl "just *throwing stones*" at his windshield and at his *body*." "Your body?" "*My car body*" (emphases mine). Just as a searchlight beacon in its 360-degree sweep simultaneously illuminates points at every radius from the center, most proximate and most distant, this single instant of perception reveals itself. And compressed within it, as within the lifetime character and symptom patterns, the day's events, the criminal act, and the attempt to explain it away through confabulation, we find the same recapitulation of familiar traumata. "It was that girl back home! And I beat her until she was a pulp and I was glad!"

This moment merits closer scrutiny. My car body = my body. A stone = a stone. A stone thrown from the hand of any little girl at my car body = the stones thrown by Beth at my naked, humiliated, impotent child-body-head-genital just before they nearly drowned me. Before the rush of accumulated affect and the pressure of the past, and facilitated by alcohol, spatial, personal and temporal distinctions dissolve into equivalences. "She was *past*, but she was *still* coming up on me."

In Shaver's case these bridging leaps in imagination—of time, place, and person—were uncorrected by realistic knowledge. They were acted upon, fatally, with an overriding conviction as to their truth.

Suppose, however, that he had had the requisite aspects of ego strength to stand off, reflect in the light of reality, and not act. Suppose, further, that he had had the talent to transform his experience into art, such as painting or writing. For example, what if he had gone drinking at the Lazy-A, had seen a little girl throw stones at the body of his car, and had later written a short story having to do with the rape and murder of a child one hot Fourth of July eve?

To be more precise, what qualities would have been required for an act of creative rather than clinical imagination, or simply normal control? To begin with, the author would have needed a dual capacity: to tap into the enormous organizing power of the unconscious, such as we have seen illustrated in the Shaver case, and at the same time be able to withstand and not be overwhelmed by the force of unconscious drives. Instead of feelings, thoughts, and perceptions, split off from history and the flow of time, seizing upon fortuitous details in order to *reenact* the traumatic past through a contemporary cast of innocent characters and events—the clinical face of imagination—still more would have been necessary for an act of creative imagination: (1) the talent to create forms that would channel the force of unconscious drives into an artistic medium, (2) transmit a sense of the scope and depth of integration taking place unconsciously, and (3) communicate a feelingful perspective that transcended the private dimensions of merely personal trauma.

As for the underlying structure of the resulting work, the fictional characters and dramatic action might well have been organized around the same traumatic elements: "horizontally" on different levels ranging from the symbolic self-beatings of the migraine to actual violence, and "vertically" in different time frames, from lifetime pattern to the day's events to a single crucial moment—each level and each time frame recapitulating the original experiences.

What effect might such a work have had on a potential audience? The emotional impact would still have been one of horror. But not only. If one may apply such a cold-blooded view to personal disaster, the aesthetic experience of the story would have been superior to the real event. For the shock of a real event tends to obliterate everything but horror, while the successful work of fiction allows other emotions to surface and coexist, each undiluted by the others. So this one, too, could have elicited a wider range of emotional reactions, together with greater understanding for the complexities involved. A reader of such a story, after richly experiencing identifications with the several characters involved, might well have been left with a more *compassionate understanding* of the nature of tragedy, the blurring of innocence and guilt, the tendency for it to perpetuate itself into the generations.

Art is superior to life. Creative imagination surpasses everyday and clinical imagination in its ability to enlarge upon life's very features and hold them up for feelingful reflection. Prominent among those features is the capacity of any mind, Shaver's included, to orchestrate diverse elements around a few unifying themes, on many levels simultaneously, and in different time frames—*unconsciously*.

Perhaps this capacity is revealed especially in traumatic themes, which determined Shaver's character, distorted his perception, made possible his crime, and lay embedded in his unconscious confession:

> Like father, like son
> Like horse, like cart . . .

POSTSCRIPT

As the summer wore on, temperatures climbed above 100. Tempers grew short, and threats were heard as rumors spread that outsiders were going to try to get the child-killer off on the basis of some "theory." A change of venue moved the trial out to a small ranching town suffering from drought and with little use for ambiguity. Within recent memory, a rancher had caught his wife *in flagrante* with the hired hand and, treating him like one of his own herd, proceeded to rope and neuter him. He was duly tried and acquitted.

Shaver's sanity trial came first. It was held in a crowded schoolroom. The judge sat in his suspenders, there were cuspidors on the floor, and many in the jury wore their customary sidearms. Testimony was heard for up to fourteen hours a day, and Shaver was never seen to move a single time. Reporters were still taking bets on whether he would move at all when the jury began its deliberations. After twenty-three hours it found the defendant sane and fit to be tried.

Then came the criminal trial. It did not take as long. After some three hours the jury returned to ask two question: (1) If Shaver were given a sentence of life imprisonment, could he ever be released from prison? and (2) if he could be released under a life term, was there any other sentence he could be given so that he would never be freed?

After being instructed by the judge, the jury returned a speedy verdict of guilty of murder with malice. The sentence of death in the electric chair was passed.

A second trial was held. Appeals to the U.S. Supreme Court were turned down. The sentence was executed close to the anniversary of the crime on the eve of the Fourth of July.

4

MULTIPLE PERSONALITY:
CHARACTERS DISOWNED BY
THEIR "AUTHOR"

Under the impact of trauma, or of a traumatic intensity of conflict, the organism is in danger of being flooded with affects. In an attempt at containment and mastery, these affects may split off. Dostoevsky's fictional character, Golyadkin, experienced a "vertical" split of consciousness to become Golyadkin plus his newly formed double; in Shaver's real-life case, affects that had become too intense for consciousness underwent "horizontal" repression—that is, they were rendered unconscious.

Golyadkin's envy and ambition had been thinly disguised behind obsequiousness; his hypocrisy was laid bare when he was spotted by his section chief in a fancy carriage pretending to be a fine gentleman. In order to disown the affects and traits that stood revealed, he pretended that "it's not I at all, it's not I—(Dostoevsky [1846] 1950, 142). Soon his own repugnant qualities became personified in the form of the "other" Golyadkin, his double. The conscious coexistence of Golyadkin and his double within a single cohesive reality became increasingly untenable and culminated in the final break from sanity.

Shaver's rage and desire for revenge were repressed into the unconscious, and turned against himself; they appeared in the disguised form of somatic and other symptomatic torments. Occasionally they would erupt through his characteristic external submissiveness and take the shape of brief, deliberate sneak attacks against the various women who dominated him. The rape and murder on the eve of the Fourth of July were acted out in a mental state dissociated from consciousness.

In both cases, the affects that became fragmented off—splitting away either within consciousness or from consciousness—did not live on in a vacuum but continued to seek discharge and, just as persistently, were defended against to avoid the danger of flooding the organism. This shifting equilibrium of affects and defense against them represents ongoing efforts at mastery; it exerts an "organizing" effect on thoughts and percepts and the behavior that flows accordingly.

Shaver's explosive episode provides a highly condensed glimpse of this ongoing struggle: on the day of the crime, Shaver's rebellion and rage grew as he became frustrated with his wife's absence; his control over these affects diminished the more he drank; when he saw a stone-throwing little girl attacking his "body," he misperceived her as his childhood tormentor and the old fear of being raped and killed finally erupted openly in a vengeful, preemptive act of rape and murder.

A clinical condition where the sequence of splitting and reintegration is slowed down and magnified affords a closer examination of the nature of trauma and mastery. Such a condition is multiple personality disorder, in which a number of repressed affects become split off from consciousness and organized into two or more distinct personalities; disowned by their "author," they interact with each other, have unique behavior patterns and social relationships, and periodically dominate the individual's thoughts, feelings, and behavior.

BACKGROUND

Multiple personality disorder figured prominently in the psychological and psychiatric literature of the late nineteenth and early twentieth centuries. It is noteworthy that Pierre Janet (1889), who was perhaps the first to formulate a theory regarding this disorder, located its cause in traumatic events of the past (as well as in heredity). Similar views were expressed by William James (1890), and by Morton Prince (1906) in his writing about his most famous patient, Christine Beauchamp.

More recently, multiple personality has attracted considerable media attention (Thigpen and Cleckley, *The Three Faces of Eve*, 1957; Schreiber, *Sybil*, 1973; Keyes, *The Minds of Billy Milligan*, 1981), and also received renewed scientific study (for example, the first conference devoted to the study of multiple personality, at Rush Medical School, Chicago, September, 1984). Surprisingly little psychoanalytic attention has been devoted to it (Lasky 1978; Marmer 1980; Berman 1981).

In this condition, the personalities other than the original, host, or presenting personality are referred to as the *alternates*. Pascal (as quoted by Bentley 1952, xxvii) said, "There is no man who differs more from another man than he does from himself at another time." Nowhere is this more true than among the alternates, who differ among themselves in almost every respect: gender, age, and sexual orientation; wardrobes and possessions; pursuits, styles, and values; manifest problems, symptoms, and diagnoses. Their psychophysiological variations are among the most striking features: presence or absence of allergies; handedness and handwriting; voices, type of accent, and speech patterns, including the presence or absence of stammering, the knowledge or ignorance of foreign languages, and the scope of vocabulary; facial expressions, movements, and talents—artistic, musical, mathematical, mechanical, and so on; even brainwave tracings (including the refined technique of visual evoked potentials). As the alternates achieve integration within one personality, visual changes include visual acuity, ocular tension, color vision and visual fields (Shepard and Braun, 1985).

A prominent and consistent finding among cases of multiple personality disorder is that more than 90 percent were victims of child abuse—physical, mental, sexual (including incest)—often verified.

The greater the severity, the earlier the onset, and the longer the duration of the abuse, the more intense the condition; the later treatment is undertaken, the poorer the prognosis.

General opinion, however, both within psychiatry and outside the field, tends to be outspokenly skeptical or politely dubious as to the existence of the condition. This contributes to the fact that the diagnosis is often overlooked; where multiple personality is alleged to exist, it is likely to be attributed to suggestion or gullibility on the part of the therapist, an unconscious collusion of therapist and patient joined in a folie à deux, or a conscious malingering attempt of the patient to avoid punishment for some crime.

Undoubtedly, it was with similar latent attitudes that I stepped into the waiting room to greet my next regular patient, whom I shall call Diana.

Long familiarity over the course of several years had taught me what to expect: a dour, unsmiling, fortyish woman, with wooden expression, slow, deliberate motions, conveying in manner and inflection heavy, unrelieved gloom together with the unshakable conviction that all efforts on her behalf were doomed in advance. Anhedonia—the absence of pleasure in acts that are normally pleasurable—her life seemed to have given new meaning to the term. Except for work. She was a gifted, competent, sensitive college teacher, beloved by her students and respected by her colleagues. Her married and family life, on the other hand, was grimly devoted to being relentlessly on guard against the dangers lurking everywhere ready to strike herself, her husband, or her children should her vigilance falter. In short, depression, anxiety, compulsions, and phobias had long dominated the clinical picture and constricted her life.

Her symptoms had defeated every attempt at treatment over the years, by myself and others, and had taught me a new respect for "negative therapeutic reaction"—a prim term to describe a dreaded treatment phenomenon in which everything that should help paradoxically serves to make matters worse. Earlier efforts at psychotherapy and psychoanalysis had bogged down in intractable silence or unresponsiveness. Results with me, first in psychoanalysis, then in psychotherapy, seemed little better. Trials with numerous drugs under the supervision of a consultant invariably led to bizarre side effects which required neurological, cardiovascular, and endocrine investigations (all negative). Deepening depression with serious suicidal risk on two occasions necessitated emergency hospitalization for about a month each time. Concomitant marital and family therapy with a male and a female therapist did little to improve the quality of the home.

And yet, in spite of the succession of one dramatic crisis after another and her insistence that each was the worst so far and truly unbearable, I had the impression of overall qualitative improvement—though I could never allude to it on pain of immediate worsening of her symptoms. The dynamics of the case were becoming increasingly clear, and though it was apparent to both of us that she could at times harbor psychotic ideation and even lose control of herself at home, there was also ample opportunity to observe that much of the time her judgment was sound and her behavior reliable.

Diana, of course, steadfastly expressed only hopelessness regarding the final outcome, but she came faithfully for her sessions and resisted my efforts to have her cut down from three to two sessions weekly. I thought that it would lessen her dependence on me, and also relieve me of some of the burden of carrying such a case.

After I returned from a short vacation, Diana said she wished she could tell me that all had gone well and that she was ready to leave treatment, but, regretfully, she could not. I said it sounded as though she would have liked to have been able to give me that as a gift. She agreed.

This is where matters stood when I went out to the waiting room to ask her in for our next treatment session.

But she was not there. Or rather, it was clearly Diana sitting there but just as clearly not Diana. The features of the woman who sat there were surely Diana's, but the expression and posture were certainly not. Sitting on the sofa in a thoroughly relaxed way with her legs curled up beneath her, she flashed me a warm, sunny, engaging smile and said, "She's not here. She left." "And who are you?" "I'm Roddy." She spoke in a tiny, child's voice, bit her lower lip, and shook her head with slow, exaggerated, up and down or sideways motions to indicate "yes" or "no." She seemed the complete image of a composed, trusting but shy, polite but forthright, charming little girl.

"Diana and I were always good friends. Then her mother told her that I was really no friend of hers and she should give me up. But Diana didn't and we remained secret friends always—until her father had a heart attack when she was eleven years old. She thought it was her fault because she had been bad and kept me as her secret friend. So she let me go. But I never went. I stayed with her. She doesn't know me, but I know her very, very well. I comforted her and would take over for her and help her out. I'm eleven years old. But when I take over I can pretend to be any age I want. Oh, no—her mother is not my mother. Who would want her for a mother? I have my own mother and father. They're real nice. I can go back to them any time I want. Why did I come today? Because she was too scared. She was scared that you are angry with her and that is why you take vacations and talk to her about cutting down to twice a week. I am her special gift to you."

I thanked Roddy for coming and said that Diana was lucky to have her as a friend and helper, and now let's bring Diana back to the session. She nodded happily and agreed to come again. Then Roddy's head dropped to her chest, she unfolded her legs from beneath her, assumed a wooden, stolid position, each hand resting on each thigh, her features took their customary heavy, stony expression, she sighed heavily, and Diana raised her head. She had no awareness of what had transpired. She looked at the clock, apologized for coming late, but things were getting to be just too much for her, time was getting away from her, and she was finding it harder and harder to keep track of things or to stay tuned in.

When I told Diana what had happened, at first she could only insist that this was bad, this was just too weird, she didn't want to have any of it, talk about it, know about it. Finally, she said she had a vague memory of having had an imaginary companion as a child. "What was her name?" "I think it was something like Roddy." "What happened?" "Mother told me I shouldn't. So I gave her up. She must have gone underground."

Thus began my acquaintance with Roddy, the first of a number of characters who began to emerge to the accompaniment of Diana's dreaming of Siamese twins, of giving birth, and similar themes.

I felt like Pirandello when he wrote his preface to *Six Characters in Search of an Author*:

> I can only say that, without having made any effort to seek them out, I found before me, alive—you could touch them and even hear them breathe—the six characters now seen on the stage. And they stayed there in my presence, each with his secret torment and all bound together by the one common origin and mutual entanglement of their affairs. . . . Born alive, they wished to live (Bentley 1952, 364).
>
> "Why not," I said to myself, "present this highly strange fact of an author who refuses to let some of his characters live though they have been born in his fantasy? . . . Having by now life in their veins, [they] do not resign themselves to remaining excluded from the world. . . . They . . . live on their own; . . . even know how to defend themselves against others. . . . Let them go where dramatic characters do go to have life: on a stage. And let us see what will happen" (p. 366).
>
> Without wanting to, without knowing it, in the strife of their bedevilled souls, each of them . . . expresses . . . the multiple personality of everyone corresponding to the possibilities of being to be found in each of us (p. 367).

The outlines of the past history were these. Diana was born in a small Midwestern town. Her father was a junior high school principal. He had courted the gym teacher for eight years before marrying her. One child, a son, died shortly after birth. Diana was the replacement for father's sake. Neither parent had family in the area, nor did they seem to have any friends. For some reason, Diana was sent away for a month to a distant aunt and uncle's at the age of two years. When she returned her disposition seems to have changed from cheerful to sad and serious. At four years of age she spent four or five weeks in bed with a fever, possibly due to cystitis. At seven she had a tonsillectomy under ether anesthesia. Until this time she slept in her parents' bedroom. She was taught to be a model child, a showpiece for the community, as befit the parents' status. She was always dressed in long stockings and gloves and was expected to remain clean at all times. Few friends were tolerated. She had dolls, but mother controlled how they were dressed and where they were to be kept at all times. Father took no part in Diana's upbringing; she was mother's project. The family would sometimes take rides in the car together, but Diana could never be part of the conversation and would always sit alone in the back seat. They went to the movies together every week faithfully. Father had a heart attack when Diana was eleven and remained confined to the home until his death four years later. Diana was not allowed to talk to him during that time. In school she was an excellent student and made close girlfriends with whom she went to the movies each week and to every play that came to town. She attended a university in a distant part of the state. There, she formed an intense attachment to her roommate. Following graduation, both young women came East and completed their postgraduate studies. Shortly after Diana took a faculty position in a church-affiliated institution, her roommate was killed in a car accident. A few years later Diana married her roommate's brother, a computer scientist. The onset of anxiety and phobic symptoms occurred following the birth of a daughter and became aggravated after the birth of a son.

Roddy and the various other characters who followed did not begin to make their appearance until after many years of treatment. As mentioned earlier, treatment began as psychoanalysis, changed to psychotherapy, was supplemented by marital, family, and drug treatment under other therapists, and was punctuated by two hospitalizations of about a month's duration each. Let us summarize the highlights.

Diana's first dream was, "I am mother's entire life." Detailing the many ways in which this was true and what it involved became the substance of her lengthy treatment. What emerged slowly and painfully was that, from her earliest years, Diana had been the subject of child abuse, both physical and emotional, was amnesic for much of it, and had escaped from it by blanking out and at the same time believed she deserved it. The abuser was her mother, who was probably psychotic, though no one ever knew.

Diana had no memory of kindness or compassion from her mother. On the contrary, it appeared that mother systematically deprived Diana of any possibility of pleasure, at the same time making Diana responsible for the deprivations. As soon as mother discovered that Diana enjoyed rubbing a piece of blanket, it was destroyed. Diana was accused of being "bad," punished by spanking, and told she had brought it on herself.

Since crying was forbidden, the more Diana cried, the more she was spanked and threatened. She finally learned never to cry. In treatment she often struggled against speaking because speaking might lead to tears, and they might never stop. She dreamed: "I was bleeding profusely and screaming because I knew I had been injured, but there was no light to see. Then the door opened and you came in and put the light on. There was no blood on my hands and no injury. I guess I had been crying and not bleeding."

The alternative to punishment and crying seemed to be silence, and that was worse. Mother would never speak to her. Diana would scream and beg to be called by name and would dream of going berserk screaming at mother. Mother refused to look at her, saying Diana did not deserve it. Or mother would say her name was "Mud." She customarily referred to Diana in the third person only, for example: "Is she going to come in for supper?"

Much of Diana's childhood was spent waiting for clues to what was coming next from mother. Mother would often leave unexpectedly at night without a word as to when or whether she would return. These departures always took place without warning; she would suddenly get up from her seat and leave a trolley car, for example, so that Diana had to keep up and not get lost. She recalled that her first anxiety attack was at about age five or six, fearing to lose mother in a department store crowd.

Could it have been that mother did not want Diana? That she did not want Diana alive? Diana was afraid to hear herself say this. She was her mother's life. Mother had almost died in giving birth to her. Mother had been told that she had given birth to a son. Diana had to be grateful for mother's sacrifices. It was just that mother did not want her to be spoiled. To care is to be indulged is to be spoiled and that is *bad*. Treatment is self-indulgence. It is disobedience to mother; it can only make things worse.

As an adult, Diana found that she could be more her own self when mother was present. When mother was away Diana would find herself yelling at her daughter and could practically hear mother's voice, but was unable to stop it. She remembered an outburst of rage at mother throwing something at the *mirror*. She feared that she would become more and more like mother, and her daughter more like herself. She was mortified to find herself beating her daughter—as mother beat her?

Dreams led Diana in the direction of memories she preferred to leave buried. "I saw a screaming, battered child on the store counter, black and blue. I wanted to comfort it, but was told that it was not allowed." Diana awoke with the pillow sopping wet with tears. Could it be that mother had been physically abusive to her?

In another dream, Diana was being locked in a closet with her daughter and fearing suffocation. Could she have been locked in a closet herself? She became afraid to sleep lest she dream. She was afraid to remember. All Hell will break loose! She did remember: she *was* locked in a closet; she *did* fear suffocating. Now she felt like vomiting. She did something terrible by telling me that. She was trained to keep secrets—above all from her father, who was too tired or too busy. Otherwise, she would *really* get it. This is "squealing." Now I will have her locked up. She never should have come here. [She looked terrified.]

Following this session, Diana got lost. When she went into a phone booth to call me she suddenly recognized her whereabouts. Such dissociation would often accompany or follow memories and confessions of having been abused. First she would consciously fight the return of the memories, then feel paranoid toward me, then become unable to hear me and fall silent. Silence, she said, had been her only defense against mother.

She began to remember that there had been many blank spells in her life, long periods without any memory: father's funeral when she was fifteen, many piano recitals over the years. As a child she remembered that a person would begin to recede before her eyes, then disappear. Diana feared that she was going blind and would practice walking around with her eyes closed to prepare herself. She had been afraid to fall asleep at night lest she wake up blind or deaf. She never told anyone this for fear of being blamed for it. After telling me, she became hypnoidally detached, seemed far away, was unresponsive, and said she could not hear me.

As memories of childhood abuse forced their way into her consciousness, Diana began to discover notes at her bedside in the morning. The first was in a handwriting not her own, unless she had written it lefty, as she used to do secretly as a child when her mother was forcing her to use her right hand. It said: "One lazy afternoon I awoke to find someone in my head." After I told her that she would have to become better friends with herself and learn to shake hands, she found a second note at her bedside the next morning: "The other other can't know the other me, we only have one hand."

Other examples of automatic writing: "I can't breathe anymore its so fast it makes me hurt and shake don't make me tell anyone anymore." And: "Sick babies cry / Don't let them die / Don't make them die / Don't make them cry." And: "It's hurting too much to do it alone." And: "I am afraid to hear her. I can't see her anymore. I won't be bad a hundred times. I can't ever be." [Printed in block print].

Diana remembered that she had had an imaginary companion named Roddy, but mother said this was silly and told her to stop it. Then Diana became unable to hear or understand me. The next morning, a note at her bedside said: "She's never there. It's so empty and bare not to care." It seemed that Diana had peopled her life with prohibited imaginary companions to fill the emptiness and to comfort herself.

The pace of memories increased and could not be slowed down or held back. Diana recalled how she would try to remain with people as long as possible and try never to be alone with mother because of the incessant punishment; she remembered that her mother kept her well-dressed and all covered up with long stockings and gloves so that there would be no visible evidence of her beatings; thus no rescue was ever possible. Along with these memories, there were mounting fears of retribution. She wanted to run away, smashed a mirror at home on some minor provocation, flung her daughter physically, struck her husband when he admonished her, and was appalled at her own behavior. Telling her that she was repeating and dramatizing her mother's irrational rages instead of remembering had no effect. Nor did daily medication with phenothiazines. She dreamed of being in a frenzy of rage against her mother, said she was afraid of herself, afraid she might kill her children and husband, and that she could not be trusted alone.

Actively suicidal and deeply depressed at the end of the second year of treatment, Diana was hospitalized for five weeks and treated with an antidepressant (Parnate) and a tranquilizer (Trilafon). She experienced the hospitalization as punishment for having been bad. It reminded her of having to be in bed every evening by 6 P.M. She said that now she no longer existed—only mother remained.

The pattern kept repeating itself during the course of the next three years: memories of child abuse coming up insistently despite great fear; "spacing out" during sessions when affect became too intense (I would fade and Diana would be unable to see or hear me); the discovery of more notes informing us of more child abuse; renewed rage at mother, followed by attempts to exonerate her and blame herself. Brief episodes of feeling somewhat better would be followed immediately by feeling worse. Recovering and sharing traumatic memories only resulted in retraumatizing herself in the process of recall. Yet, the pressure of traumatic memories demanded release.

The angrier Diana would become at her mother, the more this would trigger her own identification with her mother, and she would hate herself. The only way to be loved by mother is to be dead. [Diana began to shake uncontrollably.] Yet, it must be Diana's own fault that mother was not loving. Mother was, after all, conspicuously affectionate to other children. So Diana kept trying to transform mother into a loving person, blaming herself for failing, defending her mother. At the same time, she kept bringing in examples of mother's pathological lying, her inability to give a straight answer to anything, her irrationality, and her attempts to impose it on Diana in the past and on her grandchildren in the present. For example, mother insisted on things Diana knew to be untrue, such as that her name had always been "X" whereas Diana knew that mother's name had been "Y," having seen it as such in mother's high school yearbook.

The horror-story memories continued. While relating a dream that her air supply was being cut off, Diana would recall mother's holding her head backward under a scalding shower, telling her the water was not hot while Diana was gagging. Or of mother forcing her to drink fluids when she was ill, then forbidding her to go to the bathroom and beating her if she wet the bed.

The matter of the bathroom deserves special mention. Diana was never allowed to be in the bathroom for more than a few minutes, and the door had to remain open. She was not allowed to use the bathroom after 6 P.M. She could never use any bathroom other than the one at home, because of "germs." Therefore, Diana would rush home from school as fast as possible to get to the bathroom on time. Many of her nightmares centered on the fear of "accidents" and either beating someone for "accidents" or being beaten for them. In one dream, she knew that if she went to the bathroom to urinate she would hemorrhage to death. But if she did not go she would burst. So she did not go and remained in torment. Like crying, her fear of "letting go" was connected to the fear that she would then "go" endlessly and be punished endlessly for it.

Something further should be mentioned about mother's worldview. Happiness was too good to be true. Therefore, only the bad was real. If the weather appears to be beautiful, that is a perfect way to be taken in and get sick when the weather changes. Under no circumstances must one let down one's guard and enjoy; every apparent pleasure is a booby trap; one must always avoid hope and thus disappointment. Accordingly, if Diana began to feel somewhat better, she would become anxious. What seems good is untrue and bad; what is bad is true and good.

It was not surprising that when Diana left a session feeling good for the first time, she felt light-headed, her speech became slurred and somewhat garbled, and she developed a frontal headache of such intensity that a C-T scan was performed. (It proved negative.) Nor was it difficult to begin to understand, if almost impossible to change, her lifelong pattern of depriving herself of whatever she wanted, since getting what she wanted would only make matters worse in both the short and long run. The primitive logic was that it must have become bad because it had been good. Moral: Never let anything become good because that will make it go bad. Admitting to feeling okay was tantamount to being caught in an illicit pleasure. On one level, even being alive was getting away with something. Hence, the constant expectation of disaster and death. Once, she admitted to herself that her life had become much freer in some respects. She immediately had a panic attack together with an intense urge to cry, as though to apologize. Thus, anxiety represented self-punishment for pleasure—a way of beating mother to the punch and acquiring some degree of active mastery. (But, while pleasure was unthinkable, she was also consumed with anger and jealousy toward those who seemed to get away with it.)

Any transference gratification was at her peril. In a dream, I was pictured as calling her name repeatedly and softly, something her mother, of course, had never done. She kept screaming at me to stop, becoming angrier and angrier, and finally said that if I did not stop she would have to jump off the bridge she was standing on, into the dark, windy, cold night. And she did.

Summarizing some of the aspects of the treatment impasse: (1) Diana feared that if she were not moralistic and compulsive she might stop functioning altogether. (2) Retraumatizing herself by reliving memories of punishment was a way of punishing herself for "squealing" on mother. (3) Diana defined "really" as meaning the past; thus, her feeling that nothing can "really" change was due to her equating "really" with the past, and acting out the past in recurrent masochistic escapades made it "really" present in actuality. (4) She needed to support mother's delusion of being perfect by herself retaining the role of the evil scapegoat.

Early in the sixth year of treatment there was a sudden deterioration of the shaky equilibrium. It was triggered by nightmares, then memories of being beaten mercilessly. This was followed by rapidly escalating rage at her own daughter, and then the realization of how this was almost identical to her mother's chronic rage at her. She then remembered that as a child she used to be obsessed with thoughts of suicide and had even been actively suicidal. There was a specific memory of having deliberately walked in front of a car when she was ten years of age. The car skidded to a stop, but not before knocking her down. The driver carried her home. Her mother beat her "within an inch of my life" and refused to speak to her for days.

This memory seemed to set off a new rush of yearnings for death—the only relief she could hope for, as in childhood, and as a means of rejoining her dear, dead father. When her father had died, mother's first words to Diana had been: "You finally killed him." Diana had answered: "I'm sorry." Mother hardly ever spoke to her after that. Diana could not turn to memories of her father for comfort. There were few memories and it was just as well, for she could not take the chance of losing him. She knew he was passive and ineffectual, but he probably did all he could, and he was all she had. But he was dead. She was certain there was no other way but to put an end to the useless struggle. Diana overdosed with Valium, said goodbye to me on the phone, and had to be hospitalized again.

A few days later I received a note from the hospital. It included the following: "In spite of the garbage and anger I lay on you, I know you must understand how much I appreciate your concern, understanding, sensitivity. . . . You have helped me make some important changes (will I ever be punished for admitting that?) and seeing you [in the hospital today] did indeed breathe a little fresh air into tired lungs. Thank you. . . . In spite of these hospitalizations, I still have faith in . . . our work together. If I survive this latest episode in the ongoing soap opera of my life, I hope we can continue that work." Diana retained no memory of having written this.

After her discharge from the hospital about thirty days later, "splitting from the scene" became one of the chief themes of the next few years. It became apparent to her that this had happened far more often than she had realized. She used to be afraid to blink because she would often "awaken" days or even months later. It would come as a shock that before she "blinked" it was winter, she was in the bathtub at about five years of age and the next thing she knew she was sitting in a sandbox in the park and it was springtime. Where was she in between? Home movies proved that she swam well as a young woman, yet as far as she was aware, she did not know how to swim.

Such splitting also continued in her current life. Sometimes her handwriting would change so drastically that the bank would refuse to cash her checks. She would discover that she had done much shopping but had no memory of it. She could not recall whether she had kept her last appointment with me or had been to work. She went to wash the breakfast dishes and the next thing she knew she was standing there washing the dinner dishes and did not know what day it was. One day she discovered a large amount of cash in her purse. On another day, an expensive speeding ticket.

Diana kept finding notes everywhere. They talked about her in the third person and seemed to refer to child abuse: suggestions of oral and anal invasions of her body, gagging, choking; "The pain in her gut spreads and now she can't move her arms and legs. The tears are always salty and quiet. No one hears her." "The scissors cut too close. Glass breaks and hurts. She's bleeding again." "She's around every corner. She's in the schoolyard—in her bed—in her body." "Don't pull the blindfold off." "There is nowhere to hide. The skin looks raw." "Don't kick her. Please don't hurt her. Save her." "Under her skin she quivers. She smiles awaiting the next blow."

One note said: "She is out of step with time. Preventing her from fragmenting becomes more difficult. Her only comfort is to disappear." According to the notes, disappearing and fragmenting were related to each other: "Separate minds within a single body. Too much to endure alone." "Life on the outside differs from life on the inside. The split widens. The two worlds cannot meet."

The automatic writing and the nightmares led to more memories of abuse with further details: beatings, enemas, nose-drops, oral medications—all for Diana's own good. The beatings were always carried out without mother's raising her voice, telling her that if she cried or ever complained to father it would be much worse for her, that mother was her only friend, that Diana would appreciate it one day and love her for it because it showed mother cared no matter how bad Diana was. The only let-up was mother's silence and unresponsiveness, which were worse—or the solace of playing with dolls and, later, school, the library, the movies, or listening to music.

Aside from the realistic therapeutic alliance with me, she experienced treatment sadomasochistically. She saw me sometimes as her father, caring in some distant, ineffectual way, and would rail at me to "do" something or try to terrorize me with threats of suicide, deadlines, ultimata, crises of all sorts, while shooting down every attempt to be of help.

Alternatively, she would experience me as her mother, forcing something down her throat, which only caused her to "vomit" or "defecate" a terrible mess of more anger, necessitating more punishment. She saw me as demanding that she face intolerable memories, which only made matters worse, or tearing her away from her lifeline to her mother—namely, her pain, her neurosis.

When, at times, she would recognize that she was using treatment to retraumatize herself rather than to master the past, or was abusing me in addition to herself, she would only feel more guilty and worthless for doing nothing to protect me from her anger. "Voices" in her head, which she knew to be unreal, would warn her not to speak to me, not to listen to me, not to confide in me, because this would prove lethal for both of us.

The state of affairs just before the appearance of Roddy has already been described. By now, Diana held a responsible job and was highly respected. To the outside world she was a composed and empathic person with a well-organized life as wife, mother, daughter, community member, and hostess, as well as a successful career in academia. Few knew that her family life was turbulent, and her marriage nonsexual. Only she and I knew about her past and present panics and the way she could "drop out" or "split" from consciousness. Her functioning had improved, but treatment was at a stalemate.

Enter Roddy.

"THE OTHERS"

Roddy had been Diana's imaginary companion of childhood, probably ever since Diana had been left with her aunt and uncle for a month when she was two years of age. Until that early separation Diana had been a sunny child, but thereafter she was described as serious and sad. Roddy, on the other hand, was as cheerful and good-humored as Diana had been.

Diana's parents were not Roddy's. Roddy's parents were described in fairy tale terms—good, loving, perfect in every way. Thus Diana, was able, in effect, to disown her parents, kill them off as her parents, through Roddy. Roddy was free to express, and often did, her hatred of Diana's mother—something Diana was either totally unable to do or could do only by paying the price of intense generalized anxiety, or a crippling phobia that she and/or her immediate family were in peril of some incurable, fatal disease.

Despite mother's insistence that having an imaginary companion was silly and should cease, Roddy remained Diana's faithful fantasy-friend and comforter until Diana was eleven years of age. At that time father had the first of two heart attacks. Diana was convinced that this was due to her own disobedience in secretly keeping her companion. Thereafter, Roddy was repressed—but never "went away." She remained at age eleven and frequently "took over" for Diana and "helped her out." Diana was aware only of having blank spells—she would blink her eyes and the next thing she knew it was hours or months later. The longest blank spell lasted about a year.

Roddy served many functions. The most obvious was to permit guiltless and fearless defiance of mother. Roddy said, "Her mother didn't bother me. She wasn't *my* mother. I could leave at any time. I took Diana's mother in stride. I did not let her get to me. I could always call her names [giggles and blushes]. You know, all the names that kids pick up but that Diana never did because she was such a goody-goody."

During the course of treatment mother suffered a stroke and was partially paralyzed. Diana was almost paralyzed with guilt and walked and sat rigidly with a stony expression like mother's. I mentioned to Roddy that Diana was acting like a "mummy." Roddy enjoyed the joke immensely but said that Diana, of course, would never laugh at such a remark.

Diana was at her mother's beck and call, neglecting her own family to serve her quite slavishly. By such "dedication" she was determined to transform mother into the loving person she had always wished her to be. Diana insisted that this was working: mother was becoming kinder, warmer, more loving, and spoke warmly about her. Roddy, however, said that mother was as hateful and demanding as ever. Moreover, Roddy openly expressed the death wishes Diana must have repressed, saying, "She got what she deserved! But don't tell Diana I said so!"

In addition to being able to experience autonomy, assertiveness, and hostility, Roddy was also able to have the pleasure Diana could not permit herself. During happy occasions, celebrations, vacation, Diana would invariably blank out, leaving Roddy to enjoy the good times. Roddy would say she had a marvelous time on vacation, but Diana, of course, was miserable. "I'm not going to let her spoil things for *both* of us. She would rather die than have a good time!" When I asked her why she did mischievous things, like losing Diana's purse or buying an expensive, brightly colored leotard that could not be returned, she said it was because Diana was such a drag, no fun, much too serious for her taste. In fact, the main reason Roddy was adamantly opposed to having to grow up beyond age eleven was that she was determined not to become a sourpuss adult like Diana! She said, "You said I had to be responsible. So do I have to spend the rest of my life taking over for her? Also, what if I begin to grow up and find I am becoming like her? Can I go back to age eleven?"

Roddy retained most of the memories of happy, assertive, or angry occasions. Diana's experience and memory were limited almost wholly to depression and anxiety. Thus, Roddy was the repository of repressed memories and soon came to be my chief source of information about the traumatic past. The torment of child abuse that the anonymous notes had referred to in various generalized ways Roddy was able to disclose in detail.

In addition, Roddy would tell me the things Diana was afraid to disclose out of fear that I would become angry and abandon her. For example, that she was screaming at her child, or was taking so much medication that it was even making Roddy tired. In these ways, Roddy served to protect Diana from conscious awareness of her own anger as well as from the danger of being exposed to the anger she anticipated from me. At the same time, Roddy was ashamed of herself for "tattling." Diana, of course, was simply furious for being "ratted on."

Although it had been clearly agreed among Roddy, Diana, and myself that I would act as the faithful go-between until such time as Roddy and Diana would be in direct touch with each other, Diana felt that I was "twisting the knife." Learning some of the details of mother's abuse also made it much more difficult for her to play the role of Florence Nightingale for her convalescent mother. On the other hand, Roddy considered it ridiculous and "crazy" that Diana had to act so saintly to her mother. Rather, "she should put a clothespin on her nose" to keep out the smell of her mother's incontinence. But Roddy, too, was often very dubious about the wisdom of Diana's being in possession of her own memories and was forever cautioning me to be careful, not to tell Diana too much, to hold back until she was more ready to take it.

Ordinarily, if Roddy appeared, she would be there in the waiting room instead of Diana. However, there were a few occasions when Diana would "drop out" during the session and Roddy would make an appearance. During one session, Diana was insisting on the desirability of dying rather than living. Her face turned into a storm cloud of what appeared to be rage, then her expression suddenly changed and she transformed into Roddy—smiling, engaging, cheerful, and concerned as always. She said it was true that Diana really wanted to die and that Diana was angry and jealous of Roddy because I seemed to prefer her. After a while I said it was time to bring Diana back so that she could be the one to leave the session as usual. Roddy answered that she, Roddy, could leave for her. I asked if Diana would be safe in Roddy's care. She answered, "She's probably better off than in her own!"

Diana turned into Roddy during the course of another session when I told her she no longer had to live in terror of mother's killing her—that it was okay to wish to lose mother and even begin to tolerate pleasure. Roddy appeared and said, "That was too much for her to take."

From these two examples it is clear that it was intense emotion that brought on the appearance of Roddy. Overwhelming rage appeared to trigger the first instance. The second instance, however, is not clear. My assumption is that the prospect of living free of the fear of mother brought the anticipation of such pleasure that this immediately flooded her with the prospect of punishment and led to blanking out.

This should be spelled out in further detail. There are two reasons why Diana's sense of self was vulnerable to splitting on being flooded with intense emotion. (1) Her traumatization seems to have begun at a very early age (possibly with the separation from her parents at the age of two), before her sense of self and reality were firmly established. (2) Diana's mother appears systematically to have undermined the development of the sense of both self and reality. Her mother would insist that the milk Diana had to drink was not sour, even though it smelled bad; that the bath water was not scalding, though it was steaming. She refused to look at Diana, respond to her, or call her by name, referring to her in the third person or as "Mud" or "Miss Nobody." Diana would be tucked into bed so tightly that she could barely move, and in the morning the bedding would have to appear as unwrinkled as if "Nobody" had slept there.

Such details were supplied by Roddy. Usually, Diana had no conscious memory of them, though when they were related to her she often could supply supplementary details that served as corroboration. The stimulus for Roddy's bringing in such material would typically be some event in the present that reminded her of memories Diana had repressed.

For example, Diana was receiving 125 milligrams of Imipramine in an effort to help control her attacks of panic. Although this is considered a low to moderate dose, she developed acute urinary retention as a side effect and, after several days, required an indwelling catheter. Roddy came to one session and said: "She didn't come today. She doesn't know it but what's happening with her bladder and tubes reminds her so much of her past. I am afraid to tell because then you will have to tell her and that will make her feel bad. Also, I'm afraid you will be angry with me for being bad—I pulled the tube out last night."

Finally she told me that when Diana was three or four years old, if father was not home mother would be likely to wake Diana up at night "to clean her insides" with tubes and enemas; she would syringe her ears with hot or cold water, swab out her genitals, cut her nails to the quick, make her vomit by putting wool in her mouth and dark brown nosedrops in her nostrils. Diana developed an infection (cystitis?) with high fever that kept her in bed for many weeks. The doctor recommended hospitalization but mother refused. Instead, she "kept cleaning Diana out," telling her that it was doctor's orders. Diana tried to fight mother off, but she would tie her hands and sometimes her feet and make her sleep that way. Thereafter, Diana would hold her hands out to be tied. Mother would also keep Diana in bed till she wet the bed, then beat her and "clean her out," saying it was her own fault for being bad and dirty.

Roddy made me promise to tell Diana this only in small doses, if at all, and to help her realize that I was not mad at her. I agreed and suggested that from now on Diana should be able to void spontaneously without further difficulty. Roddy: "Do you think so? Good!" The prediction proved accurate.

Later Roddy told me that she would often stand in for Diana during those ordeals. "I would help her out by taking over and be there instead of her. It never hurt *me*, because she was not *my* mother anyway, so why should *I* care?" Had I ever read *Sybil*? "It is so much like what happened to Diana! Diana could not stand reading it until a little while ago, then I read it very carefully at the same time she did." (Diana had brought me the book and asked me to read it. I did so, underlining certain passages as I read. Diana was then able to read it, she said, because the underlinings were like aid stations along the way.)

Roddy let something slip: "Don't you think it was smart of her to invent someone to take her place—not just me—others, too? Oh! I let that out by mistake. Don't tell her there had been others, and that they became part of me and I speak for all of them."

Patsy came when Diana started school at age five. Patsy had been the name of a large doll. When Diana started school she didn't want to go because she would get beaten up. So Patsy went instead and fought back. She did not stay long. Jennifer came when Diana was nine. She stayed a long time and was able to play the piano for Diana in spite of mother's yelling and the fingers that were sore from the nail-cutting.

Unfortunately, Roddy did not now speak for all "the others." There were more alternates, which came out in the following manner. One day Diana's daughter cut her knee. Diana unaccountably delayed cleaning and dressing the wound for several hours. This was totally out of character from her usual overzealousness. When she did finish putting the dressing on, she suddenly experienced an intense suicidal urge. She attributed this to guilt for having delayed the first aid but could not explain the delay itself.

Roddy easily volunteered the explanation. It lay in a repressed memory that had been stirred by the daughter's cut knee. Diana was five. She had cut both her knees and bloodied her dress. Mother stripped her naked, beat her, yelled, and poured ammonia into the wounds. The ammonia application was repeated daily. The cuts did not heal for a long time and, when they finally did, left scars. Diana did not know the cause of the scars she still bore. Nor did she know that many of her nightly "nosebleeds" were actually caused by mother's having beaten her for sucking her lower lip. She still often sucked her lower lip in her sleep, and that was why it had been sore lately.

After I relayed this information to Diana, she remembered that as a child she would often awaken in a pool of blood caused by "nosebleeds." The next morning she found a long note at her bedside, written in an adult handwriting not quite her own:

> Looking now at my scarred knees, knowing they are the result of unmerciful, repeated applications of ammonia, remembering the pools of blood in which I found myself after each ostensible nosebleed . . . are living nightmares.
>
> Concentration camp survivors remember and move on. The criminal offenses committed against me are still "stories" that cripple me in the retelling. I try to remember instead the kindness of my father, but what I feel is the pain of that ammonia being poured on my wounds and the humiliation of my nakedness. It's just too grotesque.
>
> It embarrasses me to admit that I don't think I can continue. . . . I need to be made of sturdier stuff. Roddy appears to be my strength. But Mother will probably always stand in the way of our integration— in spite of your/our best efforts.

When I looked up after reading this letter, Roddy was there in place of Diana. She smiled and said that there was, indeed, another person who was responsible for much of the automatic writing that Diana discovered at her bedside, in her pockets, and elsewhere. Her name was Emma, she was of high school or college age, was a writer, and had kept entire diaries that Diana had thrown out.

Several weeks later, when I came out to the waiting room it was obvious that it was neither Diana nor Roddy who had arrived for the appointment. Rather, an attractive young woman, sitting rather stiffly upright, poised and self-possessed, smiled in an assured yet somewhat self-conscious manner—appearing more poised than she probably felt—and introduced herself as "Emma" and said she had been curious to meet me. She handed me a written account of a dream that Diana had had but had not remembered: it involved my coldly rejecting her outstretched hand, and her sinking to the floor, dying at my feet. The report was signed, "Emma."

Emma then told me more about herself. Speaking in a soft, cultured voice with a British-American accent, she said that she was nineteen, had grown up in England, and come here to school. Her parents were still in England; her father was similar to Diana's, but her mother was just the opposite. Emma came after Diana's father died and Diana was in danger of becoming totally dependent on her mother. Perhaps because of this, Diana became overattached to an aggressive young woman who was pursuing her and was too innocent to realize that she had nearly got manipulated into a lesbian affair.

Writing was Emma's chief interest. Whenever Emma took over she would keep copious notes. She relieved Diana of her obsessive thoughts by recording them, so that Diana could get on with the rest of her life. Writing also helped protect Diana from being disturbed by time gaps. Emma would also act as a social hostess when that was called for. "I am terribly straight, not silly like that bright child Roddy."

Emma went on to say that Diana was very concerned that, in the event that she did succeed in committing suicide, I be absolved of responsibility. Roddy did a great deal to keep Diana from suicide. Emma herself, however, did not want to be as involved as Roddy. She preferred to be somewhat more distant and aloof. She assured me that she would be around but more peripherally and would be sure to write and report her observations.

When I informed Diana of this new visitor who had taken up most of the time in her session, she exclaimed: "It is unfair that I don't get any time at all!" Roddy, for her part, said that Emma was a prim and proper snit. And even though it was tattling, she had to tell me that Emma was sixteen, not nineteen—that she just wanted me to take her more seriously.

Despite their jealousy of one another and their rivalry for my attention—played out in detail in many dreams—Roddy and Emma joined in preparing me to meet yet another character: Amanda.

Roddy expressed herself about Amanda in her usual eleven-year-old style: "Amanda came in the second grade. She blamed Diana for not being loved and was angry that Diana wouldn't do stuff like having fun and getting attention because of her mother. Diana would have liked it if her mother or father would just put an arm around her. So Amanda would go out and get attention to be loved. I won't tell you what she did. Amanda will have to tell you herself. She does what she wants—things that Diana never had the guts to ask for herself. She doesn't really care much about Diana or anybody else. She is tough, she angers easily, she yells. She is not a goody-two-shoes like Diana. She is bad sometimes. She used to get even with Diana's mother by not listening to her the way she never listened to Diana. That would make the mother wild and furious, but Amanda didn't care what happened or if someone got hurt. I would be the one to get the beating, but it didn't hurt because I just wished it away. I put myself someplace else.

"She almost came today but I told her not to because you will be going off on vacation soon. She can't stand my guts, but every family needs a boss. She is afraid that you won't like her as you do the rest of us." Roddy then gave me a call down for telling Diana too much of what *she* had told me. I defended myself, and we agreed to disagree and remain friends.

Emma, on the other hand, described Amanda in literary terms, in a written communication, contrasting her with Roddy:

"Roddy is the embodiment of youth—a time of life Diana could never know. How extraordinary that Roddy could sustain that mother's abuse and excuse Diana from so many horrendous atrocities. Roddy merely closed her eyes, obediently extended her hands, and felt nothing. Time after time after time she offered up her own body for purification to protect Diana from excruciating pain. What loyalty and endurance!

"It is Amanda, however, who feels enraged—who feels life is

unfair—who aches to love and be loved, although she desperately fears and distrusts those around her. It is Amanda who creeps out to seek some form of attention in return for a signal that someone cares.

"How sad for all of us who play a role in trying to make Diana feel whole. How tremendous our effort, and yet Diana remains so many fragile, fragmented particles."

Eventually Amanda appeared in person. She was eight or nine, as when she first came into Diana's life. (Roddy had explained that "each one stays the same age. That is how it is when one makes up any rules one likes.") Amanda looked like a young punk: her shoulders hunched up, a glowering, hostile expression, never meeting my eyes, talking in a sullen voice:

"You don't know me and I don't want to be here. Except that the others say you want to meet me. What was it like there? No fun. Diana's no fun. She's a scaredy-cat. Her mother told her not to be angry so she wasn't ever angry. She is not my mother, so I could be angry, and yell and scream. Because her mother would always lie. She would tell Diana to be in at four o'clock. When Diana came on time her mother said it should have been three. And beat her up. She was just looking for excuses to beat her. She never kissed her or anything loving. Who would want to be kissed by that woman anyway! I don't want to be here. I am not going to tell you what friends I had of my own. . . . But do you want me to come back and tell you more?"

After Diana had some dreams in which I was affectionate to everyone except her and a dream of being in a beautiful home with her father, who treated her like a stranger, Amanda again appeared:

"You said everyone liked Diana's father. That is not true. I didn't. He never showed any affection. He never touched, kissed, or hugged. I didn't like that at all! If he was such a kind, nice person, he would've done all those things. He didn't know how to act like a father, except to other kids like his nieces. They even sat on his lap! But Diana never, ever. After all, he *was* her father! Diana's mother must've told him to be that way. He had to listen to her because she was the boss of Diana and he wasn't. He treated her like she wasn't his child. *My* father hugged me plenty before he went away on important business, because he was an important person. I also got others to hug and kiss me, but I don't have to tell you. I don't even have to be here. I don't care if she does kill herself. I would just go somewhere where it is more fun, where people are happy and hug each other. Diana sits in her corner, doesn't let anyone be her friend. It's just like it always was. Because she is angry and scared, she's always dying. I won't help her kill herself, but I wouldn't save her, either. Roddy would. I am not going to tattle on her. You can talk to her now. Goodbye." She barely looked at me, glowering into her lap.

Diana said: "Amanda must have been here because my hands hurt like I have been sitting on them." I then told her what Amanda had said about her father's being affectionate to everyone except Diana, and how this jibed with her own dreams about me, and that she must have repressed the anger Amanda expressed. Diana responded that I was "hammering" at her and "twisting the knife" about her father. "He did all he could and that was more than nothing."

Diana then became unable to hear me, and Roddy appeared in her place: "Don't hold it against her father. He did do his best. It was not as much as she wanted, but it was all she did get. When you say you like her, she can't let herself hear that because it reminds her of her father and she doesn't want to feel the pain of missing him. So she checks you out. She does kind of want to talk about him, but she hears your criticism of her father as saying he was bad. She can't hear that either."

Diana reappeared: "Let me guess. Roddy was here, because look where I am sitting [on the sofa] and my posture [legs tucked under her, shoes off]. Why can't I remember what my father looked like, or what his voice sounded like? If I ever had said that I missed him or loved him, mother would have been sure to say, `He'll die.'"

Emma had more to say on the subject of Diana's father. "I knew him better than anyone because he liked me best. Diana had to take care of him all the time, set out his clothes and shaving equipment. She cleared his place after dinner, kept his desk neat, turned on his music, cared for his pipes and tobacco. He appreciated it but he never did anything for *her*. So I can understand it if she were to feel anger

91

towards him. She was just a servant for him and, for the most part, he ignored her. She was *never* treated like a child—just a miniature adult. I can well understand that she walked in front of a car when she was ten years old."

Emma then advised that it was most important that I go out of my way to show that I am different from Diana's father. She said that they were all grateful to me for being an intermediary. Maybe one day they would just go back where they came from, she said, but on no condition would they ever grow up and become Diana.

Diana made it clear that she wished to know nothing of these discussions concerning her father. For the next two sessions she sat with her eyes closed, her voice barely audible. I assured her that I would wait until she was more ready to deal with it.

One day Roddy told me that I would soon meet Miriam, another companion who was a friend to Diana, though Diana did not know it. Miriam first found a place in Diana's life when her mother bought her a pair of ice skates at seven years old. Miriam was an orphan, born of American Indian parents, and was a natural athlete, fast and graceful. She did all the athletics and helped Diana "get out" her anger that way. Although Diana would, of course, know nothing about it, Miriam got to be so good at ice skating that she even taught it for a number of years.

I explained to Diana that Miriam's function was to help her discharge anger. She asked: "Whose anger is or was it? Mine or my mother's?" Roddy later added that Amanda, too, helped discharge anger but in troublesome ways, so that Diana would beat herself up for Amanda's anger, just as mother used to. I pointed out that Diana was also in the habit of letting out on her husband much of the anger she did not let herself feel toward her father for his neglect.

Miriam finally presented herself, saying: "I know you want to meet everyone, and the others told me to come. My parents were American Indians. I lived in a big old house with lots of other children. I came to Diana when she was seven, and I am still seven because that is the rule. I would help out with anger by doing sport things like jumping rope when she was little. Now she plays tennis. I mean we play tennis together and I help her out with skiing." I asked who was the better skiier. She responded to my tactless question with silence and looked embarrassed.

Miriam continued: "I have come now because lately I help out by getting Diana to do exericse. She has been taking aerobics for two months and has not told you. I take the course for her and know the whole routine. Her mother never let her get sweaty, and would punish her with a hot, scalding bath and a hair wash for getting sweaty. Yesterday I didn't help her during the exercise course. So when she realized she did not know the routine and was getting sweaty, she panicked. I could come back to help her out again, and also tell you stories. Like how her mother made her wear strange clothes and not look pretty, because she wanted her to be serious and be good at whatever she did. She took away all the pleasure."

Regarding the aerobics course, Roddy giggled and said: "I'm helping to get her back to aerobics class. I bought her a new, expensive leotard in *my* favorite color—pink. And it is not returnable!"

One day Amanda said:

"Do you know what 'Amanda' means? It means 'worthy of love.' [Diana looked it up. It was true.] Why doesn't Diana *let* herself be loved? She is making it as miserable as it always was at home. That makes me so angry sometimes! I would let Kate kill her any time and not interfere the way Roddy always does."

I: "Who?"

Amanda: "Kate doesn't come here and talk with you? You better have her come in."

I: "How?"

Amanda: "If you don't know about her I'm not going to be the one to squeal. Anyway, Kate is shy and fearful and may not want to come in."

At the next session, Roddy said she had "listened in" and heard Amanda's slip, informing me of Kate. Roddy was concerned that I not be mad at her for having told me about Kate. She then said that Kate had arrived when Diana was seven and had had a tonsillectomy. "They were both so terrible to her that day, she just wanted to die!

Other children came in with their parents who sat with them and hugged them and were nice to them. Not Diana's parents! They just sat there for four hours and ignored her. Then when it was time to go in to the doctor's office, Diana wanted to take her red sweater with her. The doctor said that would be okay, but her mother wouldn't let her. So nothing she was wearing belonged to her. She wore the hospital gown and felt terrible. Why didn't her father say it was okay to bring in her own sweater? . . . But how can she be mad at her father? Then there would be nobody."

Diana was able to corroborate and add further details. She even appeared to hear me when I told her again that she was struggling against awareness of her anger at her father (and at me) lest it threaten her positive tie to him (and to me). She was amazed that Roddy could express anger and disagreement with me and that I did not get angry with her.

Shortly thereafter, however, Diana discovered in her coat pocket a list of characters, including many I had not met. "Will it ever come together," she asked. She feared an endless proliferation of characters and for the first time was willing to consider the use of hypnosis to facilitate integration. We discussed what integration meant: how each "character" represented a valid memory or quality of feeling that demanded recognition—for example, Amanda's standing for being "worthy of love" and the indignation for not having received it in the past. She agreed that hypnosis should be used to help her deal directly with these elements of herself rather than indirectly by hearing their "stories" through me. She also agreed that this would be more meaningful than attempting, through hypnotic suggestion, to make each character grow up and assume Diana's chronological age. Amanda's quality of indignation at injustice, Roddy's love of life, Miriam's zest for physical activity, or Emma's capacity for detached reportage may all have arisen at earlier ages, but each had an important contribution to make to Diana's adulthood.

Roddy saw it differently. She considered it important that *I* meet all the characters in due course and help Diana to accept them and still wish to live. She was firm that none of them would be willing to allow her identity to be absorbed in Diana's and become her. As for my trying to promote a conversation between any of them and Diana through hypnosis, to Roddy it sounded like hocus-pocus.

Under these uncertain auspices, the first attempt at hypnosis was not successful. The ineffectiveness reminded Diana of her father and made her uncomfortably annoyed at me.

At the next attempt to induce a hypnotic trance, Diana placed her hands on the desk in front of me and I rested my fingers lightly on hers. With this direct contact she was readily hypnotized and brought back to age eleven, when her father became ill. I told her it was not her fault that he had had a heart attack. She wept disbelievingly, saying: "But he got worse." Out of hypnosis she remembered that she used to measure her own sense of badness by his deteriorating health.

This session was followed by a rare pleasant dream of both of us being happy and pleased at a portrait of a smiling young girl named Roddy. In neither this nor the following hypnotic session were we able to bring Roddy into the conversation, however. Diana expressed the fear that, if we did, I would get sick and die.

Now Emma provided important new background, stimulated by the fact of my inducing hypnosis by touching Diana's hands. Mother had forbidden Diana to touch or be touched by anyone. This prohibition included her father. She said it would contaminate her and make her dirty. Only mother was permitted to touch Diana, and was forever scrubbing her.

Having given this background, Emma related a dream: Mother examined Diana's body carefully and determined that she had allowed someone to touch her. She became wild with anger and chopped off her hands with a cleaver, leaving a bloody mess. In the dream mother said: "Now you will never be able to touch anyone and no one will ever want to come near or touch you." Emma went on to say: "You can understand what an act of courage it has been for Diana to allow you to touch her. However, her fear of punishment is increased each time you do. That is why she is now cleansing her hands all the time—a pattern that has recurred periodically through the years."

When I informed Diana of mother's prohibition against touching and the compulsive washings, she said it was no wonder there had been so little sex in her life. Yes, she had indeed been washing her hands in scalding water lately.

Roddy added that it was Diana who was always washing her hands, but it was Kate who made it scalding water and almost made the scalding water feel good. She went on to tell me that it was not yet time for her and Diana to get together; that I should hypnotize Diana more so she was less afraid of it. Also, when I did, I should get her to remember how nice it was for her and her father to walk, hold hands, and play finger games. "But it got mixed up with mother saying she must not be touched, so Diana would scrub her hands after walking hand in hand with father, lest she find out."

During the third hypnotic session Diana was able to recall pleasant walks with her father. They would play a game in which each finger stood for certain letters, and he would tap out words to her on her fingers. But then she would rush home to scrub, in terror that her mother would "get it out of [her]." And she always did! Diana cringed and wept, remembering the tea kettle from which mother poured the hot water, telling her she was cleaning her hands for her own good.

Out of the hypnotic trance, Diana now recalled the finger games vividly, but the overriding emotion was one of terror of the tea kettle. Yet, why did the scalding water get to feel good? She was sure it was because mother had convinced her that she had been contaminated and molested and now needed to be cleansed of her sexual dirtiness.

Some time after this session a phone message was recorded on my tape: "Before the bubble bursts, I want you to know that I now have some lovely memories of my father."

Of course, the bubble did burst and Diana regretted the pleasant memories. She scrubbed, scalded, and showered, day and night. She defended her mother, wished she could cut her hands off, and dreamed of being in a oil slick. She remembered having had to wear white gloves which also had to be kept clean.

Then Kate appeared for the next session. "I met Diana the same day she went to the hospital to have her tonsils out. My father, mother, two sisters, and brother died in that same hospital on that same day. I was supposed to die then, too, but somehow I got left behind. I met her that day and went home with her. How I help her is what you won't like. I help her to want to die because I think that will be a good thing. I help her to understand that dying is good because only good things die and bad things live. For instance, her father died and her mother lived. Pretty flowers die. Diana is good and so she deserves to die, too."

My attempts to discuss this with Kate fell on deaf ears. To Diana I explained that Kate defined the core pathology: an internalization of mother's self-righteous, adamant death wish against her—an identification of Diana with the aggressor-mother. Diana's response was to dream that she had fallen into a deep ditch, that I offered her my hand to pull her out, and that she had said she was not allowed to touch my hands and thus slid further into the ditch.

Roddy encouraged me to hypnotize Diana and try again to talk with Kate, and to be firm in asking her to be fair. A fourth session of hypnosis succeeded in raising Kate, with Diana able to hear my side of the conversation only. Kate was exactly as Diana had always described her mother: totally unyielding, absolutely convinced of her view, unwilling to listen or discuss. She knew what was best, and what was best was to die. No, she would not come back again; I was nasty and only pretending to be Diana's friend. When I told her she reminded me of Diana's mother's attitude, she said: "There is good dying and bad dying. I want her to have good dying."

Following this, Kate waged a campaign against me, arguing to the others that I was no real friend. They found her more powerful than ever, and persuasive, too. Once more Diana began to have dreams of dying—in order to live happily. I told her she was in love with dying because she was dying to be loved. And afraid, because all love, including caring or accepting the helping hand of understanding through treatment, had been sexualized by her mother and rendered taboo. I told her I was not going to cave in to Kate—that I was standing up for Diana's right to live happily as she had always wished her father would stand up for her to her mother. Diana agreed that trying to fight Kate now was identical to trying to fight mother then. But her inner feeling was that both Kate and mother were right.

Another crisis appeared to be at hand.

Let us leave Diana, still shifting widely among tormented memories of the past, reliving them in the present, and periods of splitting off from consciousness—and look more closely at the phenomena of splitting and reintegration as attempts to master trauma. This will help place a bridge between two realms of timeless imagination: the multiple imaginary personalities disowned by Diana and relegated to the unconscious, on the one side, and the imaginative characters introduced into the world of literature by the work of the novelist, on the other.

ASPECTS OF SPLITTING

Usually Diana's splitting off into a dissociated state of consciousness would occur in the blink of an eye. When the onset was more gradual, she would become aware of a pervasive fear, associated with a profound feeling of weariness; voices sounded too loud; she feared she would be unable to "hold on" to her sense of self. In one instance, just prior to the split she had a dream that shed some light on what was going on. In the dream, Diana was being overlooked and treated as though she were invisible. When she got up and left, no one noticed. In another dream, she had been told to "go away," "get lost." She did go away, got lost, then found her way to my office at night, but of course I was not there.

Splitting from consciousness, then, appears to have been her way of going away, invisibly "splitting the scene" when she felt that no one was there for her, that she was effectively isolated.

I mentioned earlier that being flooded with strong emotion seemed to be the precipitant of Diana's splitting into a state of dissociation. This was easiest to document in the case of anger. One fugue state was preceded by an angry fight with her husband. She felt literally beside herself with rage and "saw" herself get up and stand behind herself and then leave. This was like a slow-motion version of the onset of a split which, in fact, followed. Other occasions were also clearly connected with anger. For example, she would hear her mother yelling, would wish that mother would die, and would then "check out." Similarly, she dreamed she was getting very angry with me, and then I began to disappear.

The question thus arises whether she was so flooded with rage every time a split would occur that she was killing someone off; then, in anticipation of being killed off herself in retaliation, did the dissociation also represent her killing herself off? Certain dreams, as well as her own written description of "re-entry" following the split, suggest that this is only a partial description. Being flooded with aggression was not the only precipitant of splitting. Diana's account of re-entry was as follows:

> The first moments of conscious awareness feel most like having been suddenly awakened from a very deep sleep—not entirely sure where I am in time and space. While my body has been carefully trained to respond in half-time, my heart beats very rapidly and my mind races to integrate with the world around me. Not until both the internal and external rhythms are synchronized do I feel grounded.
>
> During this period of re-entry, which seems interminable, I struggle on the one hand to catch up in time while simultaneously feeling strongly drawn back towards that black hole. It is the only time that I am almost aware of two separate time warps.
>
> It is a period of great anxiety—*fears of getting caught, being found out, punished*, killed, overwhelm me. I think those often *pleasurable* thoughts of suicide that I experience are particularly potent during those horrendous moments of re-entry.

What illicit pleasure does the splitting off represent—a pleasure so intense that it is carried over to color the very death sentence that it calls down upon her? Two dreams about time provide possible hints:

(1) "I found my watch in the debris around a pool. I didn't know it had been lost. In winding it, the mechanism got caught, the winding became more difficult, the face of the watch began to change into

99

clouds, outer space, symbols of galaxies, symbolizing another kind of time. It was a secret. If people knew I knew this they would think I was crazy because they did not understand."

(2) "A large man and I climbed or took an elevator up to the large face of a clock on the outside of a building—like Big Ben. We made love on the face of the clock. The hands of the clock were in motion faster than normal so we had to keep moving to let them move beneath us. We had sex there in broad daylight."

We should note that the motion of the hands, somehow related to an alteration of time, is integral to both dreams. In the first dream it was the act of hand-winding the watch that led to the entry into a secret world of time that others would equate with going crazy. The second dream is more explicit in connecting the hands (of the clock) with the passage of time and sexuality.

The first dream has to do with a "watch." Could this be a dream pun for "watching?" This possibility becomes more plausible if placed in conjunction with the "sex in broad daylight" of the second dream.

If we recall that Diana shared her parents' bedroom until the age of eight, a reconstruction of primal scene experiences would seem called for: she was repeatedly flooded with ill-defined sexual and aggressive overstimulation, sought relief through masturbation, and was incessantly punished.

Such a reconstruction allows other facts to fall into place: mother's taboo against all touching, her repeated examinations of Diana's body for evidence of contamination, her tying of Diana's hands, the cystitis at age four, the prohibition against any privacy including that of the bathroom (lest Diana touch herself?), Diana's obsessive childhood fears of blindness, and so on.

We have Roddy's word for it to resolve any doubt: mother did, in fact, threaten to cut Diana's fingers off and "tear her limb from limb" if she watched her parents have sex or ever reported what she saw. In this context, her tonsillectomy at seven was undoubtedly experienced as some kind of mutilating (castrating?) punishment about which she had been forewarned and thus brought upon herself, as mother intoned untiringly. It is not surprising that in her dreams dissociating herself from consciousness was often represented as dismemberment.

(1) Summarizing the first point that should be made about the meaning of Diana's split-off states: cutting herself off from the flow of time and becoming other personalities was Diana's response to massive sexual and aggressive overstimulation. The response had the structure of a compromise, combining both escape and expression. The former was more obvious. By means of splitting, Diana fled the grossly instinctualized environment (primal scenes and sexual-aggressive abuse) with all its secrecy, intimidation, and scapegoating. In time, this must have become a way of escaping not only from this brutalization, but also from being flooded by her own anger and sexuality whenever they might arise. At the same time, splitting was also a covert *expression* of anger and sexuality: a killing-off of her environment and a *libidinized* self-punishment in the form of *pleasurable* thoughts of suicide.

Turning now to the multiple personalities dwelling within Diana, it is apparent that they had a number of characteristics in common: probably arising from a common source, harboring repressed memories and forbidden wishes, and transfixed in time.

(2) It is likely that all arose as the familiar imaginary companions of childhood. We know that Roddy did because Diana herself remembered it. Patsy, who appeared briefly when Diana began school, was the name of a large doll. This made her particularly appropriate to become the one who fought off the attacks of other children.

(3) All the personalities shared the same affect-loaded (pleasurable and painful) memories and forbidden wishes. The chief forbidden wish expressed by the various personalities was something that Diana could not dare hope for consciously: that she had other parents or was an orphan.

(4) All the personalities remained the same age at which they first emerged from Diana's unconscious. Roddy arose consciously at an early age and was a conscious imaginary companion until age eleven, at which time she was repressed, and thus remained eleven.

It is apparent that each personality was also unique. While none of them had any use for the mother ("Who would want *her* for a mother!") they differed in the extent to which they blamed the father. Roddy defended the father as having done his best, Amanda openly expressed anger at him, while Emma said she could well understand if Diana "were to feel anger towards him."

(5) Each personality was a combination of splitting and integration (Prince 1919). That is to say, each was a fragment that had become dissociated from Diana. Once having become split off, however, each was integrated in an individual style in respect to affects and defenses—a particular degree of distance from affects, and a particular set of defenses against drives.

For example, Roddy and Diana made a contrasting pair in regard to pain and pleasure—Roddy apparently able to derive only pleasure from most anything, Diana only pain. Amanda and Kate make another contrasting pair in their attitudes toward life and death—Amanda's lust for life and love, Kate's yearning for death. Similarly, Amanda's rage at injustice might be contrasted to Kate's depressive resignation. Miriam succeeded in neutralizing aggression through her athletic skills; Emma's detached reportorial abilities might also be seen as successfully neutralizing aggression. Sexually, Emma was a "prim and proper snit," English accent and all, sixteen and never been kissed—quite at the opposite pole from Amanda with her nine-year-old-hood tastes, boasting about getting all the hugging and kissing she wanted and it's nobody's business how.

(6) Finally, the same combination of splitting and integration that molded each personality into a distinctive entity may be seen operating in another sphere—that of time. It is striking that when Diana "checked out" or "lost time," leaving a blank spell in the flow of time, the "edges" of time were melded together in a seamless web. The leading edge and the following edge seemed to move together as though nothing had happened. A fragment of time had simply dropped out; the surface was reintegrated so precisely that no sign of the lost fragment was visible. Some examples will make this clearer.

Diana, at fifteen, was in her father's funeral procession, the limousine heading for the cemetery. Suddenly she realized that the limousine was approaching her home instead of the cemetery. Had they forgotten something? Then the realization came: she had "lost time"; during the blank time the interment had taken place.

Years earlier, in elementary school, Diana had left the classroom to go to the water bubbler in the corridor; she returned to the classroom and someone else was sitting in her assigned seat. For how long had she been out?

In more recent years, she had allowed herself to enjoy a few minutes of her daughter's music recital. She came to five hours later sitting in her car in the midst of traffic. The applause of the audience at the recital had "continued" seamlessly as the noise of the traffic jam.

At her daughter's school graduation the young girls were dressed in white, the outdoor setting was beautiful on a lovely spring day, and the band had played "The Star Spangled Banner." Diana was so moved by the occasion that she wept with emotion. The next thing she knew she was in the car driving home from the graduation and tears were "still" streaming down her face. She had long since learned never to move suddenly or ask "Where am I?" but to gradually gather clues from her environment in order to "ground" herself in time after "re-entry." This time she learned that her daughter was doing a humorous parody of the graduation music, everyone in the car was laughing, and the tears streaming down her own face were tears of laughter.

In each of these examples some feature common to the moments just before and just after the "lost time"—the bubbler, the limousine, the noise, the music and tears—had been seized by the integrative function of her ego to sew together the ruptured surface of conscious time.

As for the period of time, from hours to months, that had been fragmented off and dropped out of the conscious stream of time—that was the atemporal world of Roddy and the Others. Since that world had been disowned by Diana, its unwitting author, it was consigned to the timelessness of the Unconscious. The feelings and memories there remained ever as fresh as the unchanging ages of its inhabitants.

Nonetheless, significant truths of Diana's history existed there, embodied in the multiple personalities we have met. As Pirandello says in *Six Characters in Search of an Author*, these imaginary characters were "less real perhaps, but truer!" (Bentley 1952, 217). In what sense can this be so? The facts of Diana's early life were too terrible for her conscious mind to tolerate their being real. But that did not prevent their being true, however much unacknowledged.

Again, one of Pirandellos's characters speaks: "Our reality doesn't change: it can't change! It can't be other than what it is, because it is already fixed forever. It's terrible. Ours is an immutable reality which should make you shudder when you approach us if you are really conscious of the fact that your reality is a mere transitory and fleeting illusion, taking this form today and that tomorrow." (p. 266).

5

FROM CLINICAL TO CREATIVE IMAGINATION

What is the relationship, if any, between creativity and psychopathology? One approaches this challenging terrain knowing in advance that there will be no easy trails, let alone broad vistas. Given the near-ubiquity of psychopathology, it should not be surprising that it often coexists with creativity, yet without necessarily being connected to it. On the other hand, if psychopathology and creativity appear to be related perhaps it is because they seem to share a somewhat easier access to the unconscious than that available to so-called normal and uncreative individuals.

Earlier phases of development contribute to whatever a person is—both as to creative potential, if any, as well as to a susceptibility to psychopathology. To put it the other way around, given a creative potential, it will draw upon that individual's full resources: the most differentiated skills as well as his or her least resolved conflicts. Dostoevsky's traumatic history provided the raw material for both creative transformation into literature and personal neurosis; Shaver's similar traumatic history provided the material for neurotic symptoms and psychotic reenactment.

Whether psychopathology or creativity, the determining factors lie not in id contents—which are probably universal—nor even in personal histories, but more likely in innate givens and the ways in which the ego operates defensively, integratively, and adaptively. With this in mind, a comparison of the imaginary companions of multiple personality disorder and the fictional characters of a creative writer offers us a vantage point, and the uses of the mechanism of splitting present us with a conceptual tool for entry into this area. The subject of splitting will lead us to consider the phenomenon of partnerships in the creative process and this in turn will lead us to the theme of losing and refinding as an expression of an inner split as well as an attempt to heal it.

SPLITTING AND PARTNERSHIPS

While it would seem at first to be a far reach from the bizarre world of multiple personality disorder to the special world of art or the mundane one of everyday life, the truth is less simple. Pirandello wrote that his *Six Characters* expressed "the multiple personality of everyone corresponding to the possibilities of being to be found in each of us" (Bentley 1952, 367). Likewise, Milan Kundera (1984) writes: "the characters in my novels are my own unrealized possibilities. That is why I am equally fond of them and equally horrified by them."

Residues of early phases of development exist in all of us, and may be thought of as analogous to mini-forms of multiple personalities. They lend color and variety to the various facets of even the most integrated personality. Whether these are normal or pathological depends on how flexibly and appropriately one is able to switch—for example, between more or less adult or childhood modes of feeling and expression (Lampl-De-Groot 1981). It should be stressed that this, in turn, depends on the extent to which these residues or facets of the personality are either conscious or unconscious.

The same might be said for the differences and correspondences between Pirandello's play, *Six Characters*, and Diana's actual multiple personality disorder. Each of the Pirandello characters, like Diana's alternates, represent latent aspects of the self, split off and transfixed at a time of traumatic intensity of affects and conflicts—the organism's attempt to master the danger of being flooded with overstimulation. In the case of Diana, they were split off from consciousness and, as her case illustrates, she was able time and again to remobilize, maintain, or regain mastery—at a cost of splitting consciousness and much reducing her level of awareness.

Pirandello's *Six Characters*, on the other hand, are not repressed in his own unconscious or sidetracked into the peripheral, preconscious part of his mind. In addition to being a shared rather than a private experience, Pirandello's dramatic art by its force compels the audience at large to broaden the scope of its everyday awareness and confront paradox. His art makes the audience "really conscious of the fact that [everyday] reality is a mere transitory and fleeting illusion, taking this form today and that tomorrow," while the unconscious is timeless—"it can't be other than what it is, because it is already fixed forever" (Bentley 1952, 266). It leaves an almost tangible question in the air, unasked: "Which then is the more real—the immutable unconscious or the transitoriness of everyday appearances?" And by virtue of the silent question, the audience gropes for its own answer and, searching, is left with a fuller and more meaningful awareness of the mysterious nature of reality itself. As the painter Max Beckmann said, "It may sound paradoxical, but it is, in fact, reality which forms the mystery of our existence" (quoted in Chipp 1968, p. 188).

Thus, in addition to the difference between the novelist and Diana being one of whether the splitting is conscious or unconscious, there is the use to which it is put—whether creative, meaning consciousness-expanding, or defensive, meaning consciousness-constricting. Diana's life was run to a large degree by the imaginary characters who, disowned by her, inhabited her unconscious mind. Her consciousness was split and constricted in order to defend against being flooded with overstimulation. Thus, Emma wrote defensively—that is, in order to relieve Diana of the burden of her obsessive thoughts.

The creative writer, on the other hand, consciously practices an active craft that expands awareness for himself and others. He invents characters as vehicles for his art in the shared world of literature. In contrast to Emma's need to get rid of thoughts, Keats treasured the superabundance of thought and imagery that overbrimmed his mind like rich, ripe grain:

> When I have fears that I may cease to be
> Before my pen has gleaned my teeming brain,
> Before high-piled books in charactery,
> Hold like rich garners the full ripened grain.

For Diana, the possibility of any stimulation, whether pleasurable or painful, posed the danger of being overwhelmed and had to be defended against accordingly. For example, when she attended a showing of Van Gogh paintings, she was stunned. Never consciously perceiving the color as color, she bleached it all out: the paintings came to her in black and white, and the outlines were blurred. This, incidentally, helped her to experience the brushwork more vividly. Only after she viewed the whole show was she ready to go back again and take a chance at seeing it in full color. (It was too late; the museum was closing.)

Further distinctions are in order. Diana's defensive splitting was of two types. She split consciousness "vertically:" like the two Golyadkins, the various alternates coexisted and knew one another. She also experienced a "horizontal" split from consciousness: like the murderous aspect of passive, masochistic Shaver, she was unaware of the world her alternates inhabited. Creative splitting, on the other hand, has to do with Coleridge's "willing suspension of disbelief." The reality sense is voluntarily held in temporary abeyance in order to disclose and explore imaginative possibilities. (More of this later.)

Putting aside that the creative writer and Diana make use of different types of splitting and for different purposes, there is an underlying point of similarity that makes possible their "choice" of splitting in the first place. They both treat the stuff of time and character as flexible material suitable for being shaped and molded—according to their conscious and creative or unconscious and defensive designs, respectively—and capable of undergoing endless transformations. Diana "created" unconscious alternates out of the affective and motivational material at hand; she "dropped" periods of time and patched together the remainder to provide herself with the illusion of continuity. The author fashions fictional characters and manipulates the flow of time with flashbacks and fast-forwards according to artistic requirements. In other words, character and time are treated by both author and patient as having the quality of plasticity usually associated with *aesthetic* media.

Are there other bridges which can be delineated between the imaginary world of a case of multiple personality disorder and the writer's creative imagination? They both combine splitting with integration and do so in order to regulate actual or anticipated overstimulation (approaching it from the point of view of the external world) or heightened sensitivity (viewing it from the subjective aspect). Again, this is subject to the same crucial qualification we have been stressing: the splitting and reintegration of psychopathology is automatic and unconscious; the use of these mechanisms by the creative artist may often be conscious—in *addition* to taking place unconsciously.

We have seen in some detail how Diana ingeniously, if unconsciously, combined splitting and integration to create a number of imaginary companions and wove together the fractured surface of time into an illusion of continuity (confirming Morton Prince's [1919] observation of the conjoint operation of the two mechanisms in multiple personalities). The fact that splitting is the more dramatic of the two mechanisms does not imply that the power of integration is necessarily impaired. On the contrary, the extensive use of splitting might well require special exercise and development of the capacity for integration, both within the area that has been fragmented from consciousness and in the intact areas of personality. [1]

Splitting and integration are normally available to the ego for either defensive or creative purposes. It would be a mistake to think of

1. In line with this, a recently reported case of multiple personality (Marmer 1980), though disturbed by her disordered component parts, was nonetheless able to execute paintings that demonstrated a powerful aesthetic unifying form.

splitting only as a defense mechanism in relation to repression and denial, constricting awareness of internal and external events, respectively, in order to avoid anxiety (Giovacchini 1986). Confining the use of splitting to psychopathology implies that eruptions of conflict-laden unconscious materials are ever in the offing whenever splitting is used. This overlooks the clinical observation that splitting may be used in the service of *abstraction*—a preconscious withdrawal of attention from more obvious aspects of reality in order to focus greater attention on other latent aspects that may then manifest themselves. In contrast to repression and denial, splitting in the service of abstraction is nondefensive and conflict-free. At a cultural level, such a use of splitting or abstraction is analogous to the way each of the great symbolic forms—art, language, science—pass over certain parts of immediate factuality and constitute reality from several unique directions (Cassirer [1923] 1953).

Having said this, it is necessary to note that while splitting and integration are normally available to the ego, they appear to be a predominant feature in the lives and work of creative individuals. It is as though they are embraced as a preferred pattern of repeated dissolution and reorganization, proceeding in parallel with unconscious splitting and reintegration. This may ultimately help transform ordinary work into creative work, but it may also keep disturbing the peace of conventional personal patterns with the fallout from creative *dis*organization. As a result, the life style of the artist often takes on a quality of restlessness, almost to the point of agitation.

By contrast, in the ordinary individual's history, personal revolutions may take place during the radical developmental changes of adolescence, marriage, career choice, and the like, and this may set free constructive energies (Eissler 1967); but in the overall life cycle they do not seem to occur repeatedly. In work, likewise, dissolution of established structure does not typically take place; rather, conscious reintegration produces established, useful solutions.

In the creative process, temporarily suspending traditional solutions and the established sense of reality and conscience permits the emergence of fresh imagery and fantasies from the unconscious. "The creative person [is then able to] focus his most developed mental capacities upon his world of unreality as he indifferently acknowledges his world of reality" (Weissman 1969, 117) and selects certain aspects from each world to be reintegrated and shaped into original solutions.

As a case in point, take the new field of fractal geometry. It was created singlehandedly by Benoit Mandelbrot, who trained himself *not* to reject automatically the kinds of shapes his imagination set forth when he asked himself the sorts of questions children ask: What shape is a mountain? Why is a cloud the way it is? The usual tools of classical mathematics—hand, pencil, and ruler—had initially rejected certain shapes as absurd. Yet, interestingly and perhaps not coincidentally, Mandelbrot almost depended on their aesthetic quality. He trained his imagination to accept them as obvious and found that "these shapes provide a handle to representing nature." Moreover, "intuition [imagination] can be changed and refined and modified to include them" (as quoted by Gleick, J. in *The New York Times Magazine*, December 8, 1985, 114).

When splitting and integration operate together on both conscious and unconscious levels, many layers of the personality reverberate. An overflow of raw material presses forward to be dealt with from both within and without. The artist immerses himself in sentient life, welcoming the excitation in order to master it through aesthetic form. He attends, selects, and integrates it into the forms most likely to lead to a successful aesthetic solution (Eissler 1971). His state of excitation arises from heightened perceptiveness and leads him to search and explore "the dim tangled roots of things [in order to] rise again . . . in colours" (Cezanne, as quoted by Milner 1957, 24—25). Picasso spoke of going for a walk in the forest and getting "green" indigestion. "I must get rid of this sensation into a picture. Green rules it. A painter paints to unload himself of feelings and visions" (quoted in Chipp 1968, 271). On the basis of subjective accounts of the creative process (Ghiselin 1955), such a burgeoning of thought and imagery is now generally accepted as characteristic of creative talent and due to an inborn greater sensitivity to sensory stimulation.

Greenacre (1957, 1958) has elaborated on the implications of this thesis for the childhood development and life of the artist. For one thing, she reasons, the intensity of all experience for the child of potentially great talent means that all the early libidinal phases tend to remain more lively, to overlap and communicate with each other more readily. Also, they are less decisively settled with age. When residuals of these early phases are revived in later life, they may be disconcerting in their vividness. More germane to the present discussion, they may predispose to episodes of splitting (in the sense of dissociated consciousness). Greenacre sees this as having less ominous prognostic significance than for the less gifted person. One infers that the unconscious mechanism of splitting (in the sense of suspending the reality sense) has in part become developed as a conscious ego device. The gifted person, while knowing the conventional sense of reality, is thus also able to hold it in abeyance in order to explore and concentrate full powers of integration on imaginative possibilities.

Second, the special sensitivity to inner bodily sensations and rhythms, as well as to the outer world, leads to a state of mutual permeability and oceanic feeling. It carries with it a hunger and need for completion by searching for balance between the inner and outer worlds. The force of intense body feelings, with their need for completion, responds to and brings about a sense of fusion with an increased range of outer objects (collective alternates) which come to replace parental images.

Third, the urgency of these pressures emanating from the creative self competes for attention and commitment with the person's ordinary world of social stereotype. This struggle between the conventional or social self and the creative self often causes yet another kind of split: a split in the sense of identity. It is one which may well continue into the adult life of the future artist. Depending on changing circumstances, the balance may swing now toward the urgency of creative needs, now toward the demands of ordinary life.

This final point again means that the artist's selfhood, like Diana's, is not unitary: there are two or more selves. To repeat: the artist differs from Diana, however, in that there is a lively if often adversarial

two-way conscious communication between the self-organizations—
both between the conventional and creative identity, as well as within
the private world where the reality sense is held in temporary abeyance until it is reinstated.

The idea that others may sense that the artist's self is divided
between everydailiness and creativity is well captured in *The Private
Life* by Henry James (1893), a story centering on Clare Vawdrey, the
greatest writer of his time, whose introspective and subtle works are
much admired by thoughtful readers. His public self is just the
opposite. So disappointing to his friends! His manner is unvaryingly
even and bland, his opinions second-rate and obvious, his conversation utterly without nuance, full of sound and banalities.

Vawdrey said he would write a play for an actress friend, Blanche
Adney. At first he said he had written a passage for it before dinner;
later, that he did not know whether or when he had written it; then,
that he would recite it—but as it turned out he could not remember
any of the lines; finally, that he had not written anything. When
Vawdrey did read his work to Blanche it was as if he was reading the
work of another man. It made her want to meet the *author*.

At one point during this confusing and contradictory situation,
while Vawdrey is talking to the actress, a friend goes to Vawdrey's
room to fetch the alleged manuscript. There in the darkness, to his
astonishment, he sees Vawdrey sitting at his desk writing in the dark.
It is unmistakably he, but he neither looks up nor responds. This
Vawdrey looked infinitely more like the author of Vawdrey's admira-
ble works than the Vawdrey his friends knew. It was as though there
were two of them: the private one who stayed home and wrote was the
remarkable one, the genius; the public one was a shallow mask.

For dramatic contrast James gives us another member of the circle
of friends, Lord Mellifont. He and Vawdrey had known each other all
their lives. If Vawdrey was all private and only a stereotyped shell in
public, Mellifont came alive only in public. He was always "on," full
of anecdotes for every occasion. What became of him when he was not
on stage? Was anyone there? His wife suspected that he hardly existed
in private, and she was afraid to find out. (His sexual life was hinted to

be either nonexistent or "glacial.") When he was alone nothing got done, until someone showed up. It seemed as though he was there only from the moment he knew somebody else was. Otherwise, he vanished—between the acts.

James gives us the sense that the doubleness of the writer, Vawdrey, arises from the bountifulness of his inner life—the creative person's greater sensitivity to sensory stimulation. This inner richness is highlighted by placing it next to the apparent absence of a private life of the social personage, Mellifont. Thus, if there was more than one Vawdrey, there was less than one Mellifont.

This is still a view from the outside; we do not get a glimpse of the inner picture except perhaps for a single hint about bisexuality—Vawdrey's male proper name, Clare, is a homonym of the feminine Claire. Is this an indication of still another split—in gender identity—or, as Greenacre might say, another instance of a lack of decisive closure of a developmental issue?

We know from other creative individuals that they often need to form twin-like partnerships with individuals with whom they can unconsciously feel merged. Is there a dynamic relationship between this need to form partnerships and the existence of various inner splits? If so, do the partnerships represent externalizations of the inner splits? In other words, are they the external counterparts of intrapsychic splitting and reintegration—attempts to heal *inner* splits by reenacting them *inter*personally?

The lives of Joseph Conrad and Pablo Picasso may be relevant here. Conrad wrote about doubles and in his personal life formed and lost one intense creative partnership. Picasso created a new art form in which the visual field was systematically split apart and reintegrated; both his personal and creative life depended on a series of creative partnerships, without which he fell apart and experienced creative paralysis.

Meyer's (1967) study of Joseph Conrad was perhaps the earliest discussion in the psychoanalytic literature of the artist's need for a double. This is said to have characterized Conrad throughout his life, from his early years as a motherless child dependent on a depressed father to the ultimate depression of his later years after his elder son abandoned him by eloping. Except for a close bond with fellow-author Ford Madox Hueffer, Conrad was unable to establish a deep relationship, presumably because he did not dare to relive the early relationship with his depressed father. Immediately after forming this tie to Hueffer, Conrad wrote *Heart of Darkness* (1898–99) and *Lord Jim* (1900). In the former, Marlowe recognizes himself on meeting the regressive Kurtz; in the latter, the protagonist recognizes himself when confronted by a band of criminal marauders.

The Secret Sharer (1910) was written during his intimate friendship with Hueffer, and here Conrad explicitly expressed the theme of the double already developed in his earlier novels (he had considered titling it "The Second Self" and "The Secret Self"). The story dramatizes his own intense preoccupation with mirrors and reflections, a search for the complementary role of an "other" to round out his own sense of an incomplete self (Meyer 1967).

While *Heart of Darkness* and *Lord Jim* reflect back to their protagonists aspects of themselves which are alien—regressive and criminal, respectively—*The Secret Sharer* has to do with the mysterious and immediate affinity that springs up between the young captain of a ship and the stranger, Leggatt, whom he rescues from the sea. Having always been somewhat of a stranger to himself, it seemed to the captain that when he gazed at Leggatt he saw himself reflected in the depths of an immense mirror. When he was away from Leggatt it felt as though part of himself were absent. The story ends with the captain's lowering Leggatt back down into the sea and questioning his own identity, even his own sanity.

Did Conrad need to have the young, untested captain find Leggatt in order not to feel utterly alone before his crushing responsibility? But if retaining him raised a threat from another quarter—namely, homosexual panic—did he also need to get rid of Leggatt in order to preserve the captain's sanity? And which was the greater danger in Conrad's own life—abandonment, or the possible homosexual implications of attachment? Or, from a formal point of view, whatever the content of the inner conflict, did the tenuous balance between intense engagement and necessity for disengagement from the fictional relationship reflect the delicate inner balance between splitting and integration? Meyer (1967) emphasizes that Conrad broke with Hueffer immediately after writing *The Secret Sharer* and that this estrangement was an important factor in precipitating Conrad's disintegration into psychosis.

In contrast to Conrad's sole relationship with Hueffer, Picasso was able to set up a whole string of such relationships with both sexes (M. Gedo 1980). As long as he did not feel alone—more specifically, as long as he found himself supported in a dependent relationship—he was able to continue to transform threatening inner stresses into artistic reintegrations; on the other hand, whenever a crucial relationship was interrupted or disintegrated, he reacted with the agitated paralysis of his early years.

Chief among his friends when he moved to Paris was Apollinaire, who duplicated the role Picasso's father had played during childhood and adolescence. He was Picasso's good mirror and understander. He publicly supported Picasso, defended him against hostile criticism, and interpreted the iconography of his work to the world.

When he broke with Apollinaire, Picasso formed a significant new relationship with Braque; together, they became a single superartist in a psychological twinship Braque compared to "being roped together on a mountain." Picasso, for his part, playfully called Braque "my wife" and "Madame Picasso." To signify their unity of spirit both men refused to sign their work, which was difficult to tell apart. Together they invented cubism, a radical new art style in which the subject was methodically disassembled and the illusion of fragmentation was created. While creating it, Picasso required live models, photographs, and other props to reassure himself of the continued integrity of the object in reality. He also required the presence of Braque. As long as Braque and Picasso worked together, vacationed together, the flow of work continued. When they were apart, Picasso produced a load of unfinished work which he completed quickly after reuniting with Braque.

In other words, when Picasso's partnerships fell apart, both his art and his life did also. He became obsessed with fluid, changing indentities, felt in danger of dissolution, and had to be coaxed every morning to get out of bed. At such times he suffered creative paralysis and, would try to bolster himself by turning to sculpture and indulging in passing promiscuities, all the while keeping old discarded loves installed separately nearby.

LOSS AND REDRESS: THE FRENCH LIEUTENANT'S WOMAN

When it comes to facing the blank page, the novelist may well share the feeling expressed in Keats's lines: "then on the shore of the wide world I stand alone."

Such, in fact, was the image—except it was that of a woman—that struck John Fowles, and with such force that it swept other considerations aside and led to his writing *The French Lieutenant's Woman* (1969). While he was in a half-waking state, the author "found" the future heroine of his novel; he became curious about her, explored and developed her character, and gave her up three times in alternative endings to the book before finally bringing it to a close by having her leave the protagonist forever after he lost and refound her. *The French Lieutenant's Woman* offers us the opportunity to explore the theme of loss in the creative process and speculate about its possible relationship to inner splitting and reintegration.

> It started four or five months ago as a visual image. A woman stands at the end of a deserted quay and stares out to sea. That was all. This image rose in my mind one morning when I was still in bed half asleep. . . . I ignored this image; but it recurred. . . . The woman obstinately refused to stare out of the window of an airport lounge; it had to be this ancient quay. . . . An outcast. I didn't know her crime, but I wished to protect her. That is, I began to fall in love with her. . . . This—not literally—pregnant female image came at a

2. This section is based on Gilbert J. Rose, '*The French Lieutenant's Woman:* The Unconscious Significance of a Novel to Its Author," *American Imago*, 29:165–76, 1972.

time . . . when I was already halfway through another novel. . . . It was an interference, but of such power that it soon came to make the previously planned work seem the intrusive element of my life. . . . Once the seed germinates, reason and knowledge, culture and the rest have to start to grow it (Fowles 1968).

The first sentence of the book sets the time and place: late March 1867, on a pier jutting out into Lyme Bay, "that largest bite from the underside of England's outstretched southwestern leg" (Fowles 1969, 9). It also sets the angle and object of our interest: "a local spy" might focus his telescope on a couple strolling toward a black figure of a woman who is leaning against an upended cannon barrel at the end of an ancient quay, facing the sea. She is the woman some called "whore," who had been abandoned by her lover, the French lieutenant. "There is a child?" "No. I think no child" (p. 14).

The author's imagination has taken the image and projected it a century back in time, staring out to sea, having been abandoned by her foreign lover. She, the upended cannon, and the sea form a trilogy on the ancient quay, counterbalanced by another threesome, the strolling couple and the eye of the observing spy, our narrator.

The couple are Charles and his fiancée. Charles, the protagonist, will became as obsessed with Sarah, the woman in black, as did the author, and his struggles with himself about gaining, losing, refinding, and relosing her are the substance of the novel. Charles, thirty-two, was brought up by his bachelor uncle and his widower father, his mother having died giving birth to a stillborn girl when Charles was one year of age. To block his early interest in the church he had been sent off to Paris.

When the story opens, he is a serious amateur paleontologist and collector of echinoderms. In his "lust" for finding them he explores Undercliff, a Garden of Eden on the shore where deep crevices in the lush foliage can bring disaster to the unwary. He enters and climbs a seldom used path which forks downward and then back toward the sea, up a steep small slope crowned with grass which then opens on a little green plateau; "he was about to withdraw; but then his curiosity drew him forward again . . . round the curving lip of the plateau . . . where he saw a figure," not as he thought "for one terrible moment . . . a corpse . . . but . . . a woman asleep" (p. 61)—the mysterious Sarah.

On another occasion, inevitably drawn back to the same site, he encounters her again "at the end of a tunnel of ivy. . . . She led the way into yet another tunnel . . . [from where] they came on a green slope" (p. 113). Observed emerging together it must have been assumed, wrongly the narrator tells us, that they had been in flagrante delicto.

This rather explicit body-image and the primal scene symbolism, projected onto the shore of the English motherland of long ago, is as yet only symbolism. At this point in the story, their love has not been consummated. Nor does Charles achieve a sexual connection with the prostitute he picks up at a later point in the story. It turns out that this girl has been a prostitute for two years, since she was abandoned by a soldier-lover at eighteen.

Assuming that Charles's mother had given birth to him one year after her marriage and had thus been married for two years before dying in childbirth with Charles's sister, the period of her marriage coincides with the duration of this girl's prostitution. Like Charles's mother, the prostitute also had a child, this one a girl who lay sleeping in the next room. When Charles discovers that the prostitute's name is also Sarah, he vomits up the food she has fetched him, and sex becomes out of the question; the baby awakens crying and is taken on Charles's knee and pacified by his dangling his watch before her.

When Charles and the other Sarah ultimately get together, it is in a passionate encounter of not more than ninety seconds. He is stunned to find that he has taken a virgin. He leaves, breaks off his engagement to his fiancée, but when he returns Sarah has vanished without a trace. He travels the earth searching for her without success until one day, in the French Quarter of New Orleans, he receives a telegram: "She is found" (p. 342). He sails immediately for England and arrives on the last day of May. The two years that have elapsed since he last was with her again coincide with the two years of the other Sarah's prostitution and of his mother's marriage before dying.

When he confronts Sarah, she refuses to return to him. He accuses her of giving him the coup de grace: "You have not only planted the dagger in my breast, you have delighted in twisting it." "She stood now . . . the defiant criminal awaiting sentence. He pronounced it. 'A day will come when you shall be called to account for what you have done to me. And if there is justice in heaven—your punishment shall outlast eternity' " (p. 355). Sarah answered: "There is a lady. . . . She will explain . . . my real nature far better than I can myself. She will explain that my conduct towards you is less blameworthy than you suppose.' . . . He loved her still; . . . this was the one being whose loss he could never forget" (p. 356).

The lady who can explain Sarah's adamant refusal to return to Charles turns out to be the little girl born to Sarah by Charles, unknowing. (The ninety seconds of their sexual union may be taken as prefiguring the ensuing nine-months' gestation, according to the well-known tendency of the unconscious to play with numbers; cf. Freud 1923). He picks the child up and dangles his watch for her "as he had once before in a similar predicament" (p. 358). "Sarah bowed her head. . . . Charles stared at her, his masts crashing, the cries of the drowning in his mind's ears. He would never forgive her" (p. 359). "It had to be so" (p. 360) she quietly insisted.

Why could he never forgive her? Why could the couple not be reunited, together with their child? And why had Charles to leave the house in torment? This can only be because Sarah and daughter are really ghosts—revivified images of the dead mother and sister. Charles has re-created them as he had done before in the form of Sarah the prostitute and her daughter, from whom he also fled. Mother is the one being whose loss he could never forget of forgive, and her return, except in dreams, is indeed impossible.

It is in keeping with this theme of coping with loss that the author concludes the novel with a choice of endings. The ingenious device of offering such a choice itself suggests that no ending need be considered final—that endings are negotiable and not, in fact, irremediable. Thus, the novel ends first with Charles resigning himself to marry his fiancée and forget Sarah. But Fowles himself criticizes this as "too sweet." Sixteen chapters later the novel ends a second time with Sarah agreeing to marry Charles; there is a reunion of the happy couple plus baby daughter. Finally, there is a stark ending of Sarah rejecting Charles. She has been transformed into a liberated woman; he is alone, facing the awesome and radical freedom of Existential Man.

He leaves the house in torment, "a man behind the invisible gun carriage on which rests his own corpse" (p. 366). It was "as if he found himself reborn, though with all his adult faculties and memories. But with the baby's helplessness—all to be recommenced, all to be learned again! . . . He stared down at the gray river, now close, at high tide. . . . It meant (many, many things) both prospective and retrospective" (p. 365). The river of life. His own life does not course as a single riddle or symbol toward the answer of imminent death but is to be endured in its uniqueness. "And out again, upon the un-plumb'd salt, estranging sea" (p. 366).

The novel ends, as it began, with the image of the sea, that arch-symbol of birth, which first captured the author's imagination as he emerged from half-sleep. It ends with Charles facing the impossi-bility of regaining from inexorable Fate the woman who had been his mother, yet knowing that he can never let her go from his mind and heart, and that it must be so while he endures the separateness and becomes whatever he is to be.

Let us return to Fowles's notes (1968) on writing *The French Lieutenant's Woman*.

Once the seed germinates, reason and knowledge, culture and all the rest have to start to grow it. . . .

September 2, 1967. Now I am about two-thirds of the way through. Always a bad stage, when one begins to doubt . . . the whole bloody enterprise; in the beginning one tends to get dazzled by each page, by one's fertility. . . . Some years ago I came across a sentence in an obscure French novel: "Ideas are the only mother land." Ever since, I

have kept it as the most succinct summary I know of what I believe. . . .
I loathe the day a manuscript is sent to the publisher, because on that
day the people one has loved die. . . .
  Oct. 27, 1967. I finished the first draft, which was begun on
January 25. . . . I haven't the energy.

The imagery of a seed germinating in the motherland of ideas can
be viewed with fresh clarity if we realize that the gestation period of
this first draft has been exactly nine months and two days.

Charles has become more himself, reborn, in regaining and relosing the mother of his childhood dream. He has reconstituted her in
both idealized and devalued forms, in the two Sarahs. Her daughter is
his stillborn sister, as well, perhaps, as standing for himself identified
with her and reunited with mother in death.

Pregnancy, birth, death, and rebirth. The theme reverberates
through the psychology of creativity like a leitmotif (Rank 1932)—as
insistently, in fact, as its equivalent on another level, the theme of
losing, finding, and relosing. Van Gogh's annunciation of his identity as an artist might be taken as an instance of the motif in the
symbolic mode of death and rebirth. Between October 1879 and July
1880 he was in silent misery and did not write a single letter. He
concluded this gestating silence of nine months by informing brother
Theo that he was emerging renewed like a bird after molting time,
reborn as an artist who would "re-create" rather than imitate. He
dissociated himself from the Van Gogh name, thereafter becoming
simply "Vincent" (Lubin 1972). Similarly, Picasso dropped his father's name, Ruiz, in favor of his mother's, Picasso.

Preoccupied with the oedipal constellation and problems of sexual
identification, the older analytic literatue emphasized that creative
work was the route by which the male artist was able to sublimate his
feminine wish to be reproductive like mother (Jacobson 1950). While
it is true that on an oedipal level of development such feminine
identification raises the suspicion of an unconscious flight from
heterosexuality toward a homosexual position, on an earlier, pre-

oedipal level it is at the same time consistent with the theme of loss and restitution.

To spell this out further, the urge to restore the lost unity with the primal mother and be able to do everything she can do, including having babies, is a source of power and activity—not merely a passive, receptive wish in respect to the father of the later, oedipal stage. From this earlier point of view some of the unconscious roots of an author's giving birth to a novel lie deeper than latent homosexuality based on identification with the female reproductive ability. Author and novel together are mother and child, rejoined in bodily completeness, perfection, and immortality. He is intensely attached to his work as to a part of himself, but not wholly his to control. It is not a relationship to the mother that the author is seeking but rather that oneness out of which his own newness was born. He is identified both with the creature that emerges and with the superabundant fullness that brought it forth. The author's sense of conviction, rightness, and certainty, on the one hand, and of frailty, exposure, and tenuousness, on the other, expresses this double identification with mother and child.

Another way of conceptualizing the early relationship with the mother is through Winnicott's (1953, 1966) intermediate area. Intrapsychically, an early stage of psychic organization which precedes the separation of ego from id, and the distinction between self and other, the intermediate area refers to the original space between infant and mother, at the point of the initiation of their separateness. Later, it refers to the potential or metaphorical space, between reality and fantasy, person and world (Grolnick et al. 1978). It is the site of transitional objects and phenomena—neither me nor not/me, between internal and external, animate and inanimate. Providing rich opportunity for the play of illusions and ambiguities, it is the place where play begins and where cultural experience later develops.

In addition to teddy bears and comfort blankets, Winnicott's (1953) original description of transitional phenomena included musical sounds, tunes, and words. For example, as language develops the child seems to carry words with him like objects he owns; they can be repeated in mother's absence to reassure himself and create a bridge between the familiar and the strange—between symbiosis and solitude. Thus, the child can use transitional objects and phenomena to loosen or tighten up his relationship to the mother according to need (Greenacre 1969).

The rapprochement subphase of childhood (Mahler, Pine, and Bergman 1975) is another way of conceptualizing the early relationship to the mother. The space between them is analogous to the intermediate area of Winnicott where the interplay between separateness and union, originality and tradition gives rise to the first steps in the construction of reality and the emergence of creative imagination. In this stage (15−24 months or beyond) there is a deliberate search for, and avoidance of, intimate bodily contact, an alternation between pushing mother away and clinging to her, an incessant watching of mother's every move and ducking out from her hugs. The child both exercises individuality to the limit and demands mother's constant involvement, wishing for reunion and also fearing reengulfment. The invention of play, peekaboo games, and games of imitation, social interaction and symbolic play make it possible to function at a greater distance from mother. For example, having stories read while mother is absent is of particular interest. Only toward the end of the rapprochement subphase does each child develop an unmistakable individuality and his own characteristic ways of coping.

These several perspectives on an intermediate area of fluid boundaries between the all-powerful primal mother and her infant—a potential, metaphorical space where the imagination can play with separateness and union, originality and convention—helps to bring a number of early phenomena into focus: peekaboo and mirroring; imaginary companions and doubles. They all come to focus on the common theme of loss and the various attempts to deal with it.

Is it possible that the intrapsychic mechanisms of splitting and integration are internalized forms of the rapprochement—subphase child's darting away from and rejoining mother? Just as, later, making and breaking creative partnerships may represent externalizations of these mechanisms?

In normal development, coping with loss helps set the stage for the shapes of reality to emerge, blur, reform, coalesce, and re-emerge. The shapes and shadows of oneself—attributed to others or reflected in nature at large—interact, join, support, and recede. Illusions and disillusionments help provide the raw data with which to define and redefine the self, explore the world and expand the boundaries of reality. At the same time, they help prepare the ground for retreat into psychopathology.

Loss at any time of life may be expected to reverberate with later and antecedent disappointments. This is still more likely to hold true for the experience of early loss before the person has become capable of the work of mourning with the gradual, painful disinvestment of intense feeling that this entails. Systematic studies of children who lost a parent before adolescence, for example, conclude that, as a result of the inability to mourn and gradually work through and "metabolize" the loss, the child is left with a dual and contradictory attitude: the death is intellectually accepted but emotionally denied (Wolfenstein 1966, 1969; Freud 1927, 156) conceptualized this as being due to a split within the ego itself: one current of mental life recognizes that death has occurred and takes full account of that fact; another current, however, denies it. "Wish and . . . reality exist . . . side by side."

Since the experience of loss is inevitable, why does the theme appear to be so insistent in the psychology of creativity? There are a number of factors that might account for the likelihood that a creatively endowed child could well experience early loss more intensely than an average child: (1) The more intense, sensuous engagement with the world might make for both deeper and wider rootedness of attachments. (2) Because of the lack of decisive closure of developmental stages, loss or threat of loss would reverberate and stimulate a wide range of emotional and fantasy ramifications; (3) For a creatively gifted child, the very process of individuation might be experienced as a loss—a narcissistic loss to the child's idealized sense of his own bodily and mental perfection or omnippotence. (4) Related to this, for a finely tuned child, any average mother might well be the equivalent of an insensitive one; mismatching in nonverbal responses might be inevitable and deeply wounding, leaving the child, and perhaps the caretaker, too, mutually alienated from each other (Miller 1981). (5) If, in addition, there were actual blows to such a child's narcissism, such as bodily deformations or injuries (Niederland 1967), the wound would be all the deeper and the need to build bridges to repair the gap all the greater. (6) Finally, the actual experience of childhood loss is a not infrequent finding in the lives of creative individuals.

Wolfenstein (1973) has traced the theme of loss in the work of the poet A. E. Housman and the painter René Magritte—both artists experienced the death of their mothers in boyhood. She shows in detail how opposites are fused in their poetic and painterly images: near and far, past and present, loss and denial of loss all coexist. It is as though the early loss gave rise to the splitting of the ego that Freud (1927) postulated. Moreover, in the cases of Housman and Magritte, one of the consequences of such a split appears to have been the development of a kind of mental dualism: raw, purely wishful imagination (primary process) becomes joined to highly disciplined and organized craft (secondary process) in an organically unified work of art.

The kind of dualism described by Wolfenstein as a result of loss before adolescence and consequent splitting of the ego is conducive to a particular mode of consciousness, one that is sensitized to ambiguity and the coexistence of opposites. This by itself, however, might lead merely to defensiveness. Aside from innate givens, other conditions are necessary for the ego split to be put to an adaptive and creative, as well as a defensive, use, namely, some of the elements we have already discussed: the capacity to hold the reality sense in temporary suspension, and the combined use of such splitting along with an ongoing reintegration.

If a creative piece of work were to result, one might expect that it simultaneously accorded with many functions of the mind: its form balancing the tension of strangeness with the release of familiarity; its latent content offering the wishful illusion that contradictory aims can be accommodated; and form and content together meeting high superego standards and increasing the apprehension of reality.

In summary, one might say that the unconscious reminiscence of lost unity before the birth of self and otherness is probably universal, but the creative artist is loss-sensitive and separation-prone. Therefore, his wound may be deeper; the split in the ego is such that it is set on an endless course of repeating the loss in order to repair it.

Sensitized as a child, he learns to use his talent to create imagery to defend against loss. As an adult, he uses it both defensively to cope, and nondefensively as part of his identity as an artist. The novelist, then, would be one who refinds his lost world by creating one of his own, peopled with products of self. His novel is a shadow that falls upon the present from the past and bears the shape of a former self: a self just emerging from psychic unity with the mother, he as her extension or she as his, as the novel is his; a self just unfolding into the awareness of time and separateness, mitigated somewhat by the knowledge that the temporal present, if not one's bodily self, is forever attached to the past.

Like the daughter of the French lieutenant's woman, or the daughter of that other Sarah, the novelist is the child of one parent only. Aroused from sleep or taken from his nurse's arms, with fear and curiosity, wishing both to return and to explore, he comes to sit upon the knee of the stranger who dangles a watch.

RESPONSE FROM JOHN FOWLES

Dear Dr. Rose,

Your paper interested me very much, since it confirmed my own tentative conclusions about the disease of novel-writing that I suffer from.

I think my main quarrel with your theory as applied to The FLW is the assumption that I am ignorant of Freudian ideas and therefore that the book represents clinically "true" evidence. This isn't of course to deny that images and ideas with Freudian undertones may be revealing despite conscious choice on my part, but it is false to represent them as completely unconscious elements in my writing. Two cases: one concerns Charles's younger sister who died in childbirth. Though I cannot pretend I analyzed her value as fully as you do, she was not, so to speak, inserted innocently into the story. You also mention the tunnel of foliage in the Undercliff—in that case I can quite clearly recollect altering the passage in a late draft to make the womb-vagina symbolism stronger.

I am a little dubious too of the play you make of some coincidences in elapses of time. There are good plausible technical reasons for the rash of two-year gaps you pick out. Nor can I take the nine-month gestation-period of the first draft very seriously, since the only reason it was not seven months was the very banal business of my having to spend two months during the period on other work—with considerable reluctance, but I was under contract.

The general theory of the novelist that you outline in the second half of the paper smells very probable to me, speaking out of my own experience. . . . Almost all literary accounts of novel-writing omit, or grossly under-rate, the acute pleasures of the writing of "pre-natal" or pre-separation stage, with the published book equalling full awareness of separate identity. I write far more than I publish simply because my being centres in the processus (increasingly, as I grow older) and its delights and has only a very peripheral attachment to the "born" (also "dead") book. Of course being published and moderately successful . . . is gratifying to a part of oneself. But even the greatest pleasures of that public stage cannot hold a candle to some of those one knows during the creation. Though I am sure you are right to trace the source of this back to an infant stage, it seems (at least to this conscious writer) less of a recessive. . . . experience than a kind of sideways one. I think very much of novels in process as parallel and contemporaneous worlds, as very present escapes from the real daily world; and even when story and narrative method require a "capturing" of the past, the dominant time sense is actually of a kind of futureness. This has perhaps to do with the impermanence of drafts, the knowing one will rarely get a passage right first time—or even the hundredth, alas—and the absolute need to believe in a future time when all will come good. I am trying to say that seeing one's book as a backward thing, a failure to capture an unconscious past, as a remote and now irremediable conspiracy of infantile biography, is a phenomenon of the finished, published book. The experiences of the fluid, incomplete stage are a great deal more mysterious, and I'm not convinced your account fully explains them; another very bizarre part of the writing (as opposed to written) experience is the relationship between author and characters.

"Dear Dr. Rose,

"I recently applied your theory to Thomas Hardy in an anthology on his work. . . ."

The following is an abstract of the relevant parts of the paper "Hardy and the Hag" (1977) referred to by Mr. Fowles:

The reason why most English novelists "are fanatically shy of talking of the realities of their private imaginative lives . . . is that novel-writing is an onanistic and taboo-laden pursuit" (p. 28). Like the child's creating of a "real" world, it is also heavy with the loss of illusions and desires required by adulthood and artistic good form. "The artist who does not keep a profound part of himself not just open to his past, but *of* his past, is like an electrical system without a current. . . . A seriously attempted novel is also deeply exhausting of the writer's psyche, since the new world created must be torn from the world in his head" (p. 29).

Mr. Fowles then summarizes the general theory of what produces the artistically creative mind as being the experience of the passage of the baby from merger with the mother to the awareness of separate identity and beginnings of the sense of reality:

What seemingly stamps itself indelibly on this kind of infant psyche is a pleasure in the fluid, polymorphic nature of the sensuous impressions, visual, tactile, auditory, and the rest, that he receives; and so profoundly that he cannot, even when the detail of this intensely auto-erotic experience has retreated into the unconscious, refrain from tampering with reality—from trying to recover, in other words, the early oneness with the mother that granted this ability to make the world mysteriously and deliciously change meaning and appearance. . . . He will one day devote his life to trying to regain the unity and the power by recreating adult versions of the experience . . . he will be an artist. Moreover, since every child goes through some variation of the same experience, this also explains one major attraction of art for the audience. The artist is simply someone who does the journey back for the less conditioned and less technically endowed (p. 31).

This is a plausible and valuable model because it helps explain the necessity the artist feels to return again and again on the same impossible journey. It implies "an unconscious drive towards an unattainable. The theory also accounts for the sense of irrecoverable loss (or predestined defeat) so characteristic of many major novelists. . . . Associated with this is a permanent—and symptomatically childlike—dissatisfaction with reality as it is, the 'adult' world that is the case. Here too one must posit a deep memory of ready entry into alternative worlds—a dominant nostalgia." (pp. 31–32).

The novelist longs to be in a state of being possessed, which is difficult to describe but involves a childlike fertility of imagination that takes adultly ordered ideas and sets them in flux. As the text nears completion, this state recedes and disappears. No matter how pleased one may be with the final work, this "sense of loss, or reluctant return to normality, that every novelist-child has to contend with . . . is always deeply distressing" (p. 32).

This need to transcend present reality opens many problems in more ordinary life, not the least being the complex relationship of the male writer to his wife (Rank 1932). "This relationship is . . . a far more important consideration in the writing and shaping of a novel than most critics and biographers seem prepared to allow" (Fowles 1977, 33). At the crux of the tension between creative "desire" and social "duty" is the mother-wife polarity. Setting out on a voyage of writing and shaping a novel draws on the pleasures of the primal mother-self unity. On the other side is the presence of real woman, the enemy of the mother, the ally of the conscious, outward self, the protectress against the cruel review columnists. The real woman more generally symbolizes social consensus and artistic common sense. Yet, "the writer's secret and deepest joy is to search for an irrecoverable experience [and] the ending that announces that the attempt has once again failed may well seem more satisfying . . . the doomed and illicit hunt is still far more attractive than no hunt at all" (p. 35).

If this seems paradoxical, I can call only on personal experience. I wrote and printed two [*sic*] endings to *The French Lieutenant's Woman* entirely because from early in the first draft I was torn intolerably between wishing to reward the male protagonist (my surrogate) with the woman he loved and wishing to deprive him of her—that is, I wanted to pander to both the adult and the child in myself. I had experienced a very similar predicament in my two previous novels. Yet I am now very clear that I am happier, where I gave two, with the unhappy ending, and not in any way for objective critical reasons, but simply because it has seemed more fertile and onward to my whole being as a writer (p. 35).

I realise, in retrospect, that my own book [*The Collector*] was a working-out of the futility, in reality, of expecting well of such metaphors for the irrecoverable relationship. I had the greatest difficulty in killing off my own heroine; and I have only quite recently . . . understood the real meaning of my ending. . . . It is a very grave fallacy that novelists understand the personal application of their own novels. I suspect in fact that it is generally the last face of them that they decipher (p. 38).

If in every human and daily way . . . the actual woman in a novelist's life is of indispensable importance to him, imaginatively it is the lost ones who count, firstly because they stand so perfectly for the original lost woman and secondly . . . because they are a prime source of fantasy and of guidance. . . . Because they were never truly possessed, they remain eternally malleable and acquiescent. . . . The maternal muses . . . grant the power to comprehend and palliate the universal condition of mankind . . . a permanent state of loss (p. 40).

REPRISE

Two themes run through John Fowles's discussion: (1) the private delights of the actual process of writing as against the public pleasure of the finished product and its aftermath, and (2) the problem of the split and tension between creative "desire" and social "duty."

Regarding the first, Mr. Fowles refers to the experiences of the *process* of writing as being mysterious, fluid, onanistic, and taboo-laden. It involves a bizarre relationship between the author and his characters. "The novelist longs to be in a state of being possessed. . . . [by a] childlike fertility of imagination that takes adultly ordered ideas and sets them in flux. . . . [before] complet[ing]. . . . the final work. . . . [with its] sense of loss, or reluctant return to normality."

Perhaps to some extent, *The French Lieutenant's Woman* allows the reader to sample the "fertility and flux" of the writing process, for we are given the impression of being in on a novel in-the-making, or of one that is inventing itself. This is done through the device of an interior plot, which has to do with the author's own reflections on writing the novel. This device is usually referred to as the narrator disclaiming responsibility by speaking directly to the reader, deliberately breaking the spell of the text and warning the reader not to take the story too much to heart or believe in the existence of the characters.

For example, Fowles is explicit in reminding us that this is fiction: "I do not know. This story I am telling is all imagination. These characters I create never existed outside my own mind" (p. 80). Not only does Fowles tell the story, he walks on as author and criticizes and interprets the story. He makes fun of himself, and of Henry James; he launches into treatises on fictional technique, takes the reader on tours through Victorian London, as well as etymology. He scolds himself for using too many exclamation points. He puzzles over what to do with the sleeping face of a character in a railroad coach: "What the devil am I going to do with you?" And we have already alluded to the author's struggle with alternative endings to *The French Lieutenant's Woman*—a predicament which, he informs us, he also experienced in his previous two novels.

However, if this device serves to disclaim responsibility, in Fowles's hands, at least, it does more. It permits the reader to glimpse some of the pleasures of the act of writing. Fowles glories in the characters' freedom to talk back to him, their author: "A genuinely created world must be independent of its creator; . . . *It is only when our characters and events begin to disobey us that they begin to live* [my italics]. When

Charles left Sarah on her cliff edge, I ordered him to walk straight back to Lyme Regis. But he did not; he gratuitously turned and went down to the Dairy" (p. 81).

In other words, we are now in an intermediate world of transitional phenomena—between reality and fantasy—a world of controlled splitting. We are in dialogue with a dream. The reality-sense can be held temporarily in abeyance, allow the characters trial periods of freedom to feel and behave, in order to discover and explore their potential. They are not permitted to get up and walk off the page and take over one's life like Emma, who, we recall, wrote defensively— that is, in order to relieve Diana of the threat of being flooded by traumatic memories. On the contrary. The visual image of a woman standing at the end of a deserted quay staring out to sea did not oppress Fowles, though it kept recurring and interfered with his life. He became curious about her. He wished to protect her. He fell in love with her. And if writing *The French Lieutenant's Woman* came to dominate him for a time, as a novelist he crafted the story and the characters, making creative choices and transforming the private image into literature. The act of writing was his love affair with her.

Perhaps that is why he refers to it as auto-erotic. And in writing about Hardy (Fowles 1977), he states that it seems clear that his deepest pleasure was in postponing consummation—advancing, re-treating, unveiling, re-veiling. In *The Well-Beloved*, "gaining briefly to lose eternally is the chief fuel of the imagination in Hardy himself" (p. 37). Actual sexual consummations are often without erotic qual-ity. Tryst scenes scarcely conceal the underlying primary relationship of the child with the vanished mother. Nor is it a coincidence that incest plays so large a part in the novel.

If, as Fowles implies, the delayed and desexualized consummations are due to autoerotic and incestuous taboos, I would suggest addi-tional factors from earlier levels. Some of the mysteries of the fluid state of the creative process have to do with rapprochement with the primal mother of infancy—of longing to be possessed, as Fowles says—and also of risking reengulfment and darting away. It is a time of intercourse with reflections of oneself in mother, doubles, and imaginary companions, to say nothing of ghosts—only to avoid them (like Freud), break disastrously from them (like Conrad), lest they take over completely (Golyadkin, Shaver) or compartmentalize one's consciousness (Diana). It is a universally experienced time of playing peekaboo with sunbeams and shadows, learning the constraints and freedoms of reality. Except that the creative person seems compelled to do it again and again, relearning as if from the beginning, and sometimes learning something new.

This touches directly on Mr. Fowles second theme, that of the tension between creative "desire" and social "duty." At the crux of this, he suggests, is the mother-wife polarity; the lost woman of infancy remaining the living source of fantasy, "eternally malleable and acquiescent"; the actual woman in the novelist's life being indispensable "in every human and daily way."

The struggle between the conventional self and the creative self and how this may cause an enduring split in the future artist's sense of identity was discussed earlier in this chapter. Henry James's character, Vawdrey, in "The Private Life," was taken as an illustration of the doubleness of the writer. We mentioned that earlier stages seemed less decisively closed and that this, together with the artist's ability to suspend (split off) the reality sense temporarily while allowing integration to proceed, was perhaps sometimes responsible for disturbing the peace of his personal life. Later we discussed a third split—that of the ego itself; in response to the experience of early loss, a dual mode of consciousness develops whereby an aspect of reality is intellectually acknowledged while emotionally denied, and this leads to repetitive attempts to harmonize and reintegrate these two realms of experience.

This returns us to the question that was raised at the outset, namely, the relationship, if any, between creativity and psychopathology. As promised, there has been no easy answer. If the creative process, like psychopathology, shares an easier access to the unconscious, the umbrella concept of splitting offers a way to explore and discuss it. In the examples of psychopathology we have chosen, the splits have been "vertical", that is, involving consciousness itself, and "horizontal" splits from consciousness; they take place without awareness, in the interest of defense against overstimulation, and at the cost of constricting awareness. The splits that take place as part of the creative process are more conscious and controlled, temporary—as far as the suspension of the reality sense is concerned—and serve to expand awareness.

To the extent that the creative process involves splitting it would seem to necessitate a delicate balance with the capacity for reintegration. Furthermore, it presupposes that the material at hand is capable of undergoing endless transformations in the furtherance of the creative aim. If this way of dealing with the aesthetic medium is such an integral part of the way the artist is connected to reality, it may not be possible for him to deal with his *personal* life in any other way. Yet, obviously, however essential for performing a creative task, it is incompatible with carrying on healthy, viable personal relationships—live people, in contrast to maternal muses, do not readily lend themselves to being rendered "eternally malleable and acquiescent".

We seem to have completed a circle, but perhaps have gained higher ground. Creative work requires the ability to mold and shape, fragmentize, cut off and reunify material—repeatedly; the same form-producing procedures, when carried over to human relations, are dehumanizing. What is creative in one area is destructive in the other. Some artists seem to be able to confine the creative process to creative work; others—and some of the greatest, Picasso among them —appear to be ruled by it.

M. Gedo (1980) has noted Picasso's psychopathology was reflected in his repetitive destructive relationships with women. The data suggest still more: his disturbed relationships with women reflected his relationships in general and were perhaps even a reflection of the way he envisioned reality itself.

First let us look at some of Picasso's relationships with other men: (1) When his good friend and defender, Apollinaire, was arrested as a possible accomplice in an art theft from the Louvre, Picasso not only did not corroborate Apollinaire's story, but possibly even denied that he knew him. Years later, when Apollinaire died suddenly, Picasso painted his *own* shocked visage—and there were no further self-portraits for twenty years. (2) When his old friend Max Jacob was taken to a concentration camp in 1944, Picasso dropped him a note but took no steps to help him—for example, by corroborating that Jacob had converted to Catholicism about twenty-five years earlier. (3) When Matisse's daughter kept phoning Picasso to inform him of the funeral arrangements for her father, he refused to go to the telephone. He neither went to the funeral nor mourned in a conventional manner. Instead he began to paint à la Matisse, emulating that painter's formal elements: lyrical rhythms, bright colors, bold patterns, and careful control.

As for casual acquaintances, he became furious with his then wife, Gilot, when she gave away articles of his clothing to their crippled gardener, accusing her of doing this to turn him into a hideous cripple. And as for his own children, after his eldest child Paulo, Picasso could not integrate his subsequent offspring into his self-image: he would "trade" articles of clothing with son Claude, perhaps out of some magical wish to change places with a younger person.

This material suggests that Picasso's personal world of variable self-images and unstable outer objects was rife with anxiety—anxiety regarding the loss of the sense of self, other people, and the world itself. The very reliability of perceptual recognition, discrimination, and self-object boundaries must have remained uncertain. Mirroring and peekaboo play at losing and refinding self in others and others in self is the earliest patterned form of testing and reconfirming the shifting dimensions of reality.

The role of play in Picasso's life, as well as its relation to his work and love life, was particularly significant. His creative work-play was no child's play. Sensitized by his past, he was able to discern the permeability and inconstancy of boundaries which to everyday conventional vision appear deceptively static and stable. Thus, in his creative work he showed the play of edges "that rhyme with one another . . . or with the space that surrounds them" (Gilot and Lake 1964, 114). His art revealed the latent, polymorphous aspects of reality that lurk beneath the conscious, stable appearances at the surface.

While he played profoundly at work that endures, he labored unrewardingly at passing loves, or played around regressively with personal relationships—as though they were objects to be assembled, discarded, hoarded, fractionated, recombined. Was his tendency to treat people as things somehow related to his tendency to do the opposite with items of junk, namely to anthropomorphize them? This is posed not as a moral question but as something more basic, perhaps connected to his not being able to deal with numbers as abstract symbols but rather as concrete signs. In short, were these but different aspects of his concern with a fluid reality—reflections of that intermediate area of transitional phenomena stemming from the rapprochement subphase of development—where something can be or become other than what it seems?

We are dealing here with fundamental questions, epistemological and psychological, regarding the nature of the arts and perhaps the essence of creative imagination: a sensitivity to the interplay of malleability and integrity—or, in intrapsychic terms, of splitting and reintegration. In Picasso's case we are left with a compelling irony: his imaginative experience of the solid world of reality as being inherently shifting, perilous, and shocking could destructively impersonalize those who shared his private life; when harnessed to his creative power to disassemble and reconstitute the perceptual field, it illuminated his powers of observation—inspiriting the inanimate media of his craft, and transforming the vision of our time.[3]

3. The foregoing remarks on Picasso appeared first in my review of *Picasso: Art as Autobiography*, by M. Gedo. *Review of Psychoanalytic Books*, 1:411–18, 1982.

6

IN PURSUIT OF SLOW TIME:
MODERN MUSIC AND
A CLINICAL VIGNETTE

Moving from clinical to creative experience, our argument has stressed several points: (1) The difference between psychopathology and creativity depends less on particular mechanisms—for example, splitting—than on the use to which they are put. (2) Psychopathology represents an attempt at defensive mastery, with private and unconscious meaning for the individual concerned, and is purchased at the cost of constricted awareness and functioning. (3) The creative process contributes to the public domain by broadening the apprehension of reality. (4) In any particular case—Picasso, for example—defensive and creative purposes may and often do overlap.

The coexistence within an individual of defensive and creative purposes implies many things—among them, that an ego mechanism such as splitting may be used both to repress private unconscious conflicts and to foster abstraction of certain elements selected from a myriad reality in order to highlight them.

This is an expanded version of Gilbert J. Rose, "In Pursuit of Slow Time: A Psychoanalytic Approach to Contemporary Music," *The Psychoanalytic Study of Society*, 10:353–65, 1984. Cf. also Rose, (1980), pp. 162–66.

Whether a creative work achieves wordly success depends on many factors beyond our purview. A psychological way of explicating the factor of timing (Kubler 1962) is to say that it takes a dovetailing of personal conflict and the context of history (Erikson 1958)—a synchrony between the (latent) concerns of the individual and his society—to form a psychosocial bridge: the work transcends the private; the audience, recognizing itself in the work, resonates with it, feels affirmed and completed by it.[1]

Knowingly or unknowingly, the creative artist is often attuned to currents of unconscious thought and feeling within and around him. Thus, music, like literature and art, may well prefigure as well as reflect its times. Music is a creative transformation of feeling into form. It balances the relaxation of constancy with the tension of change. Combining defensive with creative purposes, it may also represent the wishful illusion that the flow of time is controllable—that time is cyclical as well as linear—and in this way, perhaps, serves as an unconscious defense against death.

This chapter attempts to discern what some modern music is "getting at" and foretelling—not by way of examining the personal problems that certain musicians may have attempted to master through their music—but by juxtaposing a clinical vignette to some recent innovations in the musical approach to time. It suggests that some modern music, like some traumatized patients, responds to the anticipation of imminent yet unpredictable violence by altering the perception of time. Creative and defensive aspects of mastery unite to transform and expand perception of this dimension of reality.

The art of the novel treats the stuff of personality as a malleable medium. The novelist reaches into himself to discover the raw mate-

---

1. Among the crucial elements that influence creative success—endowment, opportunity, craftsmanship, awareness of tradition and *zeitgeist*—the clinician may comment on one: the *fear* that treatment will have a negative impact on creative work. My experience suggests that this fear is the expression of some private, unconscious meaning that the individual has attributed to creative activity. Where the work per se presents no problem, the subject hardly arises for clinical exploration.

rial of memory and imagination from which to fashion characters and narrative possibilities corresponding to the potential of some of the "multiple personalities" to be found in each of us.

Music, likewise, treats its material as a malleable aesthetic medium. However, its material being time, and nonverbal, we are immediately confronted with especially formidable problems— problems regarding the nature of time, as well as the necessity of using language to discuss a nonverbal artform.

The Greeks used two different terms, *kairos* and *chronos*, to refer to different modes of experiencing time and organizing behavior in relation to it. The term *kairos* remained in classical Greek only and did not come down through Latin into the Romance languages. It denotes the human and living time of intentions or goals. It is episodic time with a beginning, a middle, and an end. It has to do with the flux of Heraclitus—a confluence of past memory, present perception, and future desire. All these coexist in the ongoing human experience, along with preconscious awareness and unconscious motivation.

Chronos, on the other hand, is clock-time. It refers to the measurable time of succession, before and after, earlier and later. It has to do with the static atomism of Parmenides, the discontinuous world of fixed and constant entities in empty space. Instead of a range of preconscious awareness and a whole field of unconscious motivational forces, there is a conscious, focused perception of the passage of units of time.

This is not to say that there are two types of time, one real and one unreal. Nor, for that matter, are there three types of time—past, present, and future. There is only one time. It is a mental abastraction, not a thing. It does not do things, such as "flow" in any direction, either linear or cyclical. There are cyclical events, like the seasons, day and night, and serial events, like growth, aging, and death. Whether one experiences time as cyclical primarily or as serial depends partly on one's attitude toward death. The cyclical experience of time denies death; the serial experience of time accepts it.

Chronos and kairos, in other words, are different ways of *experiencing* time as well as of expressing certain truths about the relations between events (Whitehead). For Newton, "true" time was absolute and mathematical time in a uniform flow. For Bergson, this so-called true time of Newton was a fiction as opposed to Bergson's *durée réelle*. For Cassirer, neither concept sufficed; each represented a partial view into a whole—a particular standpoint of consciousness. Both must be understood as *symbols* that the mathematician and the physicist take as a basis in their view of the outer world, and the psychologist in his view of the inner one.

The conception of the physical world requires only the chronological aspect of time. Both views, however, are necessary for a conception of the human world. Furthermore, while the world is both atomic and in flux, continuous and discontinuous, static and flowing, objective and subjective, concrete and abstract, universal and particular, one cannot experience both of these awarenesses of time cognitively at the same time. Instead, there is an oscillation of awareness between the two, organizing our experience of the world (Jaques 1982).

The dual experience that the cognitive mode cannot accomplish the aesthetic mode makes possible. By treating time as an aesthetic medium, music is able to bridge two different dimensions of time and harmoniously accommodate diversity and unity, change and constancy. Just as the novel treats the constituents of the person as having the plasticity of an aesthetic medium suitable for shaping into new, self-consistent characters, music deals with time as being infinitely flexible while retaining its inner integrity.

Through the use of various devices (ornamentation, the minor key, moving from one key to another, dissonance) it causes delay and arouses the tension of anticipating what will come next (L. B. Meyer 1956, 1967). At the same time, many of the melodic, rhythmic, and harmonic variations introduced for the sake of apparent variety are actually repetitions and recurrences in disguise (Bernstein 1976). Being experienced as returns to the familiar, they are associated with the reduction of tension. Thus, in music one may experience the tension of change together with the release of tension that comes with the return to constancy (G. J. Rose 1980). Moreover, since the built-in delays and concealed recurrences act as a steady stimulus to memory as well as an anticipation of what will come next, there is a conflating of past and future. In music, past and future coexist with the present as a dynamic whole. This whole is built up in an accumulation of wave after wave of intensification. In other words, instead of being viewed as a static measure—divisible into equal parts—of the transient events that give *form* to experience, time is revealed as a dynamic force, reflecting the complexity, volume, and variability of the *content* of psychic life (Zuckerkandl 1956).

How else may one account for the widespread impact of a "simple" musical structure such as the famous first movement of Beethoven's "Moonlight Sonata" (no. 14 in C-sharp minor, opus 27/2)? One of the most popular pieces of keyboard music, it has inspired at least two novels and several paintings and poems. It has even been arranged for chorus and orchestra with the words of the "Kyrie" as a text. According to Czerny, Beethoven himself resented the popularity of the work. Nor did he have anything to do with its programmatic title. The phrase, "Moonlight, or a boat passing the wild scenery of Lake Lucerne in the moonlight," was applied to the sonata by the poet-musician Rellstab thirty years after its composition.

The three-note melody is itself only a slight variation of its three-note accompaniment. The acompaniment figures gradually become an end in themselves as they rise from the middle to the upper registers of the piano and back to the role of accompaniment. The original melody then returns. The brief coda is based on the rhythm of the melodic motif, which was itself derived from the rhythm of the accompaniment.

Obviously, this structure is devoid of any referential meaning to things outside itself. It has nothing to do with either moonlight or other scenes from nature, let alone abstract concepts such as courage or longing. Rather, the accumulation of three-note wave after similar wave combines near-constancy with minute differences, and this gradual intensification of focused attentions is associated with mounting feeling.[2]

2. Music is associated with the same physological changes that occur during emotional experience: changes of pulse, respiration, blood pressure, electrical conductivity of the skin, delay in the onset of muscular fatigue (Mursell 1937).

Such emotion, according to Langer (1942, 1953), is the "meaning" of music; it is a representation of the emotional quality of subjective, lived time made audible—an auditory apparition of felt-time. Instead of vaguely sensing time as we do through our own physical life processes, we hear its passage. But it is not a trickle of successive moments as it is in the conceptual framework of classical physics with which we usually operate in practical life. "Musical time is not at all like clock-time. It has . . . voluminousness and complexity and variability that make it utterly unlike metrical time" (Langer 1957, 37). Music sounds the way feelings feel, mirroring their ups and downs, motion and rest, fulfillment and change.

Langer's distinction between discursive and presentational symbols is a helpful one. *Discursive* symbols are readily translatable and have fixed definitions. Music, on the other hand, like all the arts, expresses the quality of emotional life through *presentational* symbols. Presentational symbols are untranslatable; they are understandable only through their relations within the total structure of the work. The meaning of a piece of music lies entirely within the work—that is, in its own formal structure and inner relations. Unlike ordinary language, presentational symbols capture the flux of sensations and emotions.

For example, music can express opposites simultaneously and so capture the ambivalence of content better than words or language. In addition to such simultaneity, the linear unfolding of music in the course of time also mirrors the "shapes" of emotions. Music sets up expectations, interposes delays, and grants hidden recurrences before reaching a final resolution. The frustration of expectations is associated with rising tension, its gratification with release of tension. Tension-release embodies feeling. And it is precisely this element— the balance between tension and release—that has been called the specific dynamic of musical form (Toch 1948, 157).

Artist-analyst Marion Milner's *On Not Being Able to Paint* (1957) and musician-philosopher Victor Zuckerkandl's posthumously published *Man the Musician* (1973) provide important insights into the relationship of language to nonverbal art. Both make a clear distinction

143

between formal, logical thinking, on the one hand, and creative or aesthetic thinking, on the other. According to formal logic, all thought which does not make a total separation between what a thing is and what it is not is irrational. Thus, according to formal logic, the whole area of symbolic expression is irrational, since the point about a symbol is that it is both itself and something else. Formal logic, then, gives a false picture in aesthetics; this false picture is avoided, Milner writes, only "if we think about art in terms of its capacity for fusing . . . subject and object, seer and seen and then making a new division of these" (p. 161).

Similarly, Zuckerkandl spells out the differences between objective hearing and musical hearing. The "I" that hears music, he writes, is different from the "I" who is the subject of a sentence, who is going to attend to outside signals in order to react to them in one way or another. The listener to music is more like the swimmer who allows himself to be carried by the water as he swims. Language, being firmly tied to subject-object predicate structure, fails us here. The "I" that listens to music is no longer something that "does"—that is, hears and now "has" the results of what it has done; namely, the sensations of tones. Hearing music involves hearing not only tones but also their direction, tension, motion, organic structure. It is the kind of hearing that moves with the tones and draws the hearer into their motion. Thus, it involves an interpenetration of subject and object, within rationality, drawn into the experience of the movement of felt time (Zuckerkandl 1973, 160–62). (The similarity to psychoanalytic listening is so striking as to require no comment.)

Both Milner and Zuckerkandl make clear that aesthetic hearing or viewing is more like creative, nonlogical thinking; also, that both are quite different from objective perception and cognitive, logical thinking. The difference lies in the opposition between subject and object—their separateness—in the case of cognitive, logical thinking, and in the togetherness of thinker and thought—their mutually influential motion—in aesthetic, creative thinking.

Milner summarizes the problem neatly: "Clearly the great difficulty in thinking logically about this problem is due to the fact that we are trying to talk about a process which stops being that process as soon as we talk about it, trying to talk about a state in which the 'me/not-me' distinction is not important, but to do so at all we have to make the distinction" (p. 161).

Turning now from the psychological to the cultural pole, perhaps nothing less than profound scholarship is able to show satisfactorily how a musical style is part of the expressive life of a culture. For example, Charles Rosen (1980) considers the evolution of sonata form out of eighteenth-century arias and concertos. In the late eighteenth century sonata form changed from being music for the court or church into music for a new concert audience, the rising middle class; musical themes took on the dramatic roles and tensions found in opera and were resolved with classical order and proportion. In the nineteenth century sonata form became something else again: it provided prestige, respectability, and constraint for the romantic impulse and a vehicle for the virtuoso's performance.

A comparable study is yet to be written for modern music and contemporary times. In the meantime, two considerations seem obvious. First, the experience of time has become drastically different from what it was previously. As during other disturbed periods in history, our era is characterized by pervasive, random violence, meaningless death, and bankrupt faith. Man has long known dread of total extinction, of course, but never its actual feasibility through instruments of destruction of unprecedented speed, range, and scope. While previous ages had a wider margin of time to buffer the unpredictability of life and powerful religious ideologies to rationalize the seemingly senseless, our own age is largely lacking in both. Secondly, while it would be impossible to prove that such a profound change in our temporal experience is reflected in contemporary music, it is plausible to assume it.

As representatives of modern music I have somewhat arbitrarily selected Charlie Parker's bebop jazz and Arnold Schoenberg's twelve-tone atonal music. Both, in reflecting a new experience of time, also contributed significantly to altering the musical experience of time.

A clinical vignette that throws some light on the psychological meaning of this altered sense of time is shown by the case of a woman who thought her appointment was one hour earlier than it was, at 3:00 P.M. instead of at 4:00. She then came fifteen minutes late for the imagined appointment (at 3:15), slept in the waiting room, and left fifteen minutes before the actual appointment was about to begin (at 3:45). As I hope to show, she was uprooting time from its usual matrix in a way somewhat analagous to certain aspects of modern music. But first to Charlie Parker and Arnold Schoenberg.

At the end of World War II, highly educated black people were coming into the mainstream of American society. Even Duke Ellington was not sophisticated enough for their taste. Hindemith and Stravinsky were becoming known to innovative jazzmen. Hindemith's own instrument was the viola, but he had played drums in jazz bands in European hotels before coming to the United States in 1940, and his "Symphonic Metamorphosis on Themes by Weber" has a strong jazz flavoring. But it was Stravinsky who was the main hero to jazz musicians because he was pushing beyond conventions. The great bebop innovators in America—Charlie Parker, Dizzy Gillespie, Thelonious Monk, Art Blakey, Kenny Clarke, Max Roach—looked on him almost as a god. (As did the pioneers of modern jazz, like Miles Davis and John Coltrane, who later took their music even further out.)

Despite these connections to the past, however, bebop of the 1940s and early 1950s represents a startling break from preceding jazz styles, and one that still causes some discomfort among today's listeners. Ron Rose (1980), in an unpublished ethnomusicological paper, maintains that the musical changes brought about by the bebop movement strongly reflected the changing black self-image in America. I am indebted to him for what follows on bebop.

> Dixieland had its childhood in New Orleans. It became refined into the smoother and more "literate" styles in the years to follow, reaching its height of polish under the rule of the big band style where improvisation (the original tenet of jazz) became the exception rather than the rule. . . . Bebop . . . appears to be a clear and unsubtle black

rebellion against the white dominated swing scene, as well as the historically established caricature of the black entertainer as mindless and officiously amusing. . . . The bebop musicians were intent upon creating a music which would allow a complete break from its "illiterate" black predecessor, and their white competitors. The music itself, . . . with its difficult chord changes and rhythmic bridges, often executed at breakneck speeds, helped keep the movement "pure" of musicians not entirely competent, as well as create a new standard for the white establishment.

The leader of the bebop movement was Charlie Parker. (While he was considered one of the major innovative forces in the history of jazz, he himself said that if he could take a year off he would go to Yale to study with Hindemith.) Perhaps his major contribution was his conception of the musical phrase as tied to yet at the same time free from the limitations of meter. Specifically, while the musical phrase had previously been restricted to the bar-lines, he extended it through the bar-lines. This means that, as soloist, he would sometimes speed up, sometimes slow down, to bring the melodic line "out of sync" with the underlying metric foundation, which was all the while being provided reliably by the other instruments. The relationship between the melodic line and the rhythmic pulse was thus rendered much more ambiguous; that relationship was no longer bound to the downbeat. Instead of classic syncopation, with its stress on up or downbeats, melodic emphasis could now be placed on any division of the beat on a sixteenth- and thirty-second-note level. This led other jazz musicians to experiment with unorthodox meters, fragment the beat until the meter became indiscernible, or blur the distinction of the downbeat much as a twelve-tonist avoids the concept of a tonic.

In short, Parker's restructuring of pulse into what might be called a fluid meter superimposed on a metric foundation turned the rhythmic conventions of Western popular music on end. One far-reaching effect was to shift the functions of the other instruments. The beat could now be displaced to the lighter cymbals, freeing the drum to become a most articulate instrument on its own. Similarly, the pianist's left hand was freed to pursue a different path.

Just as Parker's rhythmic innovations loosened the relationship between the melodic line and the underlying beat, Schoenberg's twelve-tone scale had already freed musical harmonics from the concept of the tonic. This also had far-reaching effects on the musical experience of time. A brief excursion into musical theory is necessary to show how.

It is possible to consider that the most important fact about music—its basic ingredient—is not so much sound as movement (Sessions 1950). Music embodies, defines, and qualifies movement. Each musical phrase—that portion of music that must be performed in a single breath—is a unique gesture that moves constantly toward the goal of completing a cadence. Everything else—the appropriateness of harmonies, melodic intervals, the details of rhythmic elaboration—depends on it. Hearing music is hearing the dynamic quality of tones—that is, hearing their direction, their movement. (In the same way, seeing a picture involves seeing the force, direction, intention in form and color.)

A musical scale is one of the main ways of organizing the current of motion. The scale is a system of order among tones. It describes the relationship among the tones making up the musical organization of a culture. The scales are based on the physical phenomenon of overtones making up the harmonic series. (It is said that using the overtone series for musical theory actually dates back to the ancient Greeks and Chinese, who found the overtone series useful in establishing the norms of pitch relationships, scale structure, and so on.) The starting point or tonic tone in the key of C is C; the tonic tone in the key of G is G, and so forth. The main or dominant overtone of the tonic is five tones away and is called the fifth. The main overtone or dominant of C in the key of C is G. One may move from the key of C to its main overtone, G, and then take that as the starting point, or tonic, of the key of G. One may move in the key of G to its main overtone or dominant, D, and the key of D; thence to its main overtone or dominant, A, and the key of A; thus on to the keys of E, B, F#, and ultimately back to C, completing the circle. This moving from one key to another, from tonic to dominant, makes possible a circle of fifths. It is based on the underlying organization of the scale, namely, a stable relationship of tonics and dominants based on the universal *physical* phenomenon of the harmonic series of overtones.

A second point: because of the tonal organization of the scale, the tones strive in certain directions. They have driving qualities. This accounts for one of the main ways in which music sets up a current of motion, a system of expectancies. For example, the tonic tone of any key is the one of ultimate rest and stability toward which all other tones tend to move. The octave and fifths and fourths were already binding forces for the ancients. They were relationships so fundamental that they became decisive points of reference around which to organize tones. Together they defined the space within which melody could coherently move.

In the West, other intervals were gradually incorporated into the service of musical expression—thirds, sixths, sevenths, seconds—and finally, augmented and diminished intervals. Each new conquest was associated with a new struggle. The use of these intervals led eventually to the use of chords and a new dimension in music—namely, tonality—and the modulation from one key to another, as well as major and minor modes. "Tonality implies a kind of perspective in sound, sometimes compared rather shrewdly to perspective in visual art. For it makes possible a system of relations which are unequal in strength, in emphasis, or in significance" (Sessions, 1950, p. 40).

Thus, because of a combination of the universal physical phenomenon of the harmonic series together with cultural evolution, tones that come before lead the Western ear to expect that certain tones will come after. This is so even though, in order to build up tension, this motion or expectancy may be delayed in various musical ways already mentioned.

Tonal music feels like the natural experience of time flow to Western listeners because it is *learned* so early, but it is far from universal. Training and culture are important factors. For example, a Western listener interprets the vibrato (a slight fluctuation of pitch often less than a semitone) as a constant pitch with a rich sound.

An Indian musician, however, whose native music is based on micro-tones—intervals smaller than the semitone—may perceive the Western vibrato as a significant fluctuation of pitch probably meant to express agitation. Even the basic ability to distinguish the octave[3] may be lost if one is immersed long enough in another culture where such an interval is unimportant—for example, in the music of Australian aborigines.

Now, if we could set up a series of tones which was lifted out of the gravitational pull of tonics and dominants, the overtones of the harmonic series, we would no longer be in a secure circle of fifths, going from one key to another in an orderly way. Any single tone would no longer carry implications of where it came from or where it is going. In other words, we would be taken out of the ordinary flow of time—from past to expected future.

Essentially, this was what Schoenberg did with his twelve-tone scale. It represents a whole system based on rootlessness from the harmonic series. The twelve tones and their sequence are selected in such a way that no tone has any implications regarding the tone that preceded it or the tone that may follow it; much of the directedness of tones has been rendered inoperative. Each of the tones can be played forward, backward, in mirror-image, or backward *and* mirrored. Since there are twelve tones in the Schoenberg system, we now have forty-eight possible sequences. All of them alter the ordinary experience of time as we know it in the West—not, it must be stressed, by tampering with time directly (for example, through rhythmic changes) but through changes in the tonal system, setting up ambiguous expectancies.

In addition to these changes in tonality that modify our expectancies of what will follow what musically, in much of the music of the twentieth century there is a deliberate dissolution of the ordinary sequential flow of musical events as we have come to know it. Instead

3. The perception of the octave seems to be a particularly basic and primitive skill; white rats were trained to run across a grid to food only when they heard a tone one octave away from the tone they were trained to respond to, and not to other tones (summarized from Winner 1982).

of a musical event in a composition depending on at least one previous musical event in order to build up to a climax or resolve tension, each musical event arises independently. For example, the sections of a piece of music may be put together in any possible sequence from one performance to the next with no set beginning or ending. Instead of development and recapitulation as we know it in sonata form, for instance, a piece of music in so-called vertical time does not purposefully set up expectations or fulfill any that might arise accidentally. The listener is forced to give up any expectation, any implication of cause and effect, antecedents and consequents. The sounds are unhampered and also unhelped by referential meaning. The experience has been compared to looking at a piece of sculpture: each viewer is free to walk around it, view it from any angle, in any possible sequence, and linger as long or as briefly with each, leave, return, whatever. In "vertical time" there is nothing to direct the way time passes (Kramer 1981).

In other words, in the new temporalities in music, past and future have been collapsed into a present moment which floats in uncertainty. There being no impulsion from the past, the overarching present leads to no-future. More than this: the bond tieing cause and consequence together has been loosened and meanings are cast adrift.[4]

Not only music but art and literature for decades have been foretelling and mirroring a world unhinged from the conventions of time, space, and causality that had traditionally supplied order. Take art: if discontinuity is the key to the new temporalities in music, fragmentation describes much of art history after the turn of the century and before World War II. Cézanne fragmented the image; the cubists fragmented shape; the impressionists and pointillists, light and color; the surrealists, reality itself.

4. Having stated this boldly for the sake of clarity, it is now necessary to add that experienced listeners to contemporary music insist that while at first it may sound random, expectancies inevitably emerge and order the musical experience—even that of John Cage. Thus has it ever been with innovation. What is at first disturbingly new becomes even comfortably familiar. The dialectic between new and strange and good old familiar is inherent in any organically evolving process.

After World War II, abstract expressionism and then minimalist painting rejected the illusion of three-dimensionality as well as all imagery or symbolism which might permit any conventional meaning to be read into these paintings. Instead, oversize canvases and large expanses of color draw the viewer "inside" the canvas, "enclosing" him. Describing a painting by Robert Natkin, art critic Peter Fuller (1980, 179) wrote: "It is almost as if at this level of your interaction with the work the skin had reformed but this time *around you* so that you, originally an exterior observer, feel yourself to be literally and precariously suspended within a wholly illusory space which, like the unconscious itself, contains its own time." One is drawn through the skin of paint between successive gauze-like veils of color so that the viewer feels suspended within some interior, timeless space.

The sense of enclosure and oneness is the visual counterpart of auditory immersion into the "vertical time" of some contemporary music. Just as in the painting there are layers of color and light which draw one into a timeless space, in some "vertical time" music there are layers of dense sound; relationships take place between layers of simultaneous sound rather than between successive events, as in conventional music. "The result is a single present stretched out into an enormous duration . . . that nonetheless feels like an instant" (Kramer 1981, 549).

In contemporary literature, one finds analogous discontinuities and fragmentations, resulting in a similar prolongation of the present moment lifted out of the flow of past-to-future. In the handful of years since her work first began to appear in *The New Yorker*, Ann Beattie has become for many readers the representative young American writer. Here are some of the things she said in an inteview with Joyce Maynard (*New York Times*, May 11, 1980):

BEATTIE: I don't know how to write a novel. . . . I would like to take a course on that some time, if I ever take another course. . . . It's very hard for me to work on Monday and Tuesday, and on Wednesday I

wonder what I said on Tuesday, let alone what I'm moving toward. . . .
That's why all the chapters jump around. I can't think how somebody
would move from one to the next, so I have to take a breather and hope
that I come up with something. . . . I certainly listen to records a lot.
But if I write a story I tend to put on what my husband is playing on the
stereo at that moment . . . . just what's on the turntable . . . . I really
love the notion of found art. Warhol soup cans—that kind of stuff.
When I write something, I like to look out the window the night I'm
typing and see what kind of moon it was on July the 15th and put it
in. . .

INTERVIEWER: Do you write about the relationships between men
and women?

BEATTIE: I just assume that there are going to be moments. But
when I start to write it isn't with the thought that I want to communicate about the relationship between men and women. I think, "I'd really
like to work that interesting ashtray I just bought into a story about
men and women. . . ." I read a lot—mostly modern fiction, nothing
before 1960 if I can help it. I'm a great time waster. See what a shiny
coat my dog has? I go buy him vitamins. I rap with him. I brush him.

INTERVIEWER: And did you actually know somebody who did what
the two lovers in *Falling In Place* did, during the early days of their
relationship—hold hands uninterruptedly for two days?

BEATTIE: Yes—four days. They've split up now.

Does a clinical perspective give us an inkling as to the significance
of these shifts away from the usual principles of sense and sequence?
Let us turn to the woman who came late for an appointment she did
not have, slept, and left before her actual appointment was due to
start. While not "removed" from the flow of time from past to future,
this was surely a slippage—whether one thinks of it as backward or
forward—a slippage in the racheting of the cogs of time. Let me relate
more about her and the clinical situation.

I had seen her years before in analysis. Now forty-seven, she had
asked to come in for a few sessions. We greeted each other warmly. She
sat down and smiled. I asked how she had been. She struggled with
her features and said, "Since Nancy was killed it hasn't been the

same," and burst into sobs. Shocked, I blurted, "What?" Nancy was her daughter, and she would now be about twenty-two. The manner of the patient's breaking the news was not incidental, as we shall see.

Indeed, her twenty-two-year-old daughter had been killed instantly in a car accident a year earlier. The patient had managed to continue all her activities but experienced a numbing disconnection from her feelings. Not mourning her daughter, she felt, was like holding onto her, not letting her go. She had only recently begun to weep, and this brought some relief from the sense of deadness.

She had entered analysis originally saying that she rarely knew what she was feeling; whenever she was under stress she would disconnect herself from her feelings and hide inside. In this way she could fight off depression and "keep moving and smiling." Convent upbringing had taught her that it was more important to maintain a prayerful attitude than to seek to understand many things. She had cultivated a vague fogginess as a defense against sexual and aggressive impulses. This was modelled partly on her mother. Mother was remembered mostly for her bland smilingness and the way she cultivated stereotyped responses to handle any situation. Father was a powerful political figure whose family life was characterized by towering rages and emotional withdrawal. Neither parent ever exchanged a single word with their daughter after she married outside the Church. She had been temporarily expelled from the family in adolescence for always getting into "trouble," though she was not sure what the trouble was. She of course knew there was a past, but the quality of herself in it was not available to her, and when it was it was like remembering the feeling of having had a nightmare but not knowing what it was about.

She had married a driving man who became very successful. She married him to get herself "organized" by him and play out the roles he assigned her. She did this very well and became known as a sophisticated hostess, a responsive friend, a generous volunteer worker for good causes, and a natural athlete. A few close friends also knew that she was very bright, had a discerning literary and musical taste, and had graduated with high honors from a top college. She experienced modified analytic treatment as the only calm relationship she had ever known and the first time she had allowed herself to feel that she was taking something for herself instead of being selfless.

The clinical vignette relevant to our discussion has already been related. It was easy to imagine that it represented a conventional resistance of ambivalence to talking about painful matters, but the form it took seemed unusual.

At the next session, when we discussed what had happened, I asked, on the basis of what I knew about her from the past, whether having come late for an imagined appointment and having left before a real one was a way of expressing something about wanting to reverse what was real and unreal. Whether this was wrong or irrelevant, her answer in any event led elsewhere. She said that repeatedly when she met someone she had not seen for some time, the other person would "surprise" her by asking innocently and casually about her daughter, that the patient would then have to say her daughter had died, that this would always come as a shock to the other person and the patient would have to soothe *her* down. I said it seemed surprising that it always came as a surprise to her that someone should ask innocently about her daughter. Why did she not anticipate this and somehow try to cushion the news and shield both of them from the shock? She replied that everything seemed to come as a surprise to *her* nowadays; *she* was just never ready for anything. For example, although she had been an excellent tennis player, now every time the ball came to her it seemed to come from the blue; because she did not keep her eye on her opponent's movements she could not anticipate where the ball would land, and as a result her return would always be late.

I wondered if she might be turning every moment into a kind of shock and a surprise, ripping each moment out of its context in the flow of time, and in this way perhaps continuously repeating, actively, the traumatic moment when she was informed of Nancy's death. As for coming early and leaving before her appointment was due to start, we might speculate that this was a way of dislocating time, in order to correct and master it, a way of saying, "If only it had been an hour earlier, or later, Nancy would be alive now."[5]

Any analyst would wish for more data regarding this vignette, particularly the role of unresolved transference. But since the episode of the missed appointment arose out of a brief contact many years following the termination of treatment, this is not possible. This unavoidable omission, however, helps direct our attention back to a neglected area of early psychoanalytic interest: the role of reality and the effect of trauma.

We know that random, meaningless violence can destroy both the sense of self and reality. A less drastic result of trauma is that its reality may be denied and disavowed in various ways. Uprooting the connection between cause and consequence by altering the flow of time from past to future may be one means of blunting the impact of trauma. And, as we have seen in the case of Diana, one may attempt to master past trauma by reliving it in an endless repetition compulsion, transforming the present into that past, thus effectively halting the flow of time.

But what mechanisms help to master and defend against a reality that is not denied or disavowed—that remains well recognized, in other words—and yet flies in the face of common sense and logic? The patient of course understood very well that a head-on collison led to her daughter's death, but this bears so little relation to sense that the mind recoils from such "meaning" as absurd. If it cannot totally sever cause from consequence, past from future, it can at least defensively *modify the experience of time flow*—not halting it like Diana, but sometimes slowing it down and at other times speeding it up. Is this what the patient was doing in coming late for an appointment she did not have and leaving early for one she did? Or in being too slow in meeting her tennis opponent's return, too slow in preparing the

---

5. This hypothesis is supported by more extensive and systematic recent studies which have shown that following psychic trauma, disturbances in all major aspects of time functioning—rhythm, duration, simultaneity and sequence, and temporal perspective—serve adaptive and defensive functions (Terr 1984).

ground for breaking the news of her daughter's death, too quick in blurting out the news?

If this seems tenable, we might ask whether such temporal manipulation to deal with past and anticipated trauma is more widespread than is usually recognized. Are the fragmentation, discontinuity, and "timelessness" that characterize so much contemporary art a defensive cultural response to the fear of sudden death which, though largely disavowed, pervades our age?

As previously discussed, some of the new temporalities of music represent even more drastic attempts to cool the flow of time—actually to separate each moment from its historical context, deal with each like rootless tones, without implications, in the discontinuous Now. Thus, in the words of the folk ballad: "We'll make a space in the lives we've planned / And here we'll stay, / Until it's time for you to go. / Don't ask why, / Don't ask forever, / Love me now" (Buffy St. Marie).

If we were to accept the hypothesis that it was the sudden shocking death of her daughter that led the patient to defensively modify her experience of time flow, could we make a parallel hypothesis about some contemporary music? In short, the question is: should some aspects of modern music and of current clinical phenomena be bracketed together as defensive alterations in the experience of time— attempts to modify and thus "master" its inexorable passage?

The immediate musicological answer might be: "No. The new temporalities in music represent (1) experimentation, (2) reflecting the gradual absorption of music of different cultures (for instance, the Javanese gamelan), (3) making use of technological innovations like radio, records, electronics and tape-splicing" (Kramer 1981, 543−44).

Yet, if all this were true it would not negate one possible meaning of this musical experimentation: like the patient's reaction to sudden, random death, the new temporalities in music may still represent a deeply felt need to suspend time, to deal with the possibility that any succeeding moment might fracture conventional sense and flood the self. In other words, just as my patient experienced a defensive alteration in her sense of time in response to the life-threatening unpredictability of daily life, some contemporary music (and art), perhaps in similar response to shared anxieties of the age, dissolves familiar frames of reference, temporal (and spatial).

Whatever the cause, it would be misleading to dismiss such apparent dissolutions of familiar structures as simply regressive. It is a frequent analytic finding that a temporary dissolution of structure may be a prerequisite for further development. Thus, in the case of my patient, if what she went through were to lead to further growth, or in the case of music or art, if it is to be an aesthetic experience, such partial dissolution must regularly be followed by a redifferentiation of the self (G. J. Rose 1980).

This two-phase process—partial dissolution and reintegration— occurring in rapid oscillation appears to be central to creative experience. Much slowed down, it also describes the process of growth. We observe it, too, in that particular form of growth we call psychoanalysis and refer to it there as an alternating movement of therapeutic regression and working through, losing and refinding the self, emotional reliving and thoughtful reflection.

7

SHAPES OF FEELING,
SHADOWS OF MEANING

To describe the world with all the various feelings of
the individual . . . left out from the description . . .
would be something like offering a printed bill of
fare as the equivalent for a solid meal. . . . All the
various feelings of the individual . . . are strung upon
. . . the axis of reality. . . like so many beads. . . .
Individuality is founded in feeling.
William James (1902, 490−92)

Susan Langer's distinction between nonverbal, presentational symbolism and discursive symbolism was discussed in the last chapter.
Music is an example of the former—its very structure transforms
feelings into an objectified form that may be reflected upon. Discursive symbolism, on the other hand, is translatable into language and
intellectual thought.

Language and thought both develop out of an affective and bodily matrix. As a result, feelings permeate thought and perception from the beginning. Daily habit has a deadening effect on the whole-ness and sharpness of experience—turning it into a kind of half-life—and probably necessarily so in order to damp down the bright-ness of stimulation to workable proportions. But live experience is thought-feeling-perception—not conceptual dichotomies of pure reason swayed by emotions.

Two lenses—that of pathology and art—will be helpful in taking a closer look at the affective backdrop of language and thought: devel-opmental arrests magnify the contribution of feelings and physicality to language and thought; the art of language draws on the same sources and refreshes thought and perception with body-feeling.[1] "Shadows of meaning" is meant to suggest nuance and aspects of obscurity—the impossibility of seeing things directly rather than the shadows they cast on the walls of Plato's cave.

Meanings, in other words, are not self-evident. The process of interpretation and the methods by which meanings are derived is the domain of hermeneutics. The word *hermeneutics* is related via a com-mon source in Hermes (in his character of deity of speech and writing) to the ancient Greek *herma*. The *hermae* were signposts or boundary-markers protecting land and possessions and were common to both Greek and Roman culture. Its figuration was anything but neutral in tone. "It took the form of a head carved in the round surmounting a simple angular pillar, on the front of which was added a set of mal' genitals, usually erect" (Johns 1982, 52).

Thus hermeneutics has to do with meanings, but, as the phallic herma eloquently testify, meanings are embedded in imagery, and inseparable from emotions; they—the imagery and emotions—cannot be deracinated from their sources in the body, nor fully translated into words. Yet, they contribute to much of the force and power of meanings.

1. Little effort will be made to distinguish between "feeling" as awareness of affect, "affect" as the subcortical contribution to thinking, and "emotion" as the complex mixture of affect and our previous experience with a particular affect (Basch 1976)."

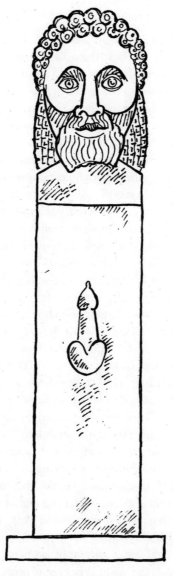

Herma with the head of Hermes. (Siphnos, c. 520 B.C.) Drawing by Gabor Peterdi.

Hermae were ancient Greek or Roman boundary markers. The word is related to *hermeneutics*, signifying the principles by which meanings are ascertained. As the hermae illustrate, meanings are not to be disembodied from feelings.

It is said that, before creating the world, Odin leaned over the bottomless chasm until the swirling mists below formed themselves into shapes. We probably all repeat this in shaping our world though we are now more inclined to think that it is a more active process of constructing forms than of passively waiting for them to shape themselves. Out of the original pandemonium of sheer impression, together with the direct physical reactions to sentient stimulation, our sense organs abstract groups and patterns of sense data and construe them as forms rather than a flux of impressions. They bring a seeming order and predictability to William James's (1892) "big booming, buzzing confusion" of sensory stimuli. These forms gradually come to include working models of self and others, by which we keep oriented in a world of shared and shifting reality.

For James, the endless subtlety and individuality of experience meant that experience was always thought-feeling, not cognition plus affect. In agreement with this, when we refer to forms we mean to indicate feeling-forms, since feeling is embodied within them. "It is entirely possible that feeling is what is given first and that all perception begins in feeling, since it may be true that we perceive forms first and that feeling is the soul of form" (Dufrenne 1953, 423).

According to Susan Langer (1942), these feeling-forms are symbols— direct metaphorical expressions of the sentient life from which they have been abstracted. They are the primitive root of the power of abstraction and constitute our first abstractions. Since abstraction is the keynote of rationality, the conditions of rationality thus lie deep in our pure animal experience of perceiving.

Every symbol refers simultaneously to the body and to the outside, hanging like a hammock between the internal, body pole and the external pole of the outside world (Kubie 1953). The first learning concerns itself with bodily things and, as it expands to the world outside, symbolic connections are etablished between our own body and the external world. Language arises out of original feeling-forms. It begins with the body—in the infant's gestures (Ferenczi 1913), sphincter activity (Sharpe 1940), and nursing patterns (Spitz 1957). The differentiaion of number and of spatial relations, and the linguistic expression of actions all start from the human body, its parts, its actions (Cassirer [1923] 1953).

In time, speech becomes increasingly practical and prosaic and ordinary language becomes well adapted for communicating the intellectual content of thought and factual observation. What had been originally the underlying *affective* matrix of language is more communicable through style—the how of language rather than the what—in short, the art of language. This early affective matrix is also discernible in magnified and distorted form in developmental arrests such as autism.

A gifted therapist identified "autistic shapes" in her work with such children (Tustin 1984). When young autistic children began to talk, they would tell her about their "shapes"—entirely personal shapes and not the objective, geometric ones located in external space that we all share, though they did involve the rudiments of the notion of boundaries enclosing a space. Furthermore, it was the "feel" of such "shapes" that mattered to the child. The feel of an object held *loosely* in the hand could be a "shape." In the younger children, touch was more important than the other senses, but all sensations, whether of sound, smell, taste, or sight, tended to be "felt" in the form of "shapes" rather than simply heard, smelled, tasted, or seen.

Early shapes apparently arise from the feel of soft bodily substances such as feces, urine, saliva, food in the mouth, and so on. However, it is the "shape" of the material rather than the bodily substance that is important to the child. (One is tempted to say that the importance of form predominates over that of content.) The child soon learns that he can make some "shapes" recur by dint of his own movements, and they become self-induced.

In normal development this capacity to make "shapes" out of sensory impressions becomes associated with the actual shapes of actual objects. Eventually they contribute to the formation of percepts and concepts and facilitate a working relationship with others in the world of shared reality.

But autistic children apparently get stuck at the level of private "shape-making." Their personal "shapes" seem more real than actual objects and certainly easier to manipulate. Thus, they may smear feces to make "shapes" on their skin. Or, once toilet-trained, they may manipulate feces internally to make "shapes" there. Or they might wriggle or rock, twirl, swing, or bubble saliva in the mouth to make "shapes." Speech is either absent or characterized by echolalia. When they do get to arithmetic and the alphabet, they use numbers and letters as contrivances to produce "shapes" rather than conceptually. Whatever the particular devices, they tend to become rigidly repetitive as they make the familiar shapes recur over and over, depending on these "shapes" to give them some sense of control.

As Tustin states, "Normal sensation shapes are the basic rudiments for emotional, aesthetic and cognitive funtioning" (p. 280). In keeping with their preoccupation and involvement with the creation of sensuous "shapes," it comes as no surprise to learn that "These children are often poetic, artistic and musical (p. 286)." It also seems likely that, whatever control or other functions are served by preoccupation with "shapes," they also reflect an expressive need.[2] This becomes the key for establishing communication. The aim of her therapy with autistic children is to make contact with their "shapes," in the hope of "chang[ing] and transform[ing] their 'shapes' into common coin, . . . enriching [the] psychological possibilities of everyday life with ordinary people" (p. 281). When successful, this leads them into the shared world of sanity and common sense while preserving their individuality.

How does this take place? (1) An essential ingredient for the mysterious transformation of private sensuous "shapes" into mean-

2. The most unusual case of artistic talent in an autistic child underlines the importance of the expressive element (Selfe 1979). Nadia's drawing skill appeared suddenly at three and a half while playing with her mother, after mother had returned from three months in the hospital because of breast cancer. As her expressive language and spontaneous speech slowly improved by age eight or nine, she seldom drew any more. Selfe points out that this flies in the face of traditional teaching (Buhler 1930) that children's drawings are graphic accounts of essentially verbal processes. It would seem, rather, that expressive need is primary and seizes upon whatever talent is available as an outlet.

ingful discourse is a caring relationship. (2) A way to get in touch with these nonverbal processes is through *metaphor*.

Tustin describes a crucial therapy session with an eight-year-old autistic child. After he had made a move toward becoming more accessible, therapist and child were able to play out and talk about his distorted body-image: he felt he had no stomach to connect his head with his bottom. In place of a middle to himself there were nameless dreads that might burst forth at any time. For example, how did food entering one end of his body turn into feces coming out the other? She writes:

> As these "nameless dreads" were "stomached" in the therapeutic ambience of the session, he no longer needed his magical envelopment by "shapes" and so we could settle down to a discussion of "growing-up" properly. This was concluded when I said that I had turned over his "shapes" in the stomach of my mind and he had turned over my "shapes" in his, and something new had come out, to which he had replied "I suppose that's thinking," to which I replied somewhat sententiously, "And you can't touch or handle thoughts" (p. 287).

The author speculates that this child's "perseverative ruminations associated with his idiosyncratic 'shapes' had been transformed [mysteriously] into 'thoughts,' through interplay with another person's 'shapes' which facilitated a process of psychological digestion" (p. 287).

Much in this account suggests Winnicott's (1953) intermediate area of experience—that of transitional objects and phenomena—the area formed when the mother is closely enough attuned to the infant's needs that the infant has the illusion that he or she has created the external correspondence. Winnicott felt that the main function of transitional objects and phenomena was to give shape to an area of illusion and serve as a bridge between the familiar and the strange, thus facilitating the acceptance of the new. On the one side transitional objects are connected to the subject and serve to allay separation anxiety; on the other, they are connected to the environment which is thus acknowledged, in part at least, to be outside the subject and not self-created.

One wonders if autistic "shapes" represent presymbolic bodily precursors of language—self-generating (autochthonous) sensations which create an independent autosensory world as a safe retreat from the external one. Perhaps the autistic child's constant handling of his "shapes" is analogous to the way a normal child in the course of early language development treats words as transitional objects. He seems to carry them with him like objects he owns—repeating them (echolalia) in mother's absence to reasure himself.

Establishing connections with the outside world depends on the therapist's tuning in so closely to the needs of the autistic child that an intermediate area, with its potential for transitional phenomena, is created. Within this privileged space, the figures of speech the therapist sends out are symbolic rescue missions, attached, like all symbols, to the body of the therapist and reaching out toward the isolated, autistic child for use as transitional objects. An effective vehicle of such symbolic speech is metaphor because its very nature is to bridge. Its vital support is the affective ambience of a trusting relationship. Sensorimotor, presymbolic, and preverbal elements intertwine inseparably with cognitive and affective meanings to form the hammock, the bridge, for the child to connect with and traverse with transitional language.

While images may be skillfully conveyed in metaphorical language to help deliver a psychotic child from its autistic "shapes," images may also be automatically perceived metaphorically with traumatic results. We have already seen in chapter 3 how the perception, "She's throwing stones at my car" was instantly translated into, "She's throwing stones at my body." Combining with traumatic childhood memories of sexual assault, it erupted psychotically into rape and murder.

The reverse process—translating a symptom into a metaphor and replacing that symptom with discourse—was, of course, the key discovery of Breuer and Freud (1893−95). If a metaphor could be discovered lying embedded in a symptom, symptoms could now begin to make sense and be made amenable to treatment through the use of words: the unconscious metaphor could be made explicit by translating it into words and this new verbal construction could serve as a brige between an unconscious thought-feeling and conscious thought. Not only lengthy psychoanalysis but immediate analytic first-aid became possible.

For example: A happy, healthy three-year-old girl, Lolly, suddenly developed a phobia of taking walks, becoming acutely anxious when she and her nursery school companions were to take a "trip" through the woods to see the ducks in the pond.[3] At the same time she developed a facial tic consisting of a tight closing and wide opening of her eyes. The disturbance seemed to be spreading further when she showed panic at being asked to paint Easter eggs in school. When she was shown the other children painting the eggs, she seemed momentarily bewildered and then, vastly relieved, was able to participate.

What proto-metaphor lay hidden in the symptoms of tic and phobia? A single conversation with Lolly brought out that she and her older brother took walks in the woods. One day the two chiildren had come across a dead bird. On another "trip" they had found a dead rabbit. They brought it home and buried it. Lolly had been struck by the wide-open, fixed eyes.

In the light of this, she was able to speak about fears of death in connection with "trips," including the vacation trip her parents were planning to take. Thereupon the facial tic disappeared and never recurred. Her sunny disposition returned. The fear of "trips" subsided within a few months.

Evidently, the rapid blinking of the eyes expressed in metaphorical body language both the fear of dying and the self-reassurance that she was, indeed, alive. The solution to the sudden panic when Lolly had been asked to help paint Easter eggs was this: The teacher had not asked the children to paint the eggs; what she had said was, "Let's *dye* some eggs."

While many individuals take pleasure in pictorial imagery and tropes of all kinds, others find them not merely pleasing but essential.

---

3. The following vignette is based on Rose 1960b.

It would be no exaggeration to say that some patients come to treatment craving appropriate metaphors as lifelines to make sense of their thoughts and feelings. A woman who happened to be a professional photographer put it this way:

> PATIENT: Somehow I have to create an image to get me out of the tight places I get into. Or I need you to give me verbal images when I get confused and I'm afraid the fuses will blow and I'm in disarray. The images are much richer than you think, and so for me to explore them is enlightening. It's almost primitive, like a ritual. I hook everything up visually. I need to understand them because they are in my head anyway and I can only do this with certain people who also think with images. Sometimes I think of myself as just a leaf in the wind. But then, if I think of myself as the skipper of my own sailboat, it narrows things down. In the first place, the boat has everything it needs. It is not a mess. All I have to do is know its qualities. Is it a keel boat or a centerboard? If it has a keel, I'm going to get hung up if I try to go over the sandbar. And if it's a centerboard, I better get it down if I'm going to sail into the wind. I cannot change the wind. I only have to have a destination, know the boat, and trim the sails. That's all. The beauty of the image is that I don't have to do or know everything. Now, take my husband. I cannot expect him to do what he can't do. A turtle can't lift its leg to pee, because that big shell is right there hanging over it. He's inside his shell, too. Kicking won't make any difference. He's insensitive. [Long pause] Sometimes the things he says and does just blow me away.
>
> THERAPIST: Is that when you see yourself as a driven leaf?
>
> PATIENT: Say! That's OK!

The way ahead now lay a bit more open to interpret the connection between her sense of disarray and confusion and the underlying anger at her husband.

THE LIMITATIONS OF WORDS

Several things should be noted about all the examples that have been given—from the autistic child with his "shapes," through the child-murderer, to the child with the facial tic and phobia of "trips," to the woman photographer. (1) In contrast to the presentational symbolism of music, where the formal structure and inner relations of the work express the quality of emotional life, these are all examples of discursive symbolism. (2) The operative questions have been, "What is the underlying metaphor that might serve as a clue to the latent thought-feeling? How might the metaphor be translated into words so as to form a bridge between this subjective and possibly unconscious thought-feeling on the one hand and objective meaning and discourse on the other?" (3) The metaphors are inseparable from pictorial imagery. (4) They and the imagery are imbedded in intense affect. This holds irrespective of whether they are used consciously (by the therapist with the autistic children, or the photographer searching for images and metaphors with which to rescue herself) or are formed unconsciously (the child-murderer, or the child with the tic).

This calls our attention to the potency of metaphorical language itself, whether consciously crafted or unconsciously shaped. Whence comes its power? Metaphorical language sweeps in fast waves over deep currents of feeling and taps their force. It is the power of this underlying feeling that determines what meanings, conscious or unconscious, progressive or regressive, will be ascribed to the metaphor. It will influence how or even whether the pictorial imagery will be consciously perceived. All this is so contrary to common sense and surface, rational appearances that perhaps it explains why metaphorical language often seems suspect—even subversive.

In the seventeenth century it was thought that the mathematical and physical sciences might provide a logically appropriate language that might once and for all sweep out the obscurities and cant of the schoolmen. Such was the immense prestige of scientific method that it seemed plausible to consider real only those things to which mathematical principles were applicable. The inherent imprecision of words was the enemy of reason. Leibniz believed in the possibility of constructing a logically perfect language—one that would truly reflect the structure of reality as revealed by science.

As this new rationalism spread into the creative arts, the Royal Society in England came out against metaphor and a proposal was made in Parliament (1670) to outlaw "fulsome and luscious" metaphors. Hobbes and Locke saw metaphor as moving passions and thus misleading judgment into wrong ideas. In France, too, writers were to be plain, literal, and precise, and were to avoid embellishments.

In order to correct these "imperfections" and transform language into an ideal instrument for describing truth and reality, some philosophers and logicians closer to our own time express their ideas through mathematical signs. This does succeed in conveying ideas of quantity and dimension, relation and probability; it organizes and communicates facts without feelings. However, it necessarily places a mathematical imprint upon the world so described, and thus distorts it precisely to the extent that everything else has been left out.

Even within such a mathematically described world, uncertainty creeps in. For example, the goal of Russell and Whitehead's *Principia Mathematica* was to derive all mathematics from logic without contradictions. The effort floundered when Gödel showed that there were *undecidable* propositions in the *Principia Mathematica* and related systems. (No axiomatic system whatsoever could produce all number-theoretical truths unless it were an inconsistent system. If a proof of the consistency of a system such as that presented in the *Principia Mathematica* could be found using only methods inside the *Principia*, then the *Principia* itself wou d be inconsistent! Cf. Hofstadter 1979.)

Philosophical idealism attacks the reliability of physics as the royal road to truth. It argues that the question of meaning in the exact sciences boils down to how space, time, and matter are defined. They are defined operationally in terms of their measurement. However, measurement requires acts of human judgment and discrimination; it is itself a value judgment created by the human mind. Thus, quantification is no guarantee of an objective physical world. There is not even any meaningful boundary between a subjective and an objective approach to things. As Poincaré maintained, mathematical truth is based not in reality but in convenience. Facts are selected to fit in with one's intuitive sense of the harmonious order of nature. They are chosen according to a hierarchy based on certain aesthetic criteria—

simplicity, elegance, symmetry, economy—as well as on the basis of what seems to have the highest frequency of recurrence. Our views of space and time are nothing more than *metaphors* to ward off specific anxieties as to merging and unpredictability. They are matters of conviction—essentially, of faith. In sum, science is the modern religion designed to ameliorate the human condition and allay the fear of chaos. "It is we, not nature, who abhor the vacuum" (Jones 1982, 48).

Lying at the opposite pole from the rationalist distrust of metaphorical language is the tendency on the part of social scientists to overemphasize verbal thinking as being *the* characteristic of normal thought. This prejudice may be accounted for by the fact that this occupational group is itself significantly more inclined toward verbal thinking than are experimental and theoretical scientists such as biologists and physicists (Roe 1952; Bush 1968).

It is easy to overestimate the importance of words. Yet, anyone who takes language seriously in the conduct of his life's work is consistently up against its limitations. As clinicians well know, many compulsively articulate people use words to comfort themselves with sound, massage the silence, and drain words of their meanings through intellectualization. In short, language may be used to conceal as much as to reveal. "Because one has only learnt to get the better of words" (Eliot 1940, 188).

Lazar (1982) has written: "At best, words can only spy on the inner world and send out abbreviated Telex messages about what is briefly glimpsed." He quotes Ionesco (1971): "I am lost in the thousands of words . . . that are my life. . . . How, with the aid of words, can I express everything that words hide?"
Again (Ionesco 1968):

> I ought to have embarked long ago on this stubborn quest for knowledge and self-knowledge. . . . Instead of writing literature! What a waste of time; . . . indeed, it is because of literature that I can no longer understand anything at all. It's as though by writing books I had worn out all the symbols without getting to the heart of them.

> They no longer speak to me with living voices. Words have killed images or concealed them. . . . These words were like masks, or else like dead leaves fallen to the ground.

The current linguistic reformulation of psychoanalysis can be viewed as part of the overemphasis on the centrality of language for thought. It receives its impetus largely from Lacan, whose central thesis is that the unconcious is structured like a language. This effort includes the attempt to break with drive theory, biologism, and economics attributed to ego psychology. It aims to "return to Freud" by situating the analytic situation and the operations of the unconscious within the field of speech and language (Ricoeur 1978).

Ironically, this "return to Freud" comes very close to one of the main tenets of *Jung's* psychology. It holds that the unconscious directly represents itself in metaphor; it assumes that some innate, conflict-free symbolic function of the psyche is given over to representing the self in the form of metaphor; this symbolic function precedes repression, may be distorted by repression, but is not a consequence of repression (Satinover 1986).

In a similar vein, a recent paper argues that a basic metaphor is far more than an analogy. Rather, some metaphors derive from structural properties of the human mind. They are generative cognitive structures which represent part of reality; they help accommodate language to the causal structure of the world (Michon 1983).

In any event, the linguistic reformulation of psychoanalysis should not blind us to the fact that less than the full content of thought resides in language, and more than language to what comprises therapy. Since linguistics tends to neglect the pictorial and sensuous aspects of words, it has little to say about affect and subjectivity (which is more the domain of rhetoric). Yet, it is precisely these matters that are relevant to psychoanalysis. In psychoanalysis meanings depend more on affects than words (Modell 1984). Linguistic competence is surely important for the proper conduct of psychoanalytic therapy, but is likely to be sterile in the absence of affective attunement.

Linguists as well as modern philosophers have been rediscovering what poets knew and complained about two thousand years ago: language conveys only very partial truth. For one thing, words clutter up the communication of facts by transmitting too many feelings along with the facts. On the other hand, a message may convey feelings irrespective of the words. For example, experimental evidence confirms common knowledge that the tone of voice tells far more than the content of an utterance (Argyle et al. 1970). Indeed, subjects can reliably interpret the emotion of a recorded utterance even when the words have been electronically masked and rendered unintelligible (Dawes & Kramer 1966; Scherer et al. 1972).

If there is much more to thought than words, what is thought composed of? Someone once compared thought to the flowing river while language gives only the contours of the river bed. This is not the place to go into the differences between primitive and developed thought but only to stress their common origin in and of the body. From the autistic child's "shapes," to the concrete thought of the psychotic person, to the raw physicality of street-talk,[4] to the conscious and unconscious metaphors of ordinary language, to the creative thought of science and art, much thought seems to be embedded in a sensuous matrix which includes visual imagery and kinesthetic impulses.

Sensitive observers of their own thought sometimes report a backdrop of muscle tonus patternings. This may be a dim reflection of the microscopic impulses toward trial action that lie remotely behind thought—a description of thought in its preverbal state. Nor should this be surprising. It is psychoanalysis itself which holds that motoric impulses toward action lie behind thought; that thought is trial action using minute quantities of energy. Why is acting-out discouraged in analysis? In order to block discharge in action and foster the

---

4. I am indebted to Dr. Ruth Lidz for telling me the way one says "piano" in pidgin in New Guinea: "Big-Fellow-Brother-Belong-Box-You-Hit-Him-In-Teeth-He-Cry."

development of verbalizable thought. By detouring motoric impulses away from action it is hoped that the formation of primitive ideation, dreams, images, and finally verbalizable thought will be driven forward, providing material for analysis.

Einstein (1955) was explicit in describing the muscular as well as visual elements that were essential in his own productive thought processes. It was only when they were sufficiently established in a "combinatory play" that he could begin the laborious search for words or signs which would communicate their discursive content—if not his experience of them—to others. One would assume that the original sensuousness of the experience of his own thoughts in their early form found no representation in their final communication through conventional language.

Creative writing restores the affective matrix of thought by drawing on this underlying physicality of thought—exploiting the weight, texture, and motoric rhythm and cadences of words against silences. Many poets—Valéry, Shelley, Eliot—have testified that a poem often first appears in the mind of its author not in the form of words but with an awareness of rhythm (Burnshaw 1970). Dylan Thomas (1951 147, quoted by Hamilton 1975) wrote: "I wanted to write poetry in the beginning because I had fallen in love with words. The first poems I knew were nursery rhymes, and before I could read them for myself I had come to love just the words of them, the words alone. What the words stood for, symbolized, or meant, was of secondary importance. What mattered was the sound of them. . . . I knew that I had discovered the most important things, to me, that could be ever. . . "

The wife of Russian poet Mandelstam described his experience of writing poetry as follows (I am indebted to Martin Bergmann for the reference):

A poem begins with a musical phrase ringing insistently in the ears; at first inchoate, it later takes on a precise form, though still without words. I sometimes saw M. trying to get rid of this kind of "hum," to brush it off and escape from it. He would toss his head as though it could be shaken out like a drop of water that gets into your ear while bathing. But it was always louder than any noise, radio or conversation in the same room. . . . The "hum" sometimes came to M. in his sleep, but he could never remember it on waking. . . . The whole process of composition is one of straining to catch and record something compounded of harmony and sense as it . . . gradually forms itself into words. The last stage of the work consists in ridding the poem of all the words foreign to the harmonious whole which existed before the poem arose. Such words slip in by chance, being used to fill gaps during the emergence of the whole. They become lodged in the body of the poem, and removing them is hard work. I noticed that in his work on a poem there were two points at which he would sigh with relief—when the first words in a line or stanza came to him, and when the last of the foreign bodies was driven out by the right word. Only then is there an end to the process of listening in to oneself. . . . The poem now seems to fall away from the author and no longer torments him with its resonance (Mandelstam 170, 70—71).

Perhaps to the poet the completed poem brings relief as it "seems to fall away from the author"; but its words and images give life to drooping thoughts, as illustrated by the following lines by the Welsh poet, W. H. Davies (1963):

My mind has thunderstorms,
  That brood for heavy hours:
Until they rain me words,
  My thoughts are drooping flowers
And sulking, silent birds.

(I am indebted to Daniel Haberman for the reference.)

Closer to home, a woman intuitively turned to poetry to shape and convey the feelings that accompanied a difficult period of analysis. *Mindsong (for G. J. R.)* (quoted by permission of the author):

The seagulls that circle the widening sky
  and the canvas that billows and bellies so high
    and the steadying waves on the hurrying keel
will be gone in an instant: the mainsail will fly
  and go flapping forever, the sea will congeal
    and be lava, the birds in the blistering sky

will become pterodactyls, unless I can feel
  your breathing behind me, your hand on the wheel,
    and the world turning back again, letting me feel
the steadying waves on the hurrying keel
  and see canvas that billows and bellies so high
    to the seagulls that circle the widening sky.

The violent content of the verbal metaphors equate the author's state of mind with her fear of being stranded alone and helpless in a floundering sailboat about to be incinerated in a volcanic sea. The form of the poem, however, imposes order which contains the turbulence. The unfailingly regular pulse of the meter bespeaks control. Moreover, there is a visual metaphor in addition to the verbal ones: the lines are indented obliquely like waves in groups of three, depicting in graphic form the unhurried and absolutely uniform motion of waves in an untroubled sea. The poem as a whole, in form and content, thus embodies (internalizes) the therapeutic interaction between patient and therapist.

The fact that this poem, like many others, makes a visual point by the placement of the lines on the page, turns our attention to the importance of pictorial elements in language. According to Spence (1982), because so much thought is composed of visual images, and because words inevitably misrepresent pictures, putting thoughts into words at best yields only a coarse translation. Language is simply unable to capture the quality of visual truth; it muddies as much as it mediates.

For the same reason, Spence claims, telling a dream cannot possibly convey an accurate description of the dream: much is lost in the quantum leap from the visual-plus-feeling mode of the dream to its verbal narration. As he makes amply clear, the situation is not as simple as Freud sometimes implied when he made it sound as if the dream were a rebus and each dream-thought had a word attached to it.[5]

5. Spence goes on to question the reliability of dream interpretation to undo memory distortions and the manifest content of the dream and return us unerringly to the latent content of underlying thoughts and feelings. But, of course, in the actual

Thoughts contain pictures, pictures cannot be translated into words, neither pictures nor language can be matched against reality in a precise and objective way (as Wittgenstein discovered when he later rejected his book *Tractatus*, on which his reputation still rests). While a visual image is unsurpassed in its ability to arouse the viewer, it has serious limitations both in its capacity to express the artist's own state of mind or to transmit any other information. The theory that holds art to be a form of expressive communication has been termed an unwarranted transphenomenal leap from the linguistic model (Casey 1971).

One example (Gombrich 1972) is particularly well suited to illustrate the limitations of art in expressing the artist's state of mind. Van Gogh, in several letters to Gauguin and to his brother Theo, clearly establishes his expressive intent on painting *Bedroom at Arles* (1888). The portrayal of this little bedroom of his was intended to depict a haven of tranquility: "absolute calm," "simplicity," "suggestive of rest and sleep," "the picture should rest the head, or rather the imagination," "should express undisturbed rest." Van Gogh compared *Bedroom at Arles* with *The Night Café*, in which he wished to show that the café was a place where one could go mad. In still another letter to his brother he stressed that in *Bedroom* there was no stippling or hatching, nothing but flat areas in harmony. Gombrich concludes: "It is this . . . that Van Gogh experiences as being expressive of calm and restfulness. Does the painting of the bedroom communicate this feeling? None of the naive subjects I have asked hit on this meaning . . . . Not that this failure of getting the message speaks against the artist or his work. It only speaks against the equation of art with communication (p. 96)."

No image tells its own story either in reflecting the artist's state of mind or in transmiting any other information. It depends mostly on the viewer's ability to "read" the image—and this involves many

---

conduct of contemporary analysis one relies at least as much on the dream as part of a process, and on the *way* it is narrated, and its nonverbal and transferential context, as on the dream simply as a rebus message carved in stone.

elements of knowledge as to the code and context. Mostly, however, it depends on the images already stored in the mind of the viewer. These are of preeminent importance and depend, in turn, largely on previous emotional experience.

The newest research suggests that early affective responses are among the key events of infancy. These first emotional "attunements" in the interplay between mother and child influence the quality of later affective attachments and character development (Stern 1983). They also strongly influence the selectivity of perception, determining what kinds of percepts will be augmented, minimized, distorted, or totally denied. One of the far-reaching results of trauma appears to be that, thereafter, rapid subliminal scanning will take place for potentially threatening stimuli: anything that may lead to further trauma tends to be defensively screened out. Since perception and affect are interrelated with cognition and memory, the clinical syndromes of traumatic origin may include an intolerance of *any* affect (Krystal 1984).

Art regularly stimulates feelings that unconsciously influence the way it is perceived. Diana's reaction to the Van Gogh paintings—bleaching out all color and transforming them into black-and-white compositions—is only an extreme example of what happens more or less regularly. Less dramatic and more usual is the experience of most viewers of Picasso's seven-foot-tall bronze nude statue *Man with a Sheep*: they do not consciously perceive that the man is clearly portrayed as emasculated (Legault 1981).

Conversely, viewers often do not see male genitals where they are just as clearly present. Recent art-historical research has uncovered more than a thousand Renaissance images which insistently emphasize the genitalia of Christ both as an infant and as an adult; yet, heretofore, these have been just as persistently overlooked or explained away (Steinberg 1983). Some examples: a theme of the Madonna exposing the child's sex, always ceremoniously; artists as diverse as Roger van der Weyden and Antonio Rossellino have the infant Christ pulling his dress aside to flaunt his penis and parade his nakedness; others have the Christ child touch himself, or have his genital solemnly manipulated by St. Anne while Joseph looks on (Hans Baldung Grien's woodcut of the "Holy Family," 1511); the emphasis on the genitalia recurs in images of the dead Christ, with repeated groin-searching gestures and erections.

Steinberg's thesis is that these images are not the product of runaway naturalism or irreverence but, rather, indicate that it was Christ's "humanation"—his partaking of humanity—that was being declared. His divinity was taken for granted. Why was all of this tactfully overlooked or explained away for half a millennium? Carefully excluding psychological factors from consideration, Steinberg refers to it as a "mystery"—on the same order of "mystery," in fact, as Renaissance art's refusal to acknowledge Christ's (or David's) circumcision. Such visual denial of circumcision, he points out, is hardly attributable to ignorance or indifference, since Catholic theologians of that time were hotly debating the fate of Christ's foreskin, assigning it as a relic to several churches or awarding it to St. Catherine of Siena as a mystical betrothal ring. "The reason for the Child's apparent uncircumcision," he offers weakly, "must lie in the artists' sense of the body's perfection" (p. 159).

It would seem, rather, that however ingenious the theological reasons for the emphasis on Christ's genitals, the explanation for the five hundred years of silence and failure to note his clearly portrayed genitals is identical with that of the refusal to acknowledge visually his circumcision. Both lie less in the realm of mystery than the necessity for mastery of castration anxiety. Unveiling, touching, presenting, and peering at the Christ child's genitalia as the main action of devotional imagery, or celebrating the dead Christ's genitals by focusing attention on it even when, as sometimes happens, it throws the pictorial economy off balance, serves the same purpose as re-endowing his penis with a foreskin: it allayed the castration anxiety of the Renaissance audience. Except for this interlude, normative Christian culture disallows direct reference to the genital as unmentionable and undepictable. For subsequent audiences, therefore, the overemphasis of the genitals represented an especially bold violation of the taboo against looking. Castration anxiety was restimulated; the offending perception of the *conspicuousness* of the genitals needed to be repressed—just as in *Man with a Sheep* it is the anxiety-provoking *absence* of the genitalia that is repressed.

Many of the issues of the foregoing discussion with its emphasis on the co-mingling of feelings with thought and perception are condensed in the following clinical vignette:

A painter dreamed: "Water was coming down inside the wall of a closet. It made the wall look better than my own painting which happened to be stored in that closet." The particular painting was a reference to a painful episode in that it was a painting similar to one he had given to his ex-fiancée; she had broken their engagement shortly before their marriage was to have taken place. The closet was a reference to still earlier experience, and of the same nature. It had been his sister's closet. She had been his mother-surrogate since his father died. The patient was four at the time. This early loss of his father had been compounded by his mother's emotionally abandoning the family by taking a lover and becoming alcoholic. When the patient was ten, the sister, now sixteen, left the family, and he had fended for himself, more or less, ever since. The water running down the walls of the closet reminded him of tears.

It was easy for both of us to suppose that the images formed on the inside wall of the closet by the symbolic "weeping" limned his sorrow at the loss of the most significant women in his life—from first to last. Since the teary images on the wall of the closet "looked better" than the painting stored in the closet, we could also glimpse some of his efforts to put a good face on his mourning. The symbolism of being "in the closet" combined a sexual meaning with the attempt to deny all feelings. All this suggested the depth and nature of the emotions and defenses that lay behind his painting: feelings about early parental abandonment, sexual longings, and attempts at active mastery and control over earlier helplessness. Finally, it is worth mentioning that there was *nothing* in his oeuvre, which was nonrepresentational, that gave a hint of this underlying personal architecture. It found no "expression" in his painting.

Immediately following this session the patient had another dream that appeared to confirm our mutual work: "I was working on a painting with a brush. I cleaned off the center with a palette knife and suddenly, where I cleaned it, it became a window. The rest of the canvas was fogged like on a winter's window pane. I thought, 'Finally, I can see! Or at least, I can see through it!' " Without pause, he related this to beginning to see more clearly how his past lived on within his present—and lay, invisibly, behind his painting.

It would seem that the awareness of the shapes of old feeling was indeed enhancing the perspective of his world with new light and shadow.

8

THE RELEVANCE OF
ART TO MASTERY

We all know that Art is not Truth. Art is a lie that makes us realize
Truth, at least the Truth that is given us to understand.
Pablo Picasso, 1923 (quoted in
Chipp 1968, 264)

The equation of science with objective truth is deeply ingrained in
contemporary thought; a symmetrical article of belief equates art with
subjective escape. Little wonder that psychoanalysts from Freud on
have valued the scientific aspect of their identity and downplayed the
artistic. The dread of feeling at a remove from the scientific community is based largely on the perceived threat of being disconnected
from objective truth and order. Worse still, perhaps, it could mean
the risk of being lumped together with the other historical victims of
attractive but deceptive illusions.

Science, however, brings order to only a fraction of the world. It
organizes facts and, to the extent that it does, it allays anxiety
regarding disorder. But art makes its own unique contribution to the

truth. It has more to do with feelings about facts. And psychoanalysis? Perhaps one might say that it is concerned primarily with facts about feelings. One thing that does seem certain is that the facile dichotomies of an earlier time do not hold. "[May] we begin to recognize that science and art are not as far apart from one another as Freud and his scientific age liked to assume? . . . Science is itself a form of reality . . . and does not not necessarily manifest the culmination of mental development or represent any absolute standard of truth, as [Freud] assumed" (Loewald 1975, 278, 291).

The same Age of Reason that produced the ban on metaphor as an obstacle to the truth sowed the seeds of doubt about such blissful simplicity. It saw the emergence of Vico (1668—1744) and the birth of an opposite current of thought. Rebelling against the all-powerful Cartesian movement, Vico held that the search for a neutral style robbed the mind of its imaginative power. Language, he maintained, shaped minds, which in turn shaped language. There is no universal speech denoting a timeless reality. The forms of speech express specific kinds of vision. He extolled the power of imaginative insight to feel and enter into other minds and situations and know them from within. He delineated this mode of understanding as distinct from a body of knowledge of facts and events. It depended on the capacity for conceiving more than one way of categorizing reality. Implicit in this, it seems to me, was the teaching of Aquinas that whatever is known is known according to the manner of the knower.

This was to be distinguished from a priori truth such as that attained in mathematical reasoning, where every step is demonstrated. A priori knowledge can extend only to what the knower himself has created (an old Augustinian proposition). Mathematical knowledge is irrefutable because man himself has created it, not—as Descartes supposed—because it represents some objective, eternal aspect of reality. The mode of understanding that Vico was adumbrating had not been sketched before. It was dependent neither on perception nor fantasy; it was neither deductive nor inductive. It depended, rather, on memory and imaginative insight. Fallible though it might be, it was a new realm of thought opposed to that of Descartes (Berlin 1980, 119).

Radical doubts about the nature of reality have never ceased to grow, while the necessity for at least the illusion of stability in the midst of flux has never begun to wane. Pascal wagered, James willed, Heidegger leaped to faith—faith in the existence of meaningfulness—to support the workings of knowledge and imagination as inseparable parts of intellectual vision. Einstein, like many creative scientists before and since, was aesthetically attached to the idea of the existence of internal harmony. Artists, whether "believers" or not, spend their lives creating it.

As disturbing questions are raised by historians, metahistorians, existentialists, relativists, perspectivists, hermeneuticists, and deconstructionists, significant changes continue to take place in our understanding of the nature of truth and of the relation between reality and imagination, objectivity and subjectivity.

A pragmatic view holds that the world consists of many "interpenetrating spheres of reality" that can be approached according to many systems of ideas—aesthetic, scientific, religious. Reality is more fluid and elusive than reason and has many dimensions. We work over the contents of the world selectively, counting and naming whatever lies upon the special lines we trace, while all the while there is an infinite chaos of relations that has not yet attracted our attention. Order and disorder are human inventions that correspond to what happens to interest or not interest us. Disorder is not the absence of order but only the disappointment of a certain expectation (James 1902).

It still remains valid, however, to make certain distinctions between art and science. Science aims at the highest order of intellectual abstraction that will cover the most nearly objective and universal generalization. It thus tends to be antipathetic to the individual, subjective, and emotional elements. These are seen as impeding the work of the intellect.

Art, on the other hand, aims at something quite different. Instead of attempting to eliminate the emotional, subjective, and individual elements, it strives for a balance between the objective and the subjective, halfway between the intellect and emotion. While it must be unique and individual, to be sure, it must not be so removed from the general as to be uncommunicable.

As an example of art striking a balance between emotion and intellect, in contrast to science which attempts to bar the emotions, take Bach's *Art of the Fugue*, which is built according to principles of constructivism. This refers to the conception of music, handed down from medieval times, that music is a mathematical discipline—according to Leibnitz, "a secret exercise of arithmetic during which the mind is unaware that it is counting." At the same time, however, it is written in the undeviating key of D-minor around a single theme based on a minor triad with narrow intervals around it. This practically amounts to a formula for conveying pathos. Thus, the rational principle of mathematic-like constructivism is joined with highly emotional musical material to form a dynamic union between Ratio and Pathos while at the same time preserving a mutual tension between them.

To the extent that we consider psychoanalysis an art or a science we expect different things of it, and this also influences the way it is practiced. For example, the famous "blank screen" approach was based on the scientific metaphor of aseptic technique and the concern with "contaminating" the growth of a pure culture of transference neurosis. Whether "true" transference neurosis exists at all, let alone as a necessary outgrowth of the unfolding of psychoanalytic treatment, is questioned by many experienced analysts. As far as the "blank screen" is concerned, it is probably not possible except for practitioners who are characterologically so predisposed, is frequently neither feasible nor therapeutically desirable, and, as mounting archival evidence indicates, was not practiced by Freud, who advocated it.

Another aspect of the scientific metaphor of psychoanalysis was Freud's comparison of the recovery and reconstruction of the past in the manner of archaeology. We psychoanalysts have long been accustomed to telling ourselves that we unearth and reconstruct the subjective truth of a patient's personal past via fragments of memory and transferences, much as Sir Arthur Evans believed he was doing with the archaeological fragments of the palace complex at Knossos in Crete. However, as any archaeologist now knows, what Evans succeeded in accomplishing was less a reconstruction of what *was* than a new creation embodying old building blocks. He did bring intelligent, plausible, coherent "narrative" meaning to what had been fields of ruins. But "historical" truth?

As I have stressed earlier, Breuer and Freud's (1893—95) epochal discovery that hysterical symptoms could be translated into metaphors and replaced by discourse makes it easy to overestimate the importance of language in psychoanalysis. However, Spence (1982) has argued that the nature of language is such as to seriously question whether it has the capacity to unearth "objective" historical truth or, more likely, to create a coherent but essentially narrative truth. He points out that it leaves out more than it includes, yet it includes so much that any number of connections can be made among the elements that are encompassed.

As Spence indicates, it is especially the *flexibility* of language that lends itself to the creation of correspondences between the patient's material and the analyst's interpretation. By choosing the right words, a lexical overlap can be made between what the patient is or has been talking about and a given interpretation. The formal match or similarity, as by punning, is enough to convey plausibility, whether or not it is "demanded" by the material, especially if it also includes a number of known facts that have not otherwise been accounted for.

This "flexibility" of language touches on a fundamental *aesthetic* property, namely, the plasticity of a medium. Aesthetic plasticity refers to the capacity of something to undergo endless transformations without rupturing the inner connection between its elements. Take time, for example. Music treats time as having both inner consistency and malleability; it remains the same and is forever changing. By treating time as plastic material capable of undergoing transformations while retaining its integrity, and addressing both of these characteristics of aesthetic plasticity, music is able to reconcile or bridge between the two aspects of time—constancy and variability (G. J. Rose 1980).

The plasticity of words is seen in the fact that their separate aspects of physical sound, intellectual content, and affective weight may be elaborated almost independently. Poetry recombines their physical attributes, emotional overtones, and semantic meanings. In poetry, words are the plastic, malleable medium, as spatial forms are in painting, and time is in music (G. J. Rose 1980).

The relevance of this for psychoanalysis is that the aesthetic plasticity of words makes it possible to correlate and link various dichotomies, thus objectifying them and making them available for conscious reflection. One such linking, fundamental to both art and science, is that between a (hidden, latent) inner unity, of meaning, for example, amid the outer changeability. Conversely, the aesthetic property of plasticity makes it possible to experience that something familiar can assume quite other aspects, or take on an unusual character.

Another way of stating this is that concern with a thing not being what it was, and with its becoming something other than what it is, is common to both art and psychoanalysis. When an analyst uses words "flexibly" to show correspondences and suggest new connections between the familiar and unfamiliar, he is, knowingly or not, exploiting the aesthetic plasticity of words and acting as an artist.

Aesthetic considerations may also play some part in the recall and reconstruction of the past. It is quite possible that when memories are recalled or reconstructed they are subject to preconscious aesthetic considerations of what constitutes good form. Just as gestalt principles underlie the perception of formal line patterns, if it is valid to transpose them to cognition and recollection they might help us understand the "retroactive power" of the present on the past.

For example, in the perception of patterns, other things being equal, a shape tends to be continued in its initial mode of operation. But the mind, continually striving for completeness, stability, and rest, tends to regularize what was irregular and complete what was incomplete. Thus, a system left to itself tends to lose asymmetries and become more regular. Memory reinforces this tendency; less good shapes tend to be forgotten.

It is possible that these principles governing the perception of forms are applicable to the ways in which we tend to rework the past. For example, the tendency toward regularity, symmetry, and completion in our perception of formal line drawings might well be analogous to our tendency to rework the past in terms of our need for narrative flow, plausibility, and certainty. In both areas we might be dealing with the aesthetic need for "good shape."

One might now approach the question of whether psychoanalysis is an art or a science somewhat along the lines of these general propositions. Instead of holding to the idea that there is some privileged access to an independent reality "out there," reality is always being formed and transformed rather than being discovered. Physical structures and programming, knowledge and imagination all contribute to its construction. Each of the symbolic forms—science, language, art (as well as myth and religion)—builds it from its own standpoint and leaves out as much as it includes. Aesthetic considerations of good form probably influence the construction of all symbolic forms, including art and science and psychoanalysis no less.

More specifically, psychoanalysis is a science in so far as it is based on objective, empirical data of growth and development, informed by the concept of the unconscious and the phenomenon of transference. Its indispensable instrument is ordinary language. But this must not allow us to forget that there is more to thought and meaning than language, and less to language than truth. To paraphrase Churchill on democracy, it is the worst form of communication there is—except for all the others. For purposes of communication, ordinary language leaves out too much and includes too much; when directed to the recall of the past, it probably alters the very memories it attempts to recover. Insofar as it attempts to objectify subjective feelings so that they may be reflected upon, understood, and reshaped, it depends on the aesthetic plasticity of language as an expressive art form. In so far as it makes use of an inseparable mix of objective knowledge and subjective imagination, like all cognition, it may be described in terms of the ego functioning in a "transitional process" of everyday life's creativity (G. J. Rose 1980).

Thus far, we have discussed the relevance of art in the most general terms: the relation of psychoanalysis to art and to science; the aesthetic plasticity of words; the possible influence of aesthetic form on memory.

We will now turn to other basic yet more specific considerations: the contribution that art makes to a rethinking of the customary subject/object dichotomy and, related to this, the refinement of imagination—that is, the primary process.

The idea of a dynamic tension among elements which interact to form an organic unity has always been essential to art. Such interactionism has become a key word for modern science as well. In the context of the new worldview in physics—that the universe is a dynamic web of interrelated events in which all forms are fluid and ever-changing—basic distinctions seem less absolute than formerly. For example, in metamathematics limitative theorems have mixed up subject and object. In physics, quantum mechanics has taught us that the observer is necessarily a factor interfering with what is observed. Sharp separation between the I and the world is no longer possible. Science has evolved to the point where it appears that the structures and continuities of an earlier time are fluid discontinuities. On the other hand, the logic of dichotomy, including the separateness of subject and object, seems to have given way to one that emphasizes permeability.

If science has reached this point, it must be said that art got there long ago. Art highlights that the Cartesian boundaries between inside and outside are not absolute. Langer (1957) is more precise and cogent: all the arts *objectify* subjective reality and *subjectify* the outward experience of nature.

This brings us to an important consideration: art forces us to make a distinction between two types of thinking and perception—the imaginative and nonlogical kind, on the one hand, and the cognitive, logical type, on the other. Wherein lies the difference? In the case of logical, cognitive thought and perception, subject and object are separate, opposed. In imaginative, nonlogical thought and perception, thinking and thought, subject and object are together in mutually influential motion. Within rationality, there is an interpenetration of subject and object.

All art invites a degree of fusing of subject and object, seer and seen, hearer and heard, and then a reseparation and possibly a new division. It was stated earlier that music demands a special kind of hearing—the kind that moves with the tones and draws the hearer into their motion. Modern painting, too, often requires a degree of merging and reseparation for it to be experienced. With drama and literature it is the temporary identification with the fictional characters that melts the boundaries. Not only am I, the spectator or reader, required to pretend that I am he and she and perhaps all the characters simultaneousy and in succession, but also that now is then, and here is there. These are three primary process condensations of time, place, and person.

Of course, the point of this partial merging with the art object, which any aesthetic experience requires, is not to get on a One-Way Regress Express—any more than empathic, analytic listening should lead to a mutual fusion state or folie à deux. Rather, it is to re-emerge with perception and thought refreshed.

In short, the imaginative, if nonlogical, perception and thought demanded by art are characterized by a temporary suspension and then reimposition of the usual boundaries of subject-object, time and space. The fusion and re-separation recalls the fluid temporal, spatial, and personal boundaries of the child—openness and sensuousness—but it is not itself child-like. At its most it offers new possibilities in the light of the adult's knowledge of reality; at its least, it refines sensibility and responsiveness.

In addition to making us face up more clearly to the differences between imaginative (nonlogical) thought and cognitive (logical) thought, art also forces us to reconsider the fundamental principles which govern their operation and their relationship to each other: the primary and secondary processes. There is reason to rethink Freud's statement that "a sharp and final decision" between these two processes takes place by puberty (1915, p. 195).

Let us remind ourselves of the contrast between primary and secondary processes in psychoanalytic theory. First, as regards modes of discharge, the primary process seeks immediate discharge of tension; this provides release and thereby pleasure. The secondary process is characterized by delayed discharge or—another way of saying this—greater control. This is accompanied by rising tension and also greater contact with reality.

Secondly, there is the contrast between the two as regards their different modes of organizing data. The primary process dissolves ordinary logical and perceptual and temporal boundaries and condenses things into wholes. Within these wholes, opposites can coexist. Thus, primary process organization makes it appear that this is also that, or here might at the same time be there (spatial condensation), now can simultaneously be then, or then now (temporal condensation), and I may also be he, you, she, or they, and so on (condensation of person).

According to formal logic there must be a total separation between what a thing is and what it is not. The point about a symbol, however, is that it is *both* itself and something else; and the point about a metaphor is that it asserts that this *is* (not just resembles) that. Therefore, according to the formal logic of the secondary process, the whole area of symbolic and metaphorical expression is irrational. Obviously, logic alone gives a false picture when it comes to the nonrational, imaginative primary process (Milner 1957, 161).

In addition to symbolism and metaphor, considerations of music also show that the sharp dichotomy we formerly made between primary and secondary processes is a false one. In the first place, all the perceptual configurations associated with the primary process (condensation, fragmentation, reversals, changes in size and shape, reduplication, figure-ground shifts) are embodied in music in the form of inversions, augmentation, diminution, rhythmic and thematic variations, and so on (Ehrenzweig 1953; Friedman 1960).

Secondly, the crucial characteristic that distinguishes musical and logical thought is time. Time is essential in music; it does not exist in logic. Music deals with motions that unfold in time (Sessions 1950). It then links these motions into tonal patterns which link consistency with novelty in such a way that they seem necessary—not logically necessary, but organically necessary in that the new patterns recapitulate the past and reintegrate as they move forward. We are in a realm which does not know Descartes and precedes Aristotle: neither logical nor illogical, but nonlogical. It comprises most of our existence.

The sharp distinction between primary and secondary processes is not tenable. It came about because of Freud's adherence to a closed system model of the organism, consistent with nineteenth-century physiology (Fechner's constancy principle). This began to change, however, in the 1940s and 1950s. With the theoretical work of Hartmann (1939) and Rapaport (1951) and the experimental work of Schilder (1942) and Fisher (1954, 1956) in perception, the closed model finally became an open one. As it did, the idea took hold of a continuum, rather than a sharp demarcation, between primary and secondary processes underlying all thought and perception.

Two of the implications of this shift from the closed to the open model were the increased significance of the ego as the organ of adaptation (Schur 1966, 45) and a new emphasis on object relations. The process of internalization and building of psychic structure was now perceived to be ongoing rather than essentially restricted to childhood.

Most important, since the primary process is also part of this open system, it, too, can participate in ongoing development. It is the formal organizational patterning of the primary process—condensation and displacement, for example (Holt 1967)—that develops by becoming linked with the slow discharge of the secondary process. This in turn affects the entire range of mental processes (Schur 1966).

This is where the arts are most importantly relevant: they promote this advancement of the primary process, and thus the accretion of psychic structure. They accomplish this through objectification and feedback. Objectification introduces feedback from the external world, exposing the primary process to secondary process monitoring in the light of reality (Noy 1968–69, 1969). The primary process configurations, now slowed down and scrutinized by the logic and reality considerations of the secondary process, are reinternalized. Further primary process forms may summate, be objectified, elaborated, and reinternalized in a continuous process of psychological development—in a working system *open* to the outside. The ambiguity of the primary process is tolerated within the problem-solving framework of the secondary processes. In short, under favorable conditions, primary and secondary processes may coexist harmoniously on a continuum with each other.

The work of two contrasting artists, M. C. Escher and Claude Monet, allows us to examine the interplay of primary and secondary processes.

Escher keeps creating the illusion of an illusion, yet every illusion created is the result of totally reasoned constructions. They have us moving up or down through levels of a hierarchical system, always done with correct perspective, yet always finding ourselves back where we started. Thus, they have been called pictorial parables of Gödel's Incompleteness Theorem: only by stepping out of the system may one complete it (Hofstadter 1979).

Writing of this apparent affinity between his work and the field of mathematics, Escher said: "By keenly confronting the enigmas that surround us, and by analyzing the observations that I had made, I ended up in the domain of mathematics. Although I am absolutely innocent of training or knowledge in the exact sciences, I often seem to have more in common with mathematicians than with my fellow artists" (Escher 1971, 42). (That his appeal is even broader is suggested by the fact that one drawing has been reproduced in a chemistry textbook and also on the record album cover of an American pop group.)

Some examples of the way he makes reason and imagination work together: *Day and Night* (2/38, catalogue # 303) shows the equilibrium of opposites, using the double function of black and white motifs. "It is night when the white, as an object, shows up against the

M. C. Escher. *Sky and Water*. (Reproduced by permission of Cordon Art B.V.)

black as a background, and day when the black figures show up against the white" (p. 24).

In *Sky and Water I* (6/38, catalogue # 306) birds and fish alternate foreground and background depending on where the eye concentrates. In the central portion of the print, birds and fish are pictorially equal—fitting into each other like jigsaw pieces. Birds become less three-dimensional proceeding downward and become a uniform background of water. Fish gradually lose their shape as they progress upward and become a background of sky. Thus, "the birds are 'water' for the fish, and the fish are 'air' for the birds" (p. 28).

Escher wrote:

> How subjective everything is. . . . There is no proof whatever of the existence of an objective reality apart from our senses. . . . In my prints I try to show that we live in a beautiful and orderly world. . . . My subjects are also often playful. I cannot help mocking all our unwavering certainties. It is, for example, great fun deliberately to confuse two and three dimensions, the plane and space, or to poke fun at gravity. Are you sure that a floor cannot also be a ceiling . . . that it is impossible to eat your cake and have it? I ask these seemingly crazy questions . . . and [am] not afraid to look at the relative nature of rockhard reality (pp. 6−7).

By treating everything as material for form, rather than already formed, in the process of becoming rather than already "there," as malleable and changing rather than fixed and static, Escher's art magnifies the ongoing interplay and linkage between primary and secondary processes—dramatizing that seemingly solid experience hovers in a transitional area between knowledge and imagination.

The work of the twentieth-century master Claude Monet, at the furthest possible reach from Escher, also illustrates the marriage of primary process modes of organization with the attention, concentration, and knowing deliberation of the secondary process.

Monet's landscapes and seascapes are omnidirectional and unanchored, floating free in a world of pure appearance which, in ordinary life, we glimpse only occasionally—"as perhaps when we are just rising out of sleep and the room around us drifts into view like a flotilla of nameless patches of color. Such moments do not fail to evoke memories of early childhood, of dreamy, unfocused existence when, it seems, the frontier between 'here' and 'out there' is only vaguely defined . . . . Such states are unbidden. We find ourselves in them. But when an artist moves into this state, he does so at will, through disciplined practice with nothing dreamy about it. He is a sharp-eyed specialist in vagueness" (Gordon & Forge 1983, 56).

In a traditionally composed landscape there is a concentration on certain central points of focus. The eye is led forward toward the horizon. Monet's canvases offer few such invitations for the eye to enter and explore in a pointed, directional way. Instead, the pictures face us all at once and we are "in" them at once, needing to look everywhere on the canvas.

Vetheuil in the Fog (1879), for example, refuses the viewer any pathway by which to approach it as it hovers immersed in the fog. It is there at once, and we have no choice but to be immersed in it at once. "Somehow the boundaries between subject and object, viewer and viewed, have become porous, open to a two-way exchange" (p. 142).

Likewise, in the Varengeville landscapes of 1882−83 foreground and distance interpenetrate each other—the diagonal drift of pine trees in the foreground finds a resting place on the far hillside. In between, ground we cannot see. "We need to look everywhere on the canvas without giving special value to one place over another, and it is only through this all-over reading that the great spatial drama of the cliff top comes into its own and we are able to locate and feel the vertiginous drop to the surface of the water—beyond the boundaries of the canvas" (p. 150).

This immersion and simultaneity, this conflation of time and space, everything into everywhere and at once, finds its culmination in the Water-Lily Decorations. Monet conceived it as a completely integrated environment which would interlock the paintings' and the viewers' space. In the waters, lilies are in continuous interaction with the reversed reflections of unseen trees upside down. Within the water's surface, trees, sky, and the light of day are found simultaneously condensed into all possible conjunctions. "The plane of the water brought everything, near and far, into a single pattern, combining the drive of perspective with the enveloping frontality of the sea" (p. 276).

Frontality, the absence of point of entry or exit for the eye, the lack of focus, the abrogation of near/far, up/down discrimination, the condensation of real and reflected objects on the water's plane—all make for a sense of simultaneous envelopment and limitless expansion reminiscent of the luminosity and ambiguity of early childhood.

Have the disciplined eye and hand of a master specialist in color and light ushered us back to a state of narcissistic regression? It has been suggested (Levine 1985) that Monet's lifelong attachment to the sea is reenacted in his paintings and bespeaks a maternal fixation, an oral-erotic fantasy not unlike what Freud imagined he saw in the smiles of Leonardo's figures; in current terminology, regression to self-object symbiosis.

To be sure, in Monet's canvases one experiences the momentary sense of union with the painting so characteristic of the aesthetic experience. However, instead of the constricted awareness and dreaminess of a hypnotic trance-like state of regression, what follows is the sparkling quality of hyperalertness and fresh recognition of sensuousness and affect. Moreover the heightened sense of aliveness persists after we leave the painting and may even permanently alter the way we visually experience atmosphere and light, as well as the passage of time.

If not regression, then what? Monet has made the terms of perception the subject matter of his art. His canvases confront the viewer with the normal interplay of primary and secondary processes, slowed down and magnified.

What Monet learned from the theme of the sea and rediscovered in his frontal approaches to the landscape was the redistribution and spreading of focus, the open invitation to movement, reorientation and fusion (Gordon & Forge 1983). In terms of perception, these elements describe the global, undifferentiated, primary process pre-stages of perception. Normally subliminal, these pre-stages can be recaptured in tachistocopic experiments. What Monet's paintings accomplish is to capture the rapid cycle of subliminal dedifferentiation and redifferentiation, implicit in all perception, restrain their immediate discharge, transfix them in time, and raise them to the level of full awareness.

According to the view being advanced here, there is no need to postulate a looseness of repression of id drives, or a regression in the service of the ego (Kris 1952). If the primary process can undergo development as part of an open system, neither is it necessary to assume two different types of imagination under the auspices of the primary or secondary processes and distinguished from each other according to the immediacy of delay in discharge of psychic energies and the role of ego control (Beres 1960). Nor is it necessary to assume the existence of a special cognitive process as the basis for creativity (Rothenberg 1979).

It would seem preferable to assume that an ongoing growth process includes the possibility of developing a freer access to inner and outer experience and a fuller play of all one's faculties in a more open encounter with both worlds. Microscopically, this implies a relatively free traffic of information styled differently under both the primary and secondary processes (perhaps corresponding to the cerbral hemispheres) and their collateral integration.

Factors discussed earlier would have to come into play: the capacity to hold the reality sense in temporary abeyance while an ongoing reintegration balances the tension of strangeness with the release of familiarity. This presupposes the ability to depart, at least temporarily, from the security of established dogma and the mirroring approval of those who think similarly, in order to see and think freshly. When the reality sense is reimposed, the dimensions of reality will have been enlarged—marking this as a work of creative imagination and distinguishing it from a mere private retreat from reality.

This formulation stresses that, underlying all thought and perception, there is always a fine-tuned coordination between the primary and secondary processes. Rather than a replacement of primary process by secondary process, or an occasional, privileged, creative regression to the primary process under the auspices of the secondary process, the emphasis is on a fructifying influence between both modes and their mutual development. This places creative thought in a normative, developmental, and progressive context rather than a special category of its own, or reducing it to an aberrant and regressive one. It may even enable us to talk fairly precisely of the structural dynamics of all the arts and account for their parallel effects (G. J. Rose 1980).

At this point it may be helpful to step back and remind ourselves that these rather esoteric terms—primary process and secondary process—have a direct bearing on everyday life. They are the dried out technical names for the more detailed workings of imagination and rationality. To repeat: while we may separate them theoretically for purposes of better conceptualization, in actual experience they are inseparable. Just as there is no objective perception without subjective interpretation—inferences being corrected in the light of ongoing comparisons, leading to fresh observations, inferences, and corrections (Gombrich 1960)—knowledge and imagination work together continuously. They constitute inseparable parts of intellectual or aesthetic vision (Bronowski 1978).

Furthermore, since primary imagination and secondary process rational knowledge of reality are always working together in fine-tuned coordination in thought and perception, many of the divisions we make, based upon their separateness, are convenient and familiar but essentially misleading. All the arts show that the Cartesian separations do not hold as firmly as we once thought. On the one hand, they highlight the interpenetration between inside and outside; on the other hand, they help us to generate other connections that reason alone is unlikely to anticipate.

As for science and art, they are both approaches to the mastery of reality, and psychoanalysis has features of each. In science, art, and psychoanalysis, if they amount to anything more than hack work, the norms of conventional knowledge are always being confronted with the nonlogical playfulness of imagination. Science without imagination is sterile; art without rational knowledge is wild; psychoanalysis without either is merely a cult. Only the combination of imagination and knowledge, based on an interplay between primary and secondary processes, allows one to leap—thoughtfully—toward new intellectual possibilities.

9

TO SEE FEELINGLY:
ART AND PSYCHOANALYSIS

> We shall not cease from exploration
> And the end of all our exploring
> Will be to arrive where we started
> And know the place for the first time.
>
> T. S. Eliot, "Little Gidding" (1942)

We have seen in the last chapter that (1) art anticipated both science and psychoanalysis in stressing the permeability, rather than the separateness, of basic boundaries like inside and outside, subjective and objective; (2) experimental work and theoretical refinement in psychoanalysis gradually has resulted in a change from the closed to the open system model of the organism; (3) along with this, the primary and secondary processes may be viewed as being in interaction rather than as sharply demarcated; (4) this opens the organizational mode of the primary process to the possibility of development.

This brings us to a final contribution of art. Among other boundaries that are relative rather than firm are those between affect, on the one hand, and perception and thought, on the other. Art helps restore an awareness of the degree to which feeling and sensuousness always remain integral to thought and perception. Emotion is a subject on

201

which art is especially qualified to speak because, if it has to do with anything, art has to do with emotional experience. One definition even has it: "one way of identifying a work of art [is as] an object made for emotional experience" (Kubler 1962, 80). Langer argues for the central role of feeling in aesthetic experience, as does Dufrenne. Feeling is the nodal point at which subject and object merge in a unique sort of "communion"—the aesthetic experience. "Instead of being a flight from the real . . . art illuminates the real. But it does so only through feeling. . . . In art . . . the affective and the sensuous—feeling and perceiving—adumbrate each other" (Casey 1973, xxxiii).

Clinical observation, like the experience of art, shows that thought and perception tend to be invested with feeling. But theory historically clung to the idea that affect was sequestered from thought and perception.

When, as part of the closed-system model, Freud placed the primary and secondary processes in opposition to each other, it was as part of a yet more fundamental dichotomy—that of the pleasure and reality principles. Affectivity was viewed as essentially a secretory and vasomotor discharge into one's own body without reference to the external world. Therefore, affects, along with the primary process, were subsumed together under the pleasure principle. There they long remained as second-class citizens, isolated from and alien to perception and "pure" secondary process thought, which were directly related to the outside world and firmly ensconced under the reality principle. Though Freud (1933) later recognized that anxiety was a signal of impending danger and not a transformation of libido, not until recently was it appreciated that affect is not the antithesis of thought but basic to it as an early form of communication (Modell 1973; Ross 1975; Basch 1976).

In addition, a further complication was that the province of pleasure was largely restricted to the gratification which accompanies the *lowering* of a heightened level of instinctual drive tension. There were few exceptions to this, notably a brief early reference to the pleasure inherent in *activity* (Freud 1905, 95−96). Freud maintained, moreover, "that pleasure remains throughout life what it was in the [earliest] state . . . and that development to maturity consists in the superimposition of a relatively thin layer governed by the reality principle which is an unwelcome and enforced detour" (Schachtel 1959, 62).

Infant observation, however, shows that following the first few weeks of life infants no longer experience all stimuli from the environment as disturbances leading to unpleasure. What Freud described, essentially, was not positive pleasure but relief from unpleasure. Almost from the outset, the pleasure in directed, sustained *activity* is distinct from the pleasure of a sudden *decrease* of accumulated excitation and returning to a state of untroubled rest. In contrast to the tranquility of quiescence, exploratory play and a growing relatedness to reality offer a source of inexhaustible stimuli to the senses, thoughts, and motor functions. Shortly after birth "the nature of pleasure . . . is no longer restricted to the negative experience of relief from irritating disturbance . . . but now includes positive, joyful expansion of relatedness to the new and rapidly enlarging environment. . . . The former is a return to a stable state of rest, the latter the enjoyment . . . of the process of relating to the world" (64).

More recent observations in the first year of life (Shapiro & Stern 1980) confirm the conclusion that pleasure is also derived from and embedded in stimulus-seeking. Significantly, the affective components of this are a sine qua non for establishing object ties in the outside world of reality. This means that the reality principle is *not* in fundamental opposition to the pleasure principle. On the contrary, it is pleasure-seeking that guides the developing ego toward the most gratification in its relations with the real world (Harrison 1986).

Thus, infant observation highlights the shortcomings of the closed-system model and the affect theory that is subsumed under it. This places us in a better position to appreciate that the open-system model carries its own implications for a theory of affects and, possibly, our understanding of aesthetics as well.

The primary process is associated with release of tension; the secondary process with the building of tension. If, as the open-system model holds, they are not segregated under the pleasure and reality principles, respectively, and in opposition to each other, but rather, their working together and mutual enhancement underlies all thought and perception, then their interplay entails a continuous flux of tension and release. It is precisely such tension/release that is at the core of feeling—in fact, is its central dynamic (Arnheim 1956). One must conclude, therefore, on theoretical grounds, that feeling is embodied in the interplay of primary process release and secondary process tension inherent in all thought and perception. In short, the dynamics of feeling invest thought and perception *from the outset*.

Let us spell this out more specifically. Tension reduction and "letting go" accompany the movement from secondary to primary process—departing from the stringencies of logic, knowledge of reality, delineation of sharp boundaries, and heading for the relaxation of imagination, togetherness, wholeness, dedifferentiation—and all points in the direction of quiescence, narcissistic withdrawal, and passivity. The opposite movement, from primary process to secondary process, is active, object-oriented, and associated with the stimulation and excitement of challenge. Of course, since this is a microscopic and hypothetical description of the rapid, oscillating interchange between primary and secondary processes, the actual quality of the affects would depend largely on the nature of the *ideational* components (Brenner 1982).

It should now be possible to enlarge upon Langer's philosophical proposition that the arts enable one to think and perceive more feelingly. First, however, it is necessary to clarify something that has been implicit in the discussion, which has been limited largely to form rather than content—a tactical emphasis meant to highlight the role, in theory, that form alone plays in generating affect.

However, in order to avoid the reductionist implications that such a tactic entails, let us admit that, for all practical purposes, form and content are often inseparable; content without form cannot be communicated; and form without content cannot exist because the very way the form itself is organized conveys content. Even where there is no discursive content, as in abstract art or music, the structure of the imaginative mode of the primary process bears unconscious wishes embedded within it. The principles of organization of the primary process—that opposites may coexist (as in music), or that time is reversible (as in painting, by transforming time into spatial relations) —are themselves the expression of the *content* of standard, ubiquitous, and universal unconscious wishes. Such unconscious content, embedded in the *form* of the primary process, may well account for the lowering of tension associated with the primary process.

Having made the distinction between form and content, the "how" and the "what" of a work of art, and having qualified it, let us return to the question, "How do the arts help us to perceive and think more feelingly?" The contribution that the content of a work of art makes to more feelingful thought and perception is maximal in literature or representational art and minimal in abstract art or music. In any case, whatever the art form, the enhanced interplay between the formal modes of the primary and secondary process generates a continual flux of tension, release of tension, then renewed challenge and rebuilding of tension. Since tension/release/tension is the heart of affect, such primary and secondary process interaction is associated with a flow of affect.

Moreover, just as the arts stimulate the advancement of primary process imagination by encouraging its interplay with the problem-solving logic and knowledge of the secondary process, (as we have reasoned and illustrated with examples from Escher and Monet), the arts also help *refine* the feelings that accompany this interplay. In other words, art educates the emotions; there is, therefore, a sound psychological justification for the belief that a healthy and vigorous state of the arts is of central importance not only to the individual but to society at large; for "a society that neglects [artistic development], gives itself up to formless emotion" (Langer 1957, 74).

Aside from content, the arts restore sensuousness to perception and emotional coloration to thought by speeding the traffic between primary and secondary processes. These bodily qualities are inherent in thought and perception and always remain to some extent. But in the inevitable attrition of everyday life they get calloused over. Of course, a certain amount of screening is not only useful but even

essential. Without it, one might well be flooded, that is, traumatized, by the bombardment of stimulation impinging upon one's
adaptive resources. Especially in our present world, overstimulation
leads to familiar syndromes: on the one hand, counterphobic, fre-
netic, and insatiable stimulus-hunger; on the other hand, phobic,
numbed withdrawal from all potentially threatening stimuli.

When I suggest that the arts restore the feeling and sensuousness
that were once integral to thought and perception but which were
isolated to protect against traumatic flooding, I mean to indicate that
they restore an optimal *degree* of stimulation—a balance of distance
and closeness, neither escapist nor overpowering (G. J. Rose 1980).
The various forms of art counteract some of the inevitable and
necessary jading effect of everday life. They reinvest the quality of
experience with some of the freshness it had in the beginning—but
now in the light of the broader realities and heightened awareness of
maturity.

Why is it refreshed? Because returning to the familiar we find that,
just because it had become familiar, it was no longer known. Everyday thought and perception easily slide into the misleading laziness
of common sense. The arts recover metaphorical abilities which, far
from being a substitute for reason, lie at the heart of creative thought.
The merging and reseparation from art is a way of relieving dailiness,
taking a fresh look, intuiting the possibility of new connections,
discovering the novel in the midst of the familiar, the familiar in the
strange, an unsuspected unity amid variability, and vice versa.[1]

Poetry is a way of reviving the physical and semantic resonances of a
language deadened through overuse. Martha Graham said something
similar about the function of dance: making apparent again the
hidden realities behind the accepted symbols. And Picasso spoke of
wishing to wake up the mind by drawing it in a direction that it is not
used to—setting up the most unexpected relationships possible,
provoking a movement of contradictory tensions and oppositions.

1. The Russian formalists earlier in this century put forward the idea that the
function of art is to defamiliarize or "make stranger" the world, to overcome the
deadening effect of habit in consciousness.

Finally, by facilitating the reintegration of emotion with thought and perception, art illuminates reality in a particular way—from within. This is related to the power of imaginative insight or empathy—the capacity to enter other minds and situations and intuit them from within—first set forth by Vico as a mode of understanding in its own right. The kind of illumination that art provides does not take place by virtue of the discovery of new factual knowledge or concepts but, rather, fresh percepts—without which, concepts, alone, are blind. Monet did not discover light or postulate its structure in the form of either particles or waves. His paintings of sensuous form evoke feelings that reveal light anew. Likewise, a crucifixion is not a lesson in anatomy; a Vermeer does not teach Dutch interior design— it is, more precisely, an entrée into a world of tenderness and gentleness (Dufrenne 1953, 527).

In other words, with due regard for the fact that form and content are basically inseparable, one might yet argue that a work of art is true not in what it recounts—it may, after all, be literally a lie, or surreal—but how: its sensuousness awakens feelings and reunites them with thought and perception. I suggest that it is this inner reintegration of feeling, thought, and perception in the mind of the viewer that permits a transitory sense of union with the art object— the characteritic aesthetic moment. It draws upon that earliest form of knowing: the transient blurring of the boundaries between self and other, inside and outside—"fusing" with the outside world momentarily and then reseparating. It is this type of mastery—through temporary oneness followed by redelineation—that illuminates the art work from within. It allows us to grasp its reality—not so much from the point of view of objective knowledge as from the world of feeling it opens up, having sampled it.

Toward the end of *King Lear*, the Earl of Gloster, though sightless, appears to be the only character who seems to understand what is going on. Lear, marveling at this, declares: "No eyes in your head . . . yet you see how this world goes." To which, the blind Gloster replies: "I see it feelingly."

The performance by Billy Whitelaw of Samuel Beckett's fifteen-minute play (or monologue) *Rockaby* condenses and illustrates the foregoing discussion of concept, emotion, and percept becoming one—of our becoming one with a work of art—and of knowing from within, something old yet for the first time. With almost no words, no movement, and no scenery, this great drama and interpretation compress the weight and desolation of a lonely old woman's descent to death—its banality, its horror, its peace.

She had searched for "another creature like herself"—"one other living soul." Now she sits in her mother's old rocker. The only word she speaks on stage is "More," repeated four times. The other words are scant, incantatory, colorless language, recorded by the actress on tape. The phrase, "time she stopped," serves as a refrain. Her eyes have closed. The rocking has stopped. The single light that holds her face has become almost one with the surrounding blackness.

> In the longest of Beckett pauses, we watch the light within the face's hollow eyes and chalky cheeks dim, too. During the long stillness, the actress doesn't so much as twitch an eyelash—and yet, by the time the darkness is total, we're left with an image that's different from the one we'd seen a half minute earlier. . . . What remains is a death mask, so devoid of blood it could be a faded, crumbling photograph. And somehow, even as the face disintegrates, we realize that it has curled into a faint baby's smile. . . . And there you have it. . . . We at last reach the "close of a long day." Then Mr. Beckett and Miss Whitelaw make time stop, and it's a sensation that no theatregoer will soon forget (Rich 1984).

If one reads *Rockaby* after having seen it on stage, one is forced to wonder at the near-irrelevance of the words. Would it have the same—or nearly the same—effect if it were chanted, say, in Latin? Still more would one have to wonder about the role of "facts." What are the facts? A lonely old lady dies in a rocking chair. Her spoken thoughts turn to silence. Open eyes close. Rocking motion ceases. Light turns to darkness.

True, a microanalysis of the words invites a flight of imaginative speculation. One might, exercising "analytic" ingenuity, read into the script a transition from self-object differentiation back to self-object mirroring and to rapprochement with the primal mother—the rocker serving as a transitional object. Beyond that and reaching further back one might discern the concretism of words—rocker = rock her—and fusion with the mother. "Rocker" becomes a symbol of time—life itself. *Rockaby* invites the silent association, "Rockaby baby—bough breaks—down comes baby." So, from the beginning, Rockaby foretells that life is foredoomed. And autoerotic rhythm plays accompaniment. Among the last lines are, "rock her off / stop her eyes / fuck life." Is this a masturbatory litany with "eye" a pun for "I," as a waning sense of self heralds the approaching climax of *le petit mort?* Etc., etc.

All of which, in the final "analysis," perhaps, being almost as irrelevant to the impact of *Rockaby* as moonlight to the "Moonlight Sonata."

What lies at the heart of the emotional impact of this poetic drama, I suggest, is not such inferred latent unconscious content, and least of all the conscious narrative manifest content, but, rather, the form. It resembles the spare melody and three-beat meter of the sonata. Like the sonata, an accumulation of waves of mounting feeling are concentrated within this simple constantly recurring structure; they focus intense, laser-like attention on each swollen particle of minute change—in syntax, intonation, tempo and pause, shadow and light—to the point that the boundaries between thought, percept, and feeling dissolve, illuminating and reunifying present experience.

What does the creative artist draw on from within himself? What does he attempt to shape? How? To what end?

For the creative person, the inner processes achieve objectification in the form of fictional characters and objects of art. The creative work is a building up and melting down, again and again, a losing and refinding oneself by proxy, a rapid oscillation between imagination and knowledge of reality; in more technical terms, between primary and secondary processes, and between self-images and object-images within the ego. It continues until the work itself takes on a reality and autonomy of its own, whereupon the author also becomes free, or at least freer, to go on to something else. Samuel Beckett (1955 p. 302) writes: "For to go on means going from here, means finding me, losing me, vanishing and beginning again, a stranger first, then little by little the same as always, in another place."

As Dewey (1934) emphasized, aesthetic experience is continuous with the normal processes of living. Creative work serves the same function for the artist as any person's work for himself: externalizing inner processes and connecting the person more intimately to the outside world. In addition, however, the artist draws upon his sensitivity to past experience and traumatic intensity of stimulation. He attempts to master this past by reshaping aspects of himself, of space and of time, in the externalized forms of his work. His work objectifies his experience and subjectifies his world. As a result of an interplay of imagination and knowledge, the artwork strikes a new balance between internal and external. What began as the common task of mastering one's personal past, becomes for the creative artist a process of externalizing and transcending it—to disclose new aspects of reality itself.

As I have reasoned elsewhere (G. J. Rose 1980), aesthetic form has a biological function in the sense that it helps to sharpen the coordinates of orientation as to time, place, and person. Pursuing the same direction, the present discussion explores how the arts further facilitate mastery: expediting the interaction of primary process imagination and secondary process knowledge of reality that underlies all perception and thought.

Summarizing the important consequences of this quickened interchange of knowledge and imagination: (1) The objectification of primary process modes of organization opens the imagination to the possibility of growth and elaboration in the light of secondary process knowledge of reality. (2) The flux of tension and release that accompanies the interplay of primary and secondary processes is experienced as a flow of affect; the interplay itself helps refine the quality of this affect. (3) The refined affect associated with the traffic of primary and secondary processes restores sensuousness to perception and emotional coloration to thought. (4) By this fresh integration of feeling with thought and perception, ordinary reality becomes newly illuminated from within.

Psychoanalysis, like art, also awakens one to submerged and split-off currents of feeling. As in the aesthetic experience, during the course of analysis affect also becomes more available, better tolerated, more complex, and better expressed. Both the psychoanalytic and the aesthetic experiences are conducive to a type of mastery that is characterized by the inner reintegration of feelings with thought and perception. One must therefore inquire into the differences between these two experiences, the clinical and the creative.

In the attrition of daily life, percepts are denied, or their emotional impact attenuated or isolated. These are defensive efforts to anticipate the danger of traumatic overstimulation and dampen it down in advance. Functioning is protected, but at the cost of becoming more routinized and colorless. Art counteracts these tendencies through the fresh impact of sensuous forms. The re-assimilation of emotion to thought and perception leads to the illumination of the real from within—the characteritic fusion-reseparation experience of the aesthetic moment.

And psychoanalysis? In accordance with the closed-system model of the organism, Freud theorized that affect and the primary process are sequestered together, under the auspices of the pleasure principle—in opposition to the reality principle and secondary process thought. Ego defenses are drawn up like pioneer wagons in a circle against the onslaught of stimuli and protect the mind's tendency to withdraw to the lowest level of stimulation approximating the quiescence of a state of nirvana.

In actual practice, however, it often appears that this is a secondary *re*structuring. Contemporary psychoanalysis is conducted more in accordance with the open-system model of the organism. Through the interpretation of unconscious defenses both within the ongoing patient-therapist relationship and as it unfolds in current life as well as the developmental history, memories are recovered directly and via the transference. For all that has been said against it, verbalization is, of course, the single most important instrument in this process. Since repression essentially consists of a disruption of the link between the repressed idea in the unconscious and its *verbal* representation in the preconscious system (Freud 1915), it is verbalization that restores the connection and thus undoes the repression of feelingful memories.

Both the psychoanalytic and the aesthetic experiences tend to overcome various splits that occur under the traumatic impact of inner and outer stimulation: repressed memories, isolated feelings, denied percepts. Psychoanalysis undoes repression and, largely if not wholly through verbalization, reunites memory and affect. Art counteracts denial and, through sensuous forms, reunites perception with affect. Through different routes, they both make affect available again for reintegration with thought and perception. Both the psychoanalytic and the aesthetic experiences thus tend to restore wholeness, "reuniting our original nature, making one of two, and healing the state of man" (Plato, p. 158).

To compress the issue of increased mastery into more precise intrapsychic terms: both art and psychoanalysis strengthen the integrative function of the ego; this helps overcome splits in the ego caused by denial (Freud 1940a & 1940b) and repression and broadens the scope of the ego's reality-testing, thus enhancing mastery of inner and outer reality.

Like an ongoing exploration, the problem of the overlap of the psychoanalytic and the aesthetic experiences raises fresh questions. One might ask, "Why add further, possibly needless, complexity to unresolved issues?" After all, the means by which psychoanalysis exerts its therapeutic action is still a matter of considerable debate within the field; perhaps as much so as the ways in which art brings about an aesthetic experience. Why compound the situation by adding one unsolved question upon an other?

And yet . . . one cannot help wonder: is the affect that is made available through the recovery of repressed memories by the (verbal) psychoanalytic process the "same" as that which is tapped in the aesthetic undoing of split-off percepts? Does the former represent a "horizontal" split and the latter a "vertical" one? What about the role of internalization?

Any contemporary discussion of how change takes place—whether in the course of normal growth and development or aided by psycho-analysis—must take account of the fundamental position of internalization. The central importance of internalization in current thinking has superseded the traditional faith either in insight (achieved through interpretation), or gratification (provided by a beneficent, nonjudgmental environment).

The mechanisms by which internalization operate are (1) through the establishment of a gratifying involvement followed by (2) the experience of incompatibility in that involvement (Behrends & Blatt, 1985). In other words, interactions with others that had formerly been gratifying and then disrupted are transformed into one's own enduring functions and characteristics.

One cannot help noting a striking formal similarity between the structure of internalization and that of art. For internalization to take place the *opposite elements* of gratification and incompatibility need to have been experienced *in sequence*. Art, on the other hand, is character-ized by a *dynamic equilibrium of opposites*, each needing the other for its fulfillment. Among these are tension and release, control and ambi-guity, variability and unity—but, perhaps above all, continuity and discontinuity in time, space and personal identity (G. J. Rose 1980).

Are such parallels between aesthetic form and psychic process anything more than linguistic similarities between constructs used to describe different phenomena or are they causal in nature (Spitz 1985)? This touches on the core of the deconstructionist critic's tenet that the language of a text tends to be circular and refer to itself or other languages and not some extratextual reality. It is similar to Spence's (1982) question as to whether psychoanalytic interpretation taps the "truth" or merely exploits the flexibility of language. Being beyond my philosophical expertise to judge,[2] I subscribe to Alfred

---

2. This "ontological" question is classically raised in a metaphysical context having to do with proof of the existence of God.

North Whitehead's position that the test of an idea is not its ultimate "truth" but its ability to stimulate new and interesting thought.

Putting aside the philosophical merits of the question, therefore, let us pursue a bit further one implication of the similarity between aesthetic structure and the process of internalization. In the course of normal growth and development, the child's favorable experience with the mother's responsive mirroring gradually becomes generalized through imaginary companions and transitional phenomena into the world of real relationships. Gradually experiencing an increasing discrepancy or incompatibility between inner wishes and outer reality, these interactions are internalized in the form of a trusting yet challenging and critical interplay between one's own imagination and knowledge. In psychoanalysis, too, the benevolent yet detached ambience of the analytic relationship becomes internalized in the form of an increasing freedom to experience one's thoughts and feelings and at the same time permitting them to interact in the light of judgment and experience.

Even though the concept of internalization pertains to such human relationships rather than inanimate objects, does something analogous to internalization take place in the course of repeated, intensive involvement with aesthetic experiences? Stated most baldly, can art induce inner changes in some way comparable to the emotional maturation that takes place both in psychoanalysis as well as normal development?

One hastens to add that it would be misleading to imply that the psychoanalytic and aesthetic experiences are interchangeable with each other or with normal growth. The analyst may be called upon to exercise whatever gift he may have for artistic sensitivity but his work produces no art; the creative artist may occasionally provide an experience of therapeutic value, but he undertakes no responsibility for ongoing treatment. Moreover, it is a familiar fact that emotional maturation does not necessarily take place with any of the above. Conversely, it should be no surprise that major maturation can and usually does continue to unfold well into adulthood without the benefit of psychoanalysis (Emde 1985).

To put it in literary terms: to transform tragedy, meaning inexorability, via various means including even comedy, meaning chance, into an increased measure of choice is the promise of growth. Neither art nor treatment guarantee growth. What they do is to draw on the wellsprings of feeling, via aesthetic form and memory, helping to reintegrate it with thought and perception as in the beginning. This is a form of inner mastery which is conducive to growth.

Yet, while insisting on the separate uniqueness of psychoanalysis, aesthetics and growth, would it not be a logical extension of this discussion, to wonder (if only half-aloud): Might the sentience of the aesthetic experience also lead, at least theoretically, to reviving and reintegrating dormant memories? Conversely, may the reordering of psychoanalysis also open one more fully to the aliveness of our teeming surround?

It is time to step back from the outer reaches of speculation, return to the firmer ground of clinical experience, and conclude with a final vignette.

A phone call came in from an internist colleague referring a new patient. A German-born woman with depressive symptoms, she was the daughter of a Nazi officer. I began to demur. He interrupted: "Try anyway."

We worked together over the course of several years. Much of it centered around her early identification with and idealization of her father, his skill and generosity, followed by her severe disillusionment in him. Hitler came into power when she was nine years of age. By age eleven she was detesting her father's posturing in his S.S. uniform, his vulgarity, brutality, sentimentality. As an early teenager in the Hitler Youth she knew and did not know what was going on. She befriended a Jewish girlfriend who was later sent to Dachau. She began to know about Dachau by age seventeen (1942), but denied it. The next year her fiancé was lost on the Russian front, and this she could no longer deny. By the following year, at nineteen, she was actively resisting. Tormented with guilt for not having let herself realize what she did not wish to acknowledge, she berated herself for not having resisted earlier. It was probably this factor which, after the war, led her to marrying an ex-prisoner of the Nazis. He turned out to be as much of a bully as her father, and thus her married life consisted largely of joyless, expiatory slavishness to him and their children.

The treatment was successful in large measure. It turned largely upon dealing with the split between her masochistic attachment to her father, on the one hand, and what she knew and did not want to know, on the other. Integrating memories, perceptions, and feelings, and working this through in the transference, she achieved greater mastery over her past and became freer to assert herself in her marriage and career.

She arrived for her last session and, with a good deal of feeling, said that there were many things about the treatment she deeply appreciated, but one above all. Still under the influence of earlier teaching as to the primacy of insight in the analytic process, I half-expected a tribute for a particularly canny piece of reconstruction or interpretation and the illumination it brought. I anticipated feeling proud and modest. The truth lay elsewhere.

She was now able once again, she said, to bear the intensity of highly emotional music. Instead of fearing that she might feel threatened by its intensity and compelled to avoid it (lest she be overpowered by affects, thoughts, and images flooding over her?) she could now listen with pleasure. There was one especially beautiful piece— the *Bachianas Brasileiras No. 5* of Villa-Lobos—and it so happened she had a tape of it in her car outside. Did she wish me to play it, I asked? Indeed she did! She went to get it and we listened to the first aria together.

A rich soprano voice ascends softly and lyrically, swelling, lifting, and subsiding in an unbroken romantic melodic line flowing over the pizzicato accompaniment of a dozen violincelli. The music maintains a delicately subtle tension between the continuity of the melodic voice and the discontinuity of its plucked accompaniment. One's senses are alert and soaring and, paradoxically, in a state of deep repose at the same time. In short, one experiences that remarkable characteristic of the aesthetic experience: opposite states are present simultaneously in a combination of hyperacuity and tranquility.

We sat in silence after the music ended, both of us moved. She arose, shook hands, said, "For this, I thank you." And departed.

Somewhere, William Carlos Williams wrote, "This, in the end, comes perhaps to the occupation of the physician after a lifetime of careful listening: setting down on paper the inchoate poem of the world."

Is this, in the end, what comes to the patient after successful analysis: assimilating emotion to thought and perception—feelings to meanings?

And if this mastery is the fruit of analytic integration, is it not congruent and complementary to that of the aesthetic experience?

REFERENCES

Argyle, M.; Salter, V.; Nicholson, H.; Williams, M.; and Burgess, P. 1970. The Communication of Inferior and Superior Attitudes by Verbal and Non-Verbal Signals. *British Journal of Social and Clinical Psychology*, 9:222–31.

Arnason, H. H. 1968. *History of Modern Art*. New York: Harry Abrams.

Arnheim, R. 1956. *Art and Visual Perception: A Psychology of the Creative Eye*. Berkeley and Los Angeles: University of California Press, 1957.

Basch, M. F. 1976. The Concept of Affect: A Re-Examination. *Journal of The American Psychoanalytic Association*, 24:759–77.

Beckett, S. 1955. *The Unnameable*. New York: Grove Press.

———. 1981. *Rockaby*. New York: Grove Press.

Behrends, R. S., and Blatt, S. J. 1985. Internalization and Psychological Development throughout the Life Cycle. In: *The Psychoanalytic Study of the Child* 40:11–39, ed. A. J. Solnit, R. S. Eissler, and P. B. Neubauer. New Haven: Yale University Press.

Bentley, E., ed. 1952. *Naked Masks: Five Plays by Luigi Pirandello*. New York: Dutton.

Beres, D. 1957. Communication in Psychoanalysis and in the Creative Process: A Parallel. *Journal of the American Psychoanalytic Association*, 5:408–23.

———. 1959. The Contribution of Psychoanalysis to the Biography of the Artist. *International Journal of Psychoanalysis*, 40:26–37.

————. 1960. The Psychoanalytic Psychology of Imagination. *Journal of the American Psychoanalytic Association*, 8:252—69.

Berlin, I. 1980. *Against The Current: Essays in the History of Ideas*. New York: Viking Press.

Berman, E. 1981. Multiple Personality: Psychoanalytic Perspectives. *International Journal of Psychoanalysis*, 62:283—330.

Bernstein, L. 1976. *The Unanswered Question: Six Talks at Harvard*. Cambride, Mass.: Harvard University Press.

Brenner, C. 1982. *The Mind in Conflict*. New York: International Universities Press.

Breuer, J., and Freud, S. 1893—95. Studies on Hysteria. *Standard Edition* 2. London: Hogarth Press, 1955.

Bronowski, J. 1978. *The Origins of Knowledge and Imagination*. New Haven and London: Yale University Press.

Brücke, E. 1891. The Human Figure: Its Beauties and Defects. London: H. Grevel.

Buhler, K. 1930. *The Mental Development of the Child*. London: Routledge & Kegan Paul.

Burnshaw, S. 1970. *The Seamless Web*. New York: Braziller.

Bush, M. 1968. Psychoanalysis and Scientific Creativity with Special Reference to Regression in the Service of the Ego. *Journal of The American Psychoanalytic Association*, 16:136—90.

Carr, E. Y. 1931. *Dostoevsky*. London: George Allen & Unwin.

Casey, E. S. 1971. Expression and Communication in Art. *Journal of Aesthetics and Art Criticism*, 30:197—207.

————. 1973. Translator's foreword, pp. xv—xlii. In: *The Phenomenology of Aesthetic Experience* by M. Dufrenne. Evanston: Northwestern University Press.

Cassirer, E. 1923. *The Philosophy of Symbolic Forms*, vol. 1. New Haven: Yale University Press, 1953.

————. 1944. *An Essay on Man*. New Haven: Yale University Press.

Chipp, H. B. 1968. *Theories of Modern Art: A Source Book by Artists and Critics*. Berkeley and Los Angeles: University of California Press.

Cohen, J. 1980. Structural Consequences of Psychic Trauma: A New Look at "Beyond The Pleasure Principle." *International Journal of Psychoanalysis*, 61:421—32.

Conrad, J. 1899. *Heart of Darkness*. New York: Buccaneer Books.

————. 1900. *Lord Jim*. Garden City: Doubleday.

————. 1910. *The Secret Sharer.* New York: Buccaneer Books.

Dali, S. 1942. *The Secret Life of Salvador Dali.* New York: Dial

Dalton, E. 1979. *Unconscious Structure in "The Idiot": A Study in Literature and Psychoanalysis.* Princeton, N.J.: Princeton University Press.

Dawes, R. M., and Kramer, E. 1966. A Proximity Analysis of Vocally Expressed Emotion. *Perceptual and Motor Skills,* 22: 571−74.

Dewey, J. 1934. *Art as Experience.* New York: Minton, Balch.

Dostoevsky, F. 1846. *The Double.* In: *The Eternal Husband and Other Stories,* trans. Constance Garnett. New York: Macmillan, 1950, pp. 138−284.

————. 1862. *The House of the Dead.* New York: Oxford University Press, 1956.

————. 1866. *Crime and Punishment.* New York: Random House, The Modern Library, 1950.

————. 1876a. *A Writer's Diary.* Santa Barbara and Salt Lake City: Peregrine Smith, 1979.

————. 1876b. *The Peasant Marey.* In: *The Best Short Stories of Dostoevsky.* New York: Modern Library, 1964, pp. 99−105.

Dufrenne, M. 1953. *The Phenomenology of Aesthetic Experience,* trans. E. S. Casey, A. A. Anderson, W. Domingo, L. Jacobson. Evanston: Northwest-ern University Press, 1973.

East, W. N. 1927. *An Introduction to Forensic Psychiatry in the Criminal Courts.* New York: Wm. Wood.

Ehrenzweig, A. 1953. *The Psychoanalysis of Artistic Vision and Hearing.* New York: Julian Press.

Einstein, A. 1955. A Letter to Jacques Hadamard. In: *The Creative Process,* ed. B. Ghiselin. New York: New American Library, pp. 43−44.

Eissler, K. 1967. Psychopathology and Creativity. *American Imago* 24: 35−81.

————. 1971. *Discourse on Hamlet and "Hamlet".* New York: International Universities Press.

Eliot, T. S. 1940. East Coker. In: *Collected Poems, 1909−1962* by T. S. Eliot, pp. 182−90. New York: Harcourt, Brace & World, 1963.

————. 1942. Little Gidding. In: *Collected Poems, 1909−1962* by T. S. Eliot, pp. 200−209. New York: Harcourt, Brace & World, 1963.

Emde, R. N. 1985. From Adolescence to Midlife: Remodeling the Structure of Adult Development. *Journal of The American Psychoanalytic Association,* 33 (Supplement): 59−112.

REFERENCES

Erikson, E. 1958. *Young Man Luther: A Study on Psychoanalysis and History.* New York: Norton.

Ernst, M. 1948. *Beyond Painting.* New York: Wittenborn, Schultz.

Escher, M. C. 1971. *M. C. Escher: His Life and Complete Graphic Work, The World of M. C. Escher.* Amsterdam: Meulenhoff. Reprinted by Harry N. Abrams, New York, 1983. *M. C. Escher: 29 Master Prints.*

Ferenczi, S. 1913. Stages in the Development of the Sense of Reality. In: *Sex in Psychoanalysis.* New York: Brunner, 1950, pp. 213–39.

Fisher, C. 1954. Dreams and Perception. *Journal of the American Psychoanalytic Association,* 2:389–445.

———. 1956. Dreams, Images and Perception. *Journal of the American Psychoanalytic Association,* 4:5–48.

Fowles, J. 1968. Notes on Writing a Novel. *Harper's,* July, pp. 88–97.

———. 1969. *The French Lieutenant's Woman.* Boston: Little, Brown.

———. 1977. Hardy and the Hag. In: *Thomas Hardy after 50 Years,* ed. Lance St. John Butler. Totowa, N.J.: Rowman & Littlefield, pp. 28–42.

Frank, J. 1976. *Dostoevsky: The Seeds of Revolt, 1821–1849.* Princeton, N.J.: Princeton University Press.

Freud, E. 1960. *Letters of Sigmund Freud,* ed. E. L. Freud. New York: Basic.

Freud, S. 1894. The Neuro-Psychoses of Defense. *Standard Edition* 3:45–61. London: Hogarth Press, 1962.

———. 1895. Project for a Scientific Psychology. *Standard Edition,* 1:295–397. London: Hogarth Press, 1966.

———. 1900. The Interpretation of Dreams. *Standard Edition,* 4. London: Hogarth Press, 1953.

———. 1905. Jokes and Their Relation to the Unconscious. *Standard Edition,* 8. London: Hogarth Press, 1960.

———. 1909. Analysis of a Phobia in a Five-Year-Old Boy. *Standard Edition,* 10:3–149. London: The Hogarth Press, 1955.

———. 1910. Leonardo da Vinci and a Memory of His Childhood. *Standard Edition,* 11:59–137. London: Hogarth Press, 1957.

———. 1914a. The Moses of Michelangelo. *Standard Edition,* 13:211–38. London: Hogarth Press, 1955.

———. 1914b. On Narcissism: An Introduction. *Standard Edition,* 14:73–102. London: Hogarth Press, 1957.

———. 1914c. On the History of the Psycho-Analytic Movement. *Standard Edition,* 14:7–66. London: Hogarth Press, 1957.

REFERENCES

————. 1915. The Unconscious. *Standard Edition*, 14:161—95. London: Hogarth Press, 1957.

————. 1920. A Note on the Prehistory of the Technique of Analysis. *Standard Edition*, 18:263—65. London: Hogarth Press, 1955.

————. 1921. Group Psychology and the Analysis of the Ego. *Standard Edition*, 18:69—143. London: Hogarth Press, 1955.

————. 1923. A Neurosis of Demoniacal Possession in the Seventeenth Century. *Standard Edition*, 19:73—105. London: Hogarth Press, 1961.

————. 1925. A Note upon the "Mystic Writing-Pad." *Standard Edition*, 19:227—32. London: Hogarth Press, 1961.

————. 1927. Fetishism. *Standard Edition*, 21:149—57. London: Hogarth Press, 1961.

————. 1928. Dostoevsky and Parricide. *Standard Edition*, 21:177—96. London: Hogarth Press, 1961.

————. 1933. New Introductory Lectures on Psychoanalysis. *Standard Edition*, 22:3—182. London: Hogarth Press, 1964.

————. 1936. A Disturbance of Memory on the Acropolis. *Standard Edition*, 22:239—48. London: Hogarth Press, 1964.

————. 1940a. Splitting of the Ego in the Defensive Process. *Standard Edition*, 23:271—78. London: Hogarth Press, 1964.

————. 1940b. An Outline of Psychoanalysis. *Standard Edition*, 23:141—207. London: Hogarth Press, 1964.

Friedman, S. M. 1960. One Aspect of the Structure of Music: A Study of Regressive Transformations of Musical Themes. *Journal of the American Psychoanalytic Association*, 8:427—49.

Fuller, P. 1980. *Art and Psychoanalysis*. London: Writers and Readers Publishing Coopertive.

Furst, S. 1978. The Stimulus Barrier and the Pathogenicity of Trauma. *International Journal of Psychoanalysis*, 59:345—52.

Gedo, J. 1983. *Portraits of the Artist: Psychoanalysis of Creativity and its Vicissitudes*. New York: Guilford Press.

Gedo, M. 1980. *Picasso: Art as Autobiography*. Chicago: University of Chicago Press.

Ghiselin, B., ed. 1955. *The Creative Process*. Berkeley: University of California Press.

Gilot, F., and Lake, C. 1964. *Life with Picasso*. New York: McGraw-Hill.

Giovacchini, P. 1986. *Developmental Disorders*. Northvale, N.J. and London: Jason Aronson.

REFERENCES

Glover, E. 1943. The Concept of Dissociation. *International Journal of Psychoanalysis*, 24:7—13.

Gombrich, E. H. 1960. *Art and Illusion*. Princeton, N.J.: Princeton University Press.

———. 1972. The Visual Image. In: *Scientific American*, 227, no. 3, pp. 82—96, Sept. 1972.

Gordon, R., and Forge, A. 1983. *Monet*. New York: Harry Abrams.

Greenacre, P. 1957. The Childhood of the Artist. In: *Psychoanalytic Study of the Child*, 12:47—72. New York: International Universities Press.

———. 1958. The Family Romance of the Artist. In: *Psychoanalytic Study of the Child*, 13:9—36.

———. 1969. The Fetish and the Transitional Object. In: *Psychoanalytic Study of the Child*, 24:144—64.

Grolnick, S. A., and Barkin, L., eds. 1978. *Between Reality and Fantasy: Transitional Affects and Phenomena*. New York and London: Jason Aronson.

Hamilton, J. W. 1975. Transitional Fantasies and the Creative Process. In: *The Psychoanalytic Study of Society*, 6:53—70. New York: International Universities Press.

Hanslick, E. 1885. *The Beautiful in Music*, trans. G. Cohen. New York: Liberal Arts Press, 1957.

Harrison, I. B. 1986. A Note on the Developmental Origins of Affect: In: *Psychoanalysis: The Science of Mental Conflict*, ed. A. D. Richards and M. S. Willick. Hillsdale, N.J.: Analytic Press, pp. 191—206.

Hartmann, J. 1939. Ich-Psychologie und Anpassungsproblem. *Int. Z. Psy. Imago*, 24:62—135. In: *Organization and Pathology of Thought*, trans. D. Rappaport. New York: Columbia University Press, 1951.

Hinsie, L. E. and Shatzky, J. 1940. *Psychiatric Dictionary*. New York: Oxford University Press.

Hofstadter, D. R. 1979. *Gödel, Escher, Bach: An Eternal Golden Braid*. New York: Basic.

Holt, R. R. 1967. The Development of the Primary Process: A Structural View. In: *Motives and Thought: Psychoanalytic Essays in Honor of David Rapaport {Psychological Issues*, Monogr. 18—19], ed. R. R. Holt. New York: International Universities Press, pp. 344—83.

Ionesco, E. 1968. *Fragments of a Journal*, trans. J. Steward. New York: Grove Press.

———. 1971. *Present Past, Past Present*, trans. H. R. Lane. New York: Grove Press.

Jacobson, E. 1950. Development of the Wish for a Child in Boys. *Psychoanalytic Study of the Child*, 5:139—52. New York: International Universities Press.

Jaques, E. 1982. *The Form of Time*. New York: Crane, Russak.

James, H. 1893. *The Private Life*. New York: Harper.

James, W. 1890. *The Principles of Psychology*. New York: Dover, 1950.

———. 1902. *The Varieties of Religious Experience*. New York: The Modern Library.

Janet, P. 1889. *L'Automatisme Psychologique*. Paris: Bailliere.

Johns, C. 1982. *Sex or Symbol:Erotic Images of Greece and Rome*. Austin: University of Texas Press.

Jones, E. 1953. *The Life and Work of Sigmund Freud*, vol. 1. New York: Basic.

———. 1955. *The Life and Work of Sigmund Freud*, vol. 2. New York: Basic.

———. 1957. *The Life and Work of Sigmund Freud*, vol. 3. New York: Basic.

Jones, R. S. 1982. *Physics as Metaphor*. Minneapolis: University of Minnesota Press.

Kanzer, M. 1976. Freud and His Literary Doubles. *American Imago*, 33: 231—43.

Kernberg, O. 1975. *Borderline Conditions and Pathological Narcissism*. New York: Jason Aronson.

———. 1980. *Internal World and External Reality*. New York: Jason Aronson.

Keyes, D. 1981. *The Minds of Billy Milligan*. New York: Random House.

Klein, M. 1948. *Contributions to Psychoanalysis. 1921—1945*. London: Hogarth Press.

Kramer, J. 1981. New Temporalities in Music. *Critical Inquiry*, University of Chicago, Spring 1981:539—56.

Kris, E. 1952. *Psychoanalytic Explorations in Art*. New York: International Universities Press.

Krystal, H. 1985. *Trauma and the Stimulus Barrier. Psychoanalytic Inquiry* 5:131—61. Hillsdale, N.J.: The Analytic Press.

Kubie, L. 1953. The Distortion of the Symbolic Process in Neurosis and Psychosis. *Journal of the American Psychoanalytic Association*, 1: 59—86.

Kubler, G. 1962. *The Shape of Time: Remarks on the History of Things*. New Haven: Yale University Press.

Kundera, M. 1984. *The Unbearable Lightness of Being*. New York: Harper & Row.

225

REFERENCES

Lampl-De-Groot, J. 1981. Notes on "Multiple Personality." *Psychoanalytic Quarterly*, 50:614—24.

Langer, S. 1942. *Philosophy in a New Key.* New York: New American Library, 1948.

————. 1953. *Feeling and Form.* New York: Scribner's.

————.1957. *Problems of Art.* New York: Scribner's.

Lasky, R. 1978. The Psychoanalytic Treatment of a Case of Multiple Personality. *Psychoanalytic Review*, 65:353—80.

Lazar, M. 1982. The Psychodramatic Stage: Ionesco and His Doubles. In: M. Lazar, ed., *The Dream and the Play.* Malibu, Calif.: Undena Publications.

Legault, O. 1981. Psychoanalytic Aesthetic Theory and Picasso's "Man with a Sheep." *Journal of the Philadelphia Association for Psychoanalysis*, 3:1—24.

Levine, S. Z. 1985. Monet, Fantasy, and Freud. In: *Pychoanalytic Perspectives on Art*, ed. M. Gedo. Hillsdale, N.J. & London: Analytic Press, pp. 29—55.

Lewin, B. 1946. Counter-transference in the Technique of Medical Practice. *Psychosomatic Medicine*, 8:195—99.

Loewald, H. 1975. Psychoanalysis as an Art and the Fantasy Character of the Psychoanalytic Situation. *Journal of The American Psychoanalytic Association*, 23:277—99.

Lubin, A. J. 1972. *Stranger on the Earth: A Psychological Biography of Vincent Van Gogh.* New York: Rinehart & Winston.

Mahler, M. S., Pine, F., and Bergman, A. 1975. *The Psychological Birth of the Human Infant.* New York: Basic.

Mandelstam, N. 1970. *Hope Against Hope. A Memoir.* New York: Atheneum.

Mann, T. 1940. *The Transposed Heads.* New York: Knopf, 1941.

Marmer, S. S. 1980. Psychoanalysis of Muliple Personality. *International Journal of Psychoanalysis*, 61:439—59.

Meyer, B. C. 1967. *Joseph Conrad: A Psychoanalytic Biography.* Princeton, N.J.: Princeton University Press.

Meyer, L. B. 1956. *Emotion and Meaning in Music.* Chicago: University of Chicago Press.

————. 1967. *Music, the Arts and Idea.* Chicago: University of Chicago Press.

Michon, J. A. 1983. J. T. Fraser's "Levels of Temporality" as Cognitive Representations. Paper presented at the *Fifth World Conference of the Inter-*

national Society for the Study of Time, Castello di Gargonza, Italy, 3−9 July, 1983.

Miller, A. 1981. *Prisoners of Childhood.* New York: Basic.

Milner, M. 1957. *On Not Being Able to Paint.* New York: International Universities Press.

Mochulsky, K. 1947. *Dostoevsky: His Life and Work,* trans. M. A. Minihan. Princeton, N.J.: Princeton University Press.

Modell, A. H. 1973. Affects and Psychoanalytic Knowledge. *Annual of Psychoanalysis,* 1:125−58. New York: Quadrangle/The New York Times Book Co.

—―――. 1984. *Psychoanalysis in a New Context.* New York: International Universities Press.

Mursell, J. 1937. *The Psychology of Music.* New York: Norton.

Nabokov, V. 1975. Terror. In: *Tyrants Destroyed and Other Stories.* New York and Toronto: McGraw-Hill.

Niederland, W. G. 1967. Clinical Aspects of Creativity. *American Imago:* 24:6−33.

Noy, P. 1968−69. A Theory of Art and Aesthetic Experience. *Psychoanalytic Review* 55:623−45.

―――. 1969. A Revision of the Psychoanalytic Theory of the Primary Process. *International Journal of Psychoanalysis,* 50:155−78.

Nunberg, H., and Federn, E., eds. 1974. *Minutes of the Vienna Psychoanalytic Society. Vol. III. 1910−1912.* New York: International Universities Press.

Peto, A. 1961. The Fragmentizing Function of the Ego in the Transference Neurosis. *International Journal of Psychoanalysis,* 42:238−45.

―――. 1963. The Fragmentizing of the Ego in the Analytic Session. *International Journal of Psychoanalysis,* 44:334−38.

Peyre, H. 1974. *What Is Symbolism?* trans. E. Parker. University of Alabama Press, 1980.

Plato, *The Dialogues of Plato,* trans, B. Jowett, In: *Great Books of the Western World,* vol. 7, ed. R. M. Hutchins and M. Adler. Chicago: Encyclopedia Britannica Educational Corp., 1952.

Prince, M. 1906. *Dissociation of a Personality.* New York: Meridian, 1957.

―――. 1919. The Psychogenesis of Multiple Personality. *Journal of Abnormal Psychology,* 14:225−80.

Rank, O. 1932. *Art and Artist.* New York: Knopf.

REFERENCES

————. 1971. *The Double: A Psychoanalytic Study*. Chapel Hill: University of North Carolina Press. First published as *Der Doppelgänger*. In: *Imago: Zeitschrift fur Anwendung der Psychoanalyse auf die Geisteswissenschaften*, ed. S. Freud. Leipzig, Vienna, and Zurich: Internationaler Psychoanalytischer Verlag, 1914, vol. III, pp. 97–164.

Rapaport, D., ed. 1951. *Organization and Pathology of Thought: Selected Sources*. New York: Columbia University Press.

Rich, F. 1984. Review of "Rockaby" by Samuel Beckett. *The New York Times*, C-3, Feb. 17.

Ricoeur, P. 1978. Image and Language in Psychoanalysis. In: *Psychoanalysis and Language*, ed. Jos. H. Smith. New Haven and London: Yale University Press, pp. 293–324.

Roe, A. 1952. *The Making of a Scientist*. New York: Dodd, Mead.

Romm, S. and Slap, J. W. 1983. Sigmund Freud and Salvador Dali. *American Imago*, 40:337–47.

Rose, G. J. 1960a. Screen Memories in Homicidal Acting Out. *Psychoanalytic Quarterly*, 29:328–43.

————. 1960b. Analytic First Aid for a Three-Year-Old. *American Journal of Orthopsychiatry*, 30:200–201.

————. 1971. Narcissistic Fusion States and Creativity. In: *Psychoanalysis Today: Essays in Honor of Max Schur*. New York: International Universities Press.

————. 1972a. "The French Lieutenant's Woman": The Unconscious Significance of a Novel to its Author. *American Imago*, 29:165–76.

————. 1972. Fusion States. In: *Tactics and Techniques in Psychoanalytic Therapy*, ed. P. L. Giovacchini. New York: Science House, pp. 170–88.

————. 1980. *The Power of Form: A Psychoanalytic Approach to Aesthetic Form*. New York: International Universities Press.

————. 1983. Sigmund Freud and Salvador Dali: Cultural and Historical Processes. *American Imago*, 40:139–43.

————. 1984. In Pursuit of Slow Time: A Psychoanalytic Approach to Contemporary Music. In: *Psychoanalytic Study of Society*, 10:353–65.

Rose, R. D. 1980. *An Enthnomusicological Look at Bebop Jazz*. Unpublished.

Rosen, C. 1980. *Sonata Forms*. New York: Norton.

Rosenzweig, S. 1986. *Freud and Experimental Psychology: The Emergence of Idiodynamics*. St. Louis: Rana House; New York: McGraw-Hill.

Ross, N. 1975. Affect as Cognition: With Observations on the Meanings of Mystical States. *International Review of Psychoanalysis*, 2:79–93.

REFERENCES

Rothenberg, A. 1979. *The Emerging Goddess.* Chicago and London: University of Chicago Press.

Santayana, G. 1896. *The Sense of Beauty.* New York: Modern Library, 1955.

Santinover, J. 1986. Jung's Lost Contribution to the Dilemma of Narcissism. *Journal of the American Psychoanalytic Association,* 34:401—38.

Schachtel, E. G. 1959. *Psychoanalysis Examined and Re-Examined.* New York: Basic. Reprinted by Da Capo Press, New York, 1984. *Metamorphosis: On the Development of Affect, Perception, Attention, and Memory.*

Scherer, K. R.; Koivumaki, J.; and Rosenthal, R 1972. Minimal Cues in the Vocal Communication of Affect: Judging Emotions from Content-Masked Speech. *Journal of Psycholinguistic Research,* 1:269—85.

Schilder, P. 1942. Mind: Perception and Thought in Their Constructive Aspects. New York: Columbia University Press.

Schreiber, F. R. 1973. *Sybil.* Chicago: Remeny.

Schur, M. 1966. *The Id and the Regulatory Principles of Mental Functioning.* New York: International Universities Press.

Selfe, L. 1979. *Nadia: A Case of Extraordinary Drawing Ability in an Autistic Child.* New York and London: Harcourt Brace Jovanovich. Academic Press, 1977.

Sessions, R. 1950. *The Musical Experience of Composer, Performer, Listener.* Princeton, N.J.: Princeton University Press.

Shapiro, T., and Stern, D. 1980. Psychoanalytic Perspectives on the First Year of Life: The Establishment of the Object in an Affective Field. In: *The Course of Life, Vol. 1: Infancy and Early Childhood,* ed. S. I. Greenspan and G. H. Pollock. Adelphi, Md.: U. S. Dept of Health and Human Services.

Sharpe, E. F. 1940. Psycho-Physical Problems Revealed in Language: An Examination of Metaphor. In: *Collected Papers on Psychoanalysis.* London: Hogarth Press, 1950, pp. 155—69.

Shepard, K. R., and Braun, B. G. 1985. Visual Changes in the Multiple Personality. Paper presented at the *2nd International Conference on Multiple Personality/Dissociative States.* Audio Transcripts, Ltd., 610 Madison Street, Alexandria, Va. 22314.

Spector, J. J. 1972. *The Aesthetics of Freud.* New York: McGraw-Hill.

Spence, D. P. 1982. *Narrative Truth and Historical Truth: Meaning and Interpretation in Psychoanalysis.* New York: Norton.

Spitz, E. H. 1985. *Art and Psyche.* New Haven and London: Yale University Press.

Spitz, R. 1957. *No and Yes.* New York: International Universities Press.

REFERENCES

Steinberg, A. 1966. *Dostoevsky*. New York: Hillary House.

Steinberg, L. 1983. The Sexuality of Christ in Renaissance Art and in Modern Oblivion. *October*, Cambridge, Mass.: MIT Press.

Stern, D. N. 1983. Implications of Infancy Research for Psychoanalytic Theory and Practice. In: *Psychiatry Update II*, ed. L. Grinspoon. Washington: American Psychoanalytic Association Press.

Terr, L. C. 1984. Time and Trauma. In: *Psychoanlytic Study of the Child*, 39:633−65. New Haven and London: Yale University Press.

Thigpen, C. H., and Cleckley, H. 1957. *Three Faces of Eve*. New York: McGraw-Hill.

Thomas, D. 1951. Notes on the Art of Poetry. In: *A Garland for Dylan Thomas*. New York: Clarke & Way, 1963.

Ticho, E. A. 1986. German Culture and Freud's Thought. *International Journal of Psychoanalysis*, 67:227−34.

Toch, E. 1948. *The Shaping Forces in Music*. New York: Criterion Music.

Tustin, F. 1984. Autistic Shapes. *International Review of Psychoanalysis*, 11:279−90.

Vermorel, V. and H., 1986, Was Freud a Romantic? *International Review of Psychoanalysis*, 13:15−37.

Wasiolek, E. ed. and trans. 1967. *The Notebooks for "Crime and Punishment." Fyodor Dostoevsky*. Chicago and London: University of Chicago. (Moscow and Leningrad, 1931).

Weissman, P. 1967. Theoretical Considerations of Ego Regression and Ego Functions in Creativity. *Psychoanalytic Quarterly*, 36:37−50.

―――. 1968. Psychological Concomitants of Ego Functioning in Creativity. *International Journal of Psychoanalysis*, 49:464−69.

―――. 1969. Creative Fantasies and Beyond the Reality Principle. *Psychoanalytic Quarterly*, 38:110−23.

Whorf, B. L. 1956. *Language, Thought and Reality: Selected Writings of Benjamin Lee Whorf*, ed. J. B. Carroll. Cambridge, Mass.: MIT Press.

Williams, H. W., and Rupp, L. 1938. Observations on Confabulation. *American Journal of Psychiatry*, 95:395−405.

Winner, E. 1982. *The Psychology of the Arts*. Cambridge, Mass.: Harvard University Press.

Winnicott, D. W. 1953. Transitional Objects and Transitional Phenomena. *International Journal of Psychoanalysis*, 34:89−97.

―――. 1966. The Location of Cultural Experience. *International Journal of Psychoanalysis*, 48:368−72.

Wolfenstein, M. 1966. How Is Mourning Possible? In: *Psychoanalytic Study of the Child*, 21:93—123. New York: International Universities Press.

———. 1969. Loss, Rage and Repetition. In: *Psychoanalytic Study of the Child*, 24:432—60. New York: International Universities Press.

———. 1973. The Image of the Lost Parent. In: *Psychoanalytic Study of the Child*, 28:433—56. New Haven and London: Yale University Press.

Zuckerkandl, V. 1956. *Sound and Symbol. Music and the External World.* Princeton, N.J.: Princeton University Press.

———. 1973. *Man the Musician. Sound and Symbol*, vol. 2. Princeton, N. J.: Princeton University Press.

INDEX

Abstraction, 110
Acting out, xvii, 46–63, 173–74
Aesthetic form, 210, 213–14
Aesthetic plasticity, 186–89
Affect: flow of, 210–11; as form of communication, 202; and tension, 205–07; theory of, 203
Aggression, 21–42, 98–101
Alternates: characteristics of, 101–03; collective, 112; integration and, 66; in multiple personality disorder, 81–98. *See also* Doubles
Amnesia, 50–51, 72
Anger, 92, 94, 98–101
Art: abstract, 3–4, 7, 152, 204–05; aim of, 184–85; boundaries of, 189, 199, 201; cognitive thinking and, 189–93; cubism, 116, 151; distinctions from science, 2–3, 184; emotion and, 201–03, 205; as facilitator of mastery, 210; fragmentation in, 151–53; Freud's views on, 1–4, 13–14, 18–19; German expressionism, 4, 6; humanation of Christ child

in, 178–80; imaginative thinking and, 189–93; importance of the unconscious in, 10–11; impressionism, 3–4, 151; language and, 143–45; minimalist painting, 152; naturalism, 3–4; pointillism, 151; portrayal of genitalia in, 178–80; psychoanalysis and, xi, 2, 18–21; reality and, 207; relevance of mastery to, 182–200; similarities with structure of internalization, 213; subject/object dichotomy and, 189; surrealism, 8–14, 151; symbolism, 3–4, 143, 152, 159–60
Artist: balance between the inner and outer world and the, 112; childhood development of, 112; double identifications of, 122–23; ego splitting and the, 112, 127; objectification and the, 209; in Oedipal stage, 123; struggle with sense of self, 134; two-way conscious communication and the, 113; unconscious thought and the, 139. *See also* Novelist; Writer